KW-306-292

90 0898714 3

WITHDRAWN
FROM
UNIVERSITY OF PLYMOUTH
LIBRARY

The Japanese Pharmaceutical Industry

This book explores why Japan, despite being a world leader in many high technology industries such as automobiles and consumer electronics, is only a minor player in the global pharmaceutical industry. Japan provides a huge market for pharmaceuticals as the second largest consumer of prescription drugs after the United States, and is a massive importer of prescription drugs, relying on discoveries made elsewhere. This book charts the development of the industry, from the devastation resulting from the Second World War to its performance in the present day.

Focusing in particular on antibiotics and anticancer drugs, the book analyses factors that have prevented Japan from leading the rapid advances in science and technology that have occurred globally over recent decades. Looking at the pharmaceutical industry, the book argues that the Japanese government's research and development policies were not sufficiently incentivizing. It also shows how the nature of capitalism in Japan – which featured close relations between government and industry as well as between and within firms – was appropriate for nurturing industrial development in the immediate post-war decades, but became much less effective in later years.

Maki Umemura is a lecturer in Japanese studies at Cardiff Business School, Cardiff University, UK.

Routledge Studies in the Growth Economies of Asia

The Japanese Pharmaceutical Industry

Its evolution and current challenges

Maki Umemura

Routledge
Taylor & Francis Group

LONDON AND NEW YORK

First published 2011
by Routledge
2 Park Square, Milton Park, Abingdon, Oxon, OX14 4RN

Simultaneously published in the USA and Canada
by Routledge
711 Third Avenue, New York, NY 10017

Routledge is an imprint of the Taylor & Francis Group, an informa business

© 2011 Maki Umemura

The right of Maki Umemura to be identified as author of this work has
been asserted by her in accordance with sections 77 and 78 of the
Copyright, Designs and Patents Act 1988.

All rights reserved. No part of this book may be reprinted or reproduced
or utilized in any form or by any electronic, mechanical, or other means,
now known or hereafter invented, including photocopying and recording,
or in any information storage or retrieval system, without permission in
writing from the publishers.

Trademark notice: Product or corporate names may be trademarks or
registered trademarks, and are used only for identification and
explanation without intent to infringe.

British Library Cataloguing in Publication Data
A catalogue record for this book is available from the British Library

Library of Congress Cataloging in Publication Data
Umemura, Maki.
  The Japanese pharmaceutical industry :
  its evolution and current challenges / Maki Umemura.
  p. cm. — (Routledge studies in the growth economies of Asia)
  Includes bibliographical references and index.
  1. Pharmaceutical industry—Japan—History. I. Title.
  HD9672.J29U44 2011
  338.4'761510952—dc22
  2010032865

ISBN: 978–0–415–58766–2 (hbk)
ISBN: 978–0–203–83128–1 (ebk)

Typeset in Times New Roman by Swales & Willis Ltd, Exeter, Devon

UNIVERSITY OF PLYMOUTH
9 U08987143

Printed and bound in Great Britain by the MPG Books Group

Contents

Illustrations

Figures

Tables

Acknowledgements

This book, which was based on my doctoral thesis, would not have been possible without the kind support of many individuals and organizations. I would first like to thank my PhD thesis supervisors, Janet Hunter and Patrick Wallis, for always parting generously with their time and for providing very helpful comments and support throughout course of the PhD.

This book was supported generously by the Japan Foundation Endowment Committee, the Wellcome Trust, the International Society for the History of Pharmacy, and the 20th Century Japan Foundation. I am also extremely grateful to the London School of Economics and Political Science (LSE) Radwan Travel and Discovery Fund, the LSE Research Studentship and the Central London Research Fund for their financial support.

I thank several Japanese pharmaceutical firms for providing information. The public relations departments of Takeda Pharmaceutical Co., Sankyo Co., Banyu Pharmaceutical Co. and Tanabe Seiyaku Co. sent me their corporate histories. Eisai Inc. offered a number of books written by its founder. Morinaga & Co., Toray Industries Inc. and Lion Corp. provided articles relating to penicillin production.

I am deeply indebted to many individuals who offered guidance on my research. I am particularly grateful to Yui Tsunehiko of the Japan Business History Institute, Eisuke Daito and Robert Kneller of the University of Tokyo, Ian Neary of the University of Oxford and Miyajima Hideaki of Waseda University, for providing advice and materials. I also thank Kenjirō Nagasaka, ex-chairman of Banyu Pharmaceutical; P. Reed Maurer and Robert Niemeth, previous representatives of the Pharmaceutical Manufacturers of America in Japan; Sapin Shah, president of Shionogi America; David Drutz, previous vice president of Daiichi Pharmaceutical; and Naoko Wakaomoto of the Japan Cancer Patients Association, for sharing their experiences with the Japanese pharmaceutical industry.

I also thank Hiromi Inagaki, curator at the Naito Museum of Pharmaceutical Science and Industry and Eiko Sakaguchi, curator at the Gordon W. Prange Collection at the University of Maryland, who helped to locate relevant archival material on penicillin production during the Second World War, and the Occupation era, respectively. I am also grateful to Takeo Kubo, Director of the Doshōmachi Museum of Medicine for allowing me to consult material available at the museum, and to John Parascandola, who provided information relating to the early production of penicillin.

I benefited much from the comments offered at the Newcomen Dissertation Colloquium sponsored by the Business History Conference, the Summer School sponsored by the European Business History Association, and the PhD workshop sponsored by European Association of Japanese Studies. I also thank my friends at LSE and my colleagues at Cardiff University for their suggestions and support.

Finally, I would like to thank my family, especially Andrew, without whose support none of this would have been possible.

Abbreviations

CANPS	Cancer Patients Support Organization
CPI	consumer price index
CRO	contract research organization
FDA	Food and Drug Administration
FDI	foreign direct investment
GARIOA	Government and Relief in Occupied Areas
GCP	good clinical practice
GHQ	General Headquarters
GLP	good laboratory practice
GMP	good manufacturing practice
GPMSP	good post-marketing surveillance practice
ICH	The International Conference on Harmonisation of Technical Requirements for Registration of Pharmaceuticals for Human Use
JARA	Japan Antibiotics Research Association
JPMA	Japan Pharmaceutical Manufacturers Association
M&A	mergers and acquisitions
MHW	Ministry of Health and Welfare
MITI	Ministry of International Trade and Industry
MOSS	market-oriented and sector-selective
NCE	new chemical entity
NRDC	National Research and Development Corporation
OECD	Organization for Economic Cooperation and Development
OTC	over-the-counter
PAL	Pharmaceutical Affairs Law
PhRMA	Pharmaceutical Research and Manufacturers of America
R&D	research and development
SSM	Specific Substance Maruyama

1 Introduction

Why didn't Japan become a leader in pharmaceuticals?

When a Japanese person goes abroad, they notice something interesting about Japanese firms. The names of certain Japanese firms, such as Sony and Toyota, are available and known almost everywhere. But when one goes to a pharmacy in London or New York, the familiar names of Japanese pharmaceutical firms are largely absent. Why haven't Japanese pharmaceutical firms become household names like America's Pfizer, Britain's GlaxoSmithKline or Switzerland's Novartis? This book will answer this question.

The leading Japanese drug companies such as Takeda and Eisai have expanded overseas. But their overseas presence has become known only very recently, long after Japanese carmakers and electronics firms had become household names around the world. In addition, despite the efforts of its leading firms, Japan remains a minor player in the global pharmaceutical industry.[1] The country's largest and most profitable pharmaceutical firm, Takeda, ranked only fifteenth in global pharmaceutical sales in 2009.[2] The sales of Japan's top three pharmaceutical firms in fiscal 2008 were less than a fifth of the size of leading global firms.[3] The global pharmaceutical industry is dominated by firms in the United States, Switzerland or the United Kingdom. While Japan is the world's second largest consumer of prescription drugs, after the United States, it has discovered less than a tenth of the world's internationally used drugs since 1980.[4] Blockbuster drugs of Japanese origin are rare and Japan remains a net importer of pharmaceuticals. This phenomenon requires historical explanation.

Studying the development of Japan's pharmaceutical industry is important for several reasons. First, the pharmaceutical industry is an important field of study in its own right. Alongside improvements in nutrition, hygiene and healthcare provision, the therapeutic discoveries launched by pharmaceutical firms have revolutionized health standards and have contributed significantly to quality of life as well as to economic development in Japan. Most developed economies also spend a substantial amount on pharmaceuticals. In 2007, for example, OECD countries spent an average 1.5 per cent of gross domestic product (GDP) on pharmaceuticals, and Japan spent 1.7 per cent of GDP on pharmaceuticals.[5] In the United States, people now spend more money on prescription drugs than they do on automobiles.[6]

The experience of the pharmaceutical industry also illuminates the paradox of Japan's dual economy: Japan has an internationally competitive tier of industries, such as carmakers and electronics, which coexist with non-competitive industries such as aluminium and food processing. The Japanese pharmaceutical industry straddles these two tiers, for it includes a handful of internationally competitive drug companies such as Takeda, Daiichi Sankyo and Eisai as well as a myriad of domestically oriented, small to medium size enterprises that have survived via protective government policy.

The Japanese pharmaceutical industry failed to become a global leader for a number of reasons. One of which was the weak incentives for firms to engage in research and development (R&D). Another reason was Japan's distinct medical culture, which undermined the capacity to both develop and deliver innovative drugs.

Spurred by the industry's transformation since the 1990s, academics have recently produced more works on the Japanese pharmaceutical industry. Naturally, this trend is more pronounced in fields such as economics, business and political science.[7] Economists have examined issues ranging from patents to cost containment while political scientists have emphasized issues such as industrial policy, R&D incentives and international competitiveness.[8]

In contrast, historians have written little on the Japanese pharmaceutical industry. The existing historical literature is largely confined to company histories written by company employees. Takeda, Daiichi Sankyo, Astellas and other leading Japanese pharmaceutical firms have published such histories.[9] The Japan Society for the History of Pharmacy published a history of the industry in the mid-1990s.[10] While these publications provide chronologies of firms, developments in industry and other factual information, they do not engage in rigorous analysis.

More recently, the scientist Takashi Nishikawa provided an account of how the foundations of the post-war pharmaceutical industry were created during the Occupation period.[11] The American academic Julia Yongue also recently published several articles on the history of Japan's pharmaceutical industry.[12] The amount of scholarship on this topic, however, remains limited. Incorporating the Japanese experience should allow for a more complete understanding of the global pharmaceutical industry.

Most experts agree that Japanese pharmaceutical firms are uncompetitive relative to those based in the United States, Switzerland and the United Kingdom. Beyond that, there is no consensus. Academies have provided a number of competing explanations for the industry's lacklustre performance. Some scholars attribute the weakness of the Japanese pharmaceutical industry to the first-mover advantage enjoyed by Western pharmaceutical firms. The American business historian Alfred Chandler, for example, argued that the main reason why Japan did not become a leader in this industry was simply a matter of timing. While Japanese consumer electronic firms were able to penetrate global markets because the consumer electronics industry itself was young, Japanese pharmaceutical firms, facing barriers to entry, could not penetrate the markets dominated by the long-established European and American pharmaceutical firms.[13] Chandler stated that Japan's success in consumer electronics and relative weakness in chemicals and pharmaceuticals 'cannot be explained in terms of national culture, national political processes and institutions, or national educational institutions'.[14]

The question of timing identified by Chandler, however, offers only a partial explanation. The concept of first-mover advantage, for example, has been called into question by academics who have argued that being the first mover in an industry is not necessarily advantageous.[15] Chandler neglected several other factors for the industry's underperformance.

A number of scholars have argued that the weakness of the Japanese pharmaceutical industry was due to government policy. For example, L.G. Thomas argued that flawed policies created a dysfunctional industry where drugs had short product life; uncompetitive firms developed imitative drugs; and foreign firms were excluded from the domestic market.[16] Jeremy Howells and Ian Neary also blamed the government for the industry's weakness, and argued that the development of the Japanese pharmaceutical industry was hampered by a 'distant, controlled and reactive' government administration.[17] Steven Collins shared this view, adding that the Japanese pharmaceutical industry suffered because Japan's bureaucracy was far less coherent and effective in its planning than policymakers in the United States.[18] These authors claimed that it was the bureaucrats and politicians, rather than the entrepreneurs, who were responsible for the industry's weakness. Other political scientists also suggested that the Japanese government's decision to support other industries – such as consumer electronics – disadvantaged pharmaceutical companies and kept them from developing stronger R&D capacities to create drugs that would be in demand overseas.[19]

Taking a slight variation on this theme of administrative failure, Tomofumi Anegawa and Michael Reich suggested that government policies were effective at creating the foundations of a modern pharmaceutical industry as well as achieving the government's initial public health goal of low-cost drugs. The problem was that the Japanese government failed to shift and update its policies to encourage the transition to a more mature pharmaceutical industry based on scientific innovation rather than the volume production of imitative products.[20] According to these authors, the basic issue was that the government consistently sought to contain the price of pharmaceuticals, which reduced the incentive among firms to invest in substantial R&D. The Japanese pharmaceutical industry was an infant industry that did not grow up.

Experts on Japanese education and Japan's research environment have argued that educational institutions also had a negative impact on the industry's global competitiveness. Historians of Japanese science such as Shigeru Nakayama and Morris Low stated that Japan long emphasized applied research at the expense of basic research.[21] Japanese research became path dependent in its bias against basic research – which is crucial to making breakthrough discoveries. Chie Nakane and Robert Kneller added that aspects of Japanese organizational culture, such as *keiretsu*, lifetime employment and the lack of flexible labour markets lessened Japan's research capacity by making Japanese scientists more risk averse in their research pursuits as well as reducing opportunities for inter-firm and university–industry collaboration.[22]

In addition, Japanese researchers worked with fewer foreign scientists in their laboratories and participated in fewer collaborative projects of international scale. As a result, they were less exposed to fresh ideas from foreign researchers compared to their counterparts in more advanced pharmaceutical markets.[23] Furthermore, Japanese universities have historically produced fewer doctorates in science compared to countries such as United States or Britain. A lower proportion of Japanese PhD graduates in science have been employed in industry.[24] Moreover, until the late 1990s, barriers to entrepreneurship among university academics prevented the commercialization of academic research.[25] Japan's educational institutions and research environment hindered the capacity of Japanese firms to develop drugs that would have been more marketable abroad.

Yet timing, government policy and research environment, do not provide a sufficient explanation for Japan's weak performance in pharmaceuticals. As Kenneth Lipartito has argued, we also need to consider culture to understand differences in industrial performance across nations. While definitions of 'culture' have varied, it might be defined as shared values, norms, ideas and behaviours.[26] While scholars such as Nakane examined the role of organizational culture in Japan's research environment, a number of scholars have explored its role in Japan's industrial performance.

A growing body of research has suggested that Japanese organizational culture is not conducive to the development of soft industries – which include pharmaceuticals. Steven Vogel observed that Japan's business culture long emphasized social stability over rapid or radical economic change. He stated that this desire to preserve stability discouraged quick responses in Japanese industries.[27] Marie Anchordoguy argued persuasively that Japan's style of capitalism was conducive to the development of industries where technologies could be imported, where the technological path was stable and predictable – industries that involved, low-risk, incremental innovation and constant improvement in manufacturing processes. Anchordoguy, however, maintained that Japan's economic system was ill-suited to supporting industries such as pharmaceuticals that were based on rapid, discontinuous and unpredictable advances in science and technology.[28]

The experience of Japan's pharmaceutical industry shows that Japanese medical culture also had a major and largely negative impact on its performance. The distinct features of Japanese medical culture ranged from physician dispensing and prescribing practices, particular approaches to medical therapy, to more hierarchical doctor–patient relationships. These features discouraged Japanese firms from developing innovative cancer therapies by rewarding those who developed drugs of limited efficacy.

Aim of book

This book explains why Japan was unable to develop a globally competitive pharmaceutical industry, despite its success in developing other high technology industries. While most existing works on the pharmaceutical industry tend to offer simple explanations, no single factor explains why the Japanese pharmaceutical industry did not become an export-oriented or world-leading industry. I consider a number of factors, including government policy, industrial structure and medical culture, that influenced industrial development. I aim to provide a comprehensive, multifactorial explanation for the relative weakness of the Japanese pharmaceutical industry, which include weak R&D incentives and a distinct medical culture.

My study of the Japanese pharmaceutical industry speaks to several broader themes in Japanese economic history. It addresses the role of the state in late economic development and how an industry outside the jurisdiction of the Ministry of International Trade and Industry (MITI) was shaped by government policy. It touches upon the question of whether some of the features of Japanese capitalism are conducive to the growth of a high technology industry such as pharmaceuticals. The book also shows how Japanese firms have responded to changes in intellectual property regimes and to the recent pressures of deregulation and globalization.

Case studies

My research uses two classes of medicines, antibiotics and anti-cancer drugs, as case studies for exploring the post-1945 history of the Japanese pharmaceutical industry (Chapters 3 and 4 respectively). An approach based on therapeutic sectors is useful because it sheds light on the extent to which the development of the industry was shaped by health needs at a given time, the therapeutic attributes of certain medicines and variations in approaches to medical treatment.[29] My approach also allows for a multifaceted view of the industry's development while keeping a focus on just two sectors. In total, I examine the experience of 12 different companies, from large to small and from old to newly established firms.

Japan experienced high mortality and morbidity rates from infectious disease during the early post-war period, and for diseases of affluence in the more recent period. This led to high demand for drugs to treat these conditions in the respective periods. Infectious diseases, particularly tuberculosis, were the leading cause of death in the years after the Second World War, while cancer has become the leading cause of death in Japan since 1981.[30] Given that antibiotics were important in the early post-war period and anticancer drugs became more important in subsequent decades, the two case studies encompass the entire post-war period. This book follows how the Japanese industry evolved over the post-war period by looking at how firms responded to high demand conditions during earlier and later phases of the post-war era.

A case study of the antibiotics sector sheds light on the initial course of development in Japan's pharmaceutical industry – alongside economic trends, demographic change and scientific/technological advances. In turn, a case study of the anticancer drug sector illustrates how the industry evolved in later years, in step with revisions towards stricter regulatory guidelines for drug development, advances in drug discovery methods and globalization. It reveals how differences between older drugs influence market dynamics.

There are other reasons why these two case studies are helpful in examining the historical dynamics of Japan's pharmaceutical industry. Both sectors are large: Japan's antibiotics and anticancer drug markets remain the second largest in the world.[31] As the most produced and exported pharmaceuticals in Japan for much of the post-war era, the antibiotics sector provides an ideal forum to examine the acquisition of production as well as export capacities in the pharmaceutical industry. As Japanese pharmaceutical firms have launched globally successful drugs in both sectors, a case study of antibiotics and anticancer drugs in Japan will also shed valuable insight into evolution of pharmaceutical innovation in Japan.

To a certain extent, the selection of specific firms for case studies in the antibiotics and anticancer drug sector was dictated by the source data. The firms selected were those that developed the leading drugs during a given period. It is recognized that they are not representative of the entire pharmaceutical industry; for the most part, they showed the Japanese pharmaceutical industry at its best. But by selecting the strongest of Japanese firms across time, the case studies should also provide a more convincing explanation as to why – even with its best pharmaceutical firms – Japan was not able to develop a world-leading pharmaceutical industry.

Sources

This book is based on a range of both archival and published sources generated by government, industry and academia. Archival sources were used primarily to investigate Japan's efforts to build a modern pharmaceutical industry at the end of the Second World War and during the Allied Occupation between 1945 and 1952. I also consulted a range of published sources, from official government publications, company documents, academic and trade journals, as well as the popular press. I also conducted several interviews.

In general, combined figures for both prescription and over-the-counter (OTC) drugs have been used as proxy measures of the prescription drugs industry. This is partly because the legal distinction between prescription drugs and OTC drugs was not made until the 'Basic Policies for Drug Manufacturing Approval' were introduced in 1967. It is also because official statistics have not distinguished between prescription and OTC drugs in the post-1968 period, except for production figures available in the *Yakuji Kōgyō Seisan Dōtai Chōsa Tōkei*. Production figures after 1968 in this book therefore reflect the prescription drug sector, while trade and R&D figures reflect the combined sectors. The use of combined figures, however, should remain representative of general trends observed in the prescription drugs sector, as prescription drugs account for the majority of the drugs in the pharmaceutical industry.[32]

Unless otherwise stated, figures cited in this book are given in real terms to better evaluate long-run trends, for example, in production, R&D expenditure and trade. Nominal values have been converted into 2005 values using the consumer price index (CPI). Figures in US dollars were converted into 2005 US dollars using CPI data available from the US Department of Labor, Bureau of Labor Statistics.[33] Figures in Japanese yen were converted into 2005 yen with CPI data available from Statistical Survey Department, Statistics Bureau, Ministry of Internal Affairs and Communications.[34] CPI figures have been used for conversion as a widely used measure that reasonably reflects the changes in prices over time.

Interviews and correspondence were also conducted with a range of individuals involved in the industry, including representatives of patient groups and company executives. While this book is not based primarily on oral histories, interviews and correspondence helped illuminate published archival sources and strengthen analyses from my research findings. More specifically, they helped ascertain major shifts in the research orientation and the international competitiveness of the Japanese pharmaceutical industry as firms responded to changes in government policy as well as scientific/technological advances and globalization.

Findings and policy implications

This book offers several reasons why Japan did not become a leader in the global pharmaceutical industry. Rather than invest heavily in R&D to pursue breakthrough discoveries, most companies opted to launch many new drugs with limited innovative value that could not be sold in other advanced markets. It was true that a handful of leading firms began to develop global blockbuster drugs and increase their overseas presence. But Japanese firms remained much smaller in terms of sales, workforce or R&D expenditures, and Japan remained a net importer of pharmaceuticals.

The major reasons for the weakness of the industry are: the weak incentives for pharmaceutical firms to invest in R&D, the government's protectionist policies, the poor R&D environment and Japanese medical culture. There are several factors of secondary importance that also help to explain the underperformance of Japan's pharmaceutical industry. These include differences in therapeutic demand conditions between Japan and its potential export markets; different drug standards that essentially acted as trade barriers; the historical origins of Japanese pharmaceutical firms; the industrial structure of the Japanese pharmaceutical industry; barriers to entrepreneurship among university academics; and the lack of initiative taken by Japanese firms to expand into overseas markets.

This book also offers several policy prescriptions. They are not comprehensive, as the case studies tend to highlight specific issues over others. For example, they only touch lightly upon issues relating to entrepreneurship or the nature of scientific research in Japanese universities. That is beyond the scope of this book. Nevertheless, several important lessons can be drawn:

1 *Creating strong R&D incentives*: the single most important policy prescription for developing a globally competitive pharmaceutical industry is the creation of strong R&D incentives. As a heavily regulated industry, governments must offer pharmaceutical firms with strong incentives to invest in the discovery of innovative new drugs. In industrial policy, they need to consider the optimum balance between the needs of public health and those of industry. This can be done by establishing strong intellectual property rights, rewarding innovative

drugs with adequate returns through appropriate pricing and setting rigorous criteria for what qualifies as an 'innovative' new drug. Introducing government funding and tax incentives may also be helpful.

2   *Discourage protectionism*: governments would also do well to open the domestic market to foreign competition as domestic firms become able to reproduce existing drugs. The overprotection or prolonged protection of the domestic market undermines firms' incentives to pursue the discovery of highly innovative drugs that could be marketed overseas. The lifting of capital controls, strengthening of intellectual property laws and harmonizing distinct product standards are integral to this process. The mix and degree of interventions by government need also be monitored and adjusted as the industry develops.

3   *Introduce policies targeted towards specific therapeutic sectors*: the manner of pharmaceutical R&D is not uniform across different therapeutic sectors. Certain sectors involve low-cost, labour-intensive methods of development while others require much greater investments in equipment and human capital. Governments might target the development of certain therapeutic sectors according to the comparative advantages within the domestic market to allow for more efficient and effective use of resources.

4   *Modernize the medical system*: the existence of a modern medical system allows firms to develop new and innovative drugs. Well-trained medical specialists, hospitals equipped with cutting-edge technology and the custom of proper patient diagnoses is essential to conducting accurate and credible clinical trials. This infrastructure determines not only the manner of drug development, but also the type and amount of the drug that will likely be developed. New and innovative drugs tend to have significant side effects, and require a modern medical system both for drug development and marketing.

5   *Promote the prescription of the most efficacious drugs*: physician prescribing practices vary according to medical culture. Physician prescribing behaviour is heavily influenced by idiosyncrasies in local medical practice. These range from cost containment, disclosure practices, to treatment of terminal illness. Creating incentives to prioritize the prescription of the most efficacious drugs may encourage further development of such drugs.

Plan of book

This book is organized into five chapters. This first chapter has offered a brief introduction. Chapter 2 provides a historical analysis of the Japanese pharmaceutical industry. It examines why this industry remained relatively weak, both in comparison with global leaders and with other Japanese industries. It follows the evolution of Japan's pharmaceutical industry across several phases of development, from its origins in the late nineteenth century to a modern industry in 2008. The chapter closes by suggesting several reasons for the underperformance of Japan's pharmaceutical industry.

Chapter 3 and Chapter 4 present the studies on the evolution of Japan's antibiotics sector and anticancer drug sector, respectively. Each chapter follows the evolution of the therapeutic sectors across several stages of development. Case studies of drug development at individual firms are used to gain a more intricate understanding of firm behaviour in response to government policy and changing market conditions. While Chapter 3 provides several explanations for the strong performance of Japan's antibiotics sector, Chapter 4 offers several reasons for the weak performance of Japan's anticancer drug sector.

Chapter 5 is the conclusion. The chapter opens with a summary of the reasons for the relative weakness of Japan's pharmaceutical industry, based on the studies of the antibiotics and anticancer drugs sectors. A discussion of policy implications for other countries follows. The chapter closes by considering the future prospects for the industry in light of recent changes.

2 A historical overview of Japan's pharmaceutical industry

This chapter surveys the history of Japan's pharmaceutical industry and examines why it failed to become a global leader. One of the key reasons for the relative weakness of Japan's pharmaceutical industry lay in the lack of an industrial policy designed to develop a research-intensive, globally competitive industry. The Ministry of Health and Welfare (MHW) – rather than the MITI – regulated Japan's pharmaceutical industry.[1] The government long prioritized public health agendas to produce drugs at low cost for its large population. It also long protected Japanese firms from foreign competition and allowed firms to prosper without substantial investments in R&D. Most Japanese pharmaceutical firms began to pursue R&D much later than their Western counterparts. With their belated adoption of R&D, the Japanese pharmaceutical industry had compromised their ability to compete against Western leaders in a globalizing industry.

The history of Japan's pharmaceutical industry will be examined across seven phases. The first phase was the transition from Chinese to Western medicine from the Meiji period (1868 to 1912) up to the First World War. During this time, the Japanese government adopted Western medicine at the expense of traditional Chinese medicine, and Japanese firms began to import Western, mostly German, drugs.

In the second phase, which began during the First World War, Japanese firms shifted from the import to the manufacture of Western-style drugs. This transition was prompted by the sudden end of trade with Germany during the war. Between 1915 and 1945, Japan developed a small pharmaceutical industry and expanded into mainland Asia.

The third phase began with Japan's defeat in the Second World War. Between 1945 and 1952, Japan was occupied by the Allied powers who implemented reforms that transformed Japan – including its pharmaceutical industry. Indeed, the Occupation authorities created the foundations of Japan's post-war pharmaceutical industry by enabling Japanese firms to produce drugs and establishing modern pharmaceutical regulations to support subsequent development.

The fourth phase began when Japan regained its sovereignty in 1952. Between 1952 and 1961, Japan's pharmaceutical industry began to grow by producing foreign-discovered drugs under licence in a highly protected environment. The leading drugs produced during this period were vitamins and antibiotics, which supplemented nutrients and treated infectious diseases, respectively.

The fifth phase refers to the period between 1961 and 1975, when Japan's pharmaceutical industry grew through the volume production of imitative drugs. After 1961, Japanese firms embarked upon an extraordinary pace of expansion, as the government nurtured firms through import-substitution policies and by underwriting demand through a universal healthcare system. Japan's intellectual property regime, based on process patents, also protected Japanese firms from foreign firms who would have had to disclose the research results of new drug discoveries without much reward. As the country prospered, Japan's pharmaceutical firms also began to produce drugs that would treat diseases of affluence.

The next phase began in 1975, when Japanese pharmaceutical firms shifted from volume-based growth to research-based growth. Between 1975 and 1990, Japanese pharmaceutical firms became increasingly research oriented in order to compete against new entrants from other sectors of its domestic economy and from abroad. This research orientation intensified as the government liberalized capital controls and introduced product patents.

In the most recent phase, between 1990 and 2005, Japanese pharmaceutical firms substantially increased their overseas operations. This globalization was driven by several reforms to the regulatory landscape. For example, Japan harmonized its pharmaceutical regulations with those of the United States and the European Union, which made it easier for drugs approved in Japan to be approved the United States and Europe – and vice versa. As a result, there was increasing foreign competition in the Japanese market. These competitive pressures prompted an unprecedented wave of corporate reorganizations and mergers. Combined with the escalating costs of drug R&D, leading Japanese firms such as Takeda and Daiichi Sankyo began to transfer a large part of their operations abroad.[2]

The Meiji Restoration and the beginnings of Japan's pharmaceutical industry

The Western pharmaceutical industry in Japan began in the late nineteenth century, when Japan opened its doors to the outside world after more than two centuries of seclusion and began to modernize. It emerged in the Doshomachi district of Osaka, which had long been a centre for wholesalers of Chinese herbal medicines, who gathered to examine the medicines imported from China, bargained over prices and distributed goods nationwide. Some of Japan's leading pharmaceutical firms such as Takeda and Shionogi originated as importers and distributors of Chinese medicines. In the late nineteenth century, as the Japanese government adopted policies that favoured Western medicine at the expense of traditional Chinese medicine, these companies switched into the business of importing Western – mostly German – medicines.

It should be remembered that the major aim of the Meiji government was to resist colonization by the Western powers by adopting Western learning, reforming Japan's institutions and encouraging industrialization.[3] Adopting Western pharmaceuticals was part of this larger project. Japanese firms at this time mostly imported, rather than manufactured Western pharmaceuticals. Pharmaceutical regulation in the Meiji era was therefore designed to curb the circulation of fraudulent, if not toxic, imported medicines, rather than to govern the development of new therapies.[4]

Prior to the First World War, Japanese wholesalers of Western medicine, who showed little interest in manufacture, let alone discovery, dominated the pharmaceutical industry. In Germany and the United States, pharmaceutical firms were developing a research-based industry. German pharmaceutical firms originated from academic science while American pharmaceutical firms originated from pharmacy practice.[5]

The First World War and the birth of manufacturing pharmacy

Japan began to produce Western-style drugs during the First World War, after the war cut off imports from Germany. The Japanese government's response to this crisis was similar to that of the British and American governments – its allies during this war. Japan adopted an import-substitution policy that introduced subsidies for pharmaceutical production, nullified Germany's patent rights and disclosed detailed production methods from government laboratories.[6] The government's policies gave birth to a new wave of domestic pharmaceutical firms, such as Daiichi, Yamanouchi and Banyu, which were dedicated to the production of Western medicines. These firms manufactured vitamins, hormonal preparations, anthelmintics and sulfa drugs.[7]

Japan's small pharmaceutical industry began to expand into mainland Asia in the interwar period. The industry's growth continued into the 1930s and 1940s amidst a war economy. The military supplied firms with raw materials, monitored production, purchased drugs for rationing and controlled their distribution.[8] Between 1936 and 1942, production levels grew 20 per cent from 138 billion yen to 167 billion yen.[9] Most of this growth came from sales in East Asia; exports to this region accounted for 20 per cent of Japanese production in 1936. Indeed, these exports still accounted for 17.5 per cent of production in 1943.[10]

With heavy demand for medicines in the domestic and East Asian markets, Japan's pharmaceutical industry grew rapidly during the first few years of the Second World War. But as Japan began to sustain heavy bombing damages and scarce resources were diverted into other war industries, these gains were eroded. Drug production peaked in 1942, and fell swiftly until the end of the war.[11]

The Occupation era and the rebirth of Japan's pharmaceutical industry, 1945–1952

As in other industries, the Second World War left the pharmaceutical industry devastated. In 1946, production was approximately 15 per cent of 1941 levels.[12] But Japan's pharmaceutical industry suffered much less damage than, for example, the steel and coal industries, which had been targeted by Allied bombers.[13] In fact, Japan's pharmaceutical industry had suffered much more from the loss of East Asian markets than the physical damages incurred to its domestic facilities.[14]

During the Occupation period, Japan rebuilt its pharmaceutical industry upon the rudimentary production capacities, distribution networks and human capital it had developed before the war.

The Allied Occupation was essential to this process. The Occupation authorities provided technical assistance to various sectors of the Japanese economy, including the pharmaceutical industry. There were several reasons why the Occupation's General Headquarters (GHQ) became interested in rebuilding Japan's pharmaceutical industry. The American Occupation forces believed that improving public health conditions for Japanese civilians would help to prevent social unrest, a resurgence of militarism or a turn for Communism. The GHQ also needed to supply medicines such as penicillin to American military personnel stationed in Japan.[15] The Occupation authorities believed that domestic production would enable low-cost provision of essential medicines for both civilian and military purposes while adjusting flexibly to fluctuations in demand, without the costs and risks of relying on imports.[16]

Perhaps most important in rebuilding the industry were the technology transfers involving penicillin by Jackson Foster, a former Merck scientist who was appointed by the Occupation authorities to enable penicillin production in Japan. These measures helped sustain and foster the pharmaceutical industry's growth over the following decades.

The GHQ also conducted numerous reforms that not only improved public health conditions in Japan, but also supported the growth of the pharmaceutical industry.[17] These included revisions to the Pharmaceutical Affairs Law (PAL), reforms in medical and pharmacy education, organizational reforms within ministries, as well as revisions to the Japanese Pharmacopoeia.[18] These measures – which redefined pharmaceuticals, nurtured healthcare specialists and streamlined the bureaucracy – were important to the building of Japan's post-war industry. The authoritarian nature of the Occupation regime ensured the swift and effective execution of these reforms.[19]

The pharmaceutical industry at this time attracted new entrants from various non-traditional sectors, ranging from food, beverages, confectionery and breweries to textiles. As there was weak demand for their non-essential goods after the war, many firms in these sectors sought new opportunities in the pharmaceutical industry by producing drugs at idle manufacturing facilities. Most firms were engaged in producing antibiotics and insecticides – and repackaging bulk imports. Very few companies were involved in any R&D. Firms could manufacture pharmaceuticals with little cost or risk: demand for medicines was strong, supplies were provided with government aid, technical assistance was readily available and the medicines produced were purchased under government procurement. Rather than the traditional pharmaceutical firms that, as import-distributors, had limited production capacities, it was these new entrants who pioneered the re-emergence of Japan's pharmaceutical industry.

As the Allied Occupation drew to a close, Japanese firms became more autonomous and began to arrange their own licensing agreements independently with foreign firms. Fewer firms relied upon the Occupation authorities or the Japanese government to mediate technology transfers. But the policies that were introduced encouraged firms to acquire manufacturing capacities through imported technologies – rather than nurture R&D capacities. This created the foundations of an imitative industry that relied on technology transfers and neglected the development of industrial R&D in Japan.

Import substitution policies in the 1950s

In the 1950s, the government helped Japanese firms develop through a combination of policies. In 1950, the Japanese government embarked upon an import-substitution policy that restricted capital inflows and imported foreign technology. Under the Foreign Exchange Control Law and the Foreign Investment Law of 1949 and 1950, respectively, capital controls were eased, but Japanese firms remained sheltered from foreign competition.[20] For example, imports were subject to strict quotas; firms required licenses to produce pharmaceuticals; and ceilings were capped on royalty rates. Foreign pharmaceutical firms, for example, were prevented from owning over 49 per cent of the equity in Japanese pharmaceutical companies. Moreover, they were prohibited from establishing wholly owned subsidiaries in Japan.[21] The joint ventures essentially encouraged foreign firms to disclose technologies to Japanese firms at little cost.

In addition, Japan did not recognize product patents until 1976. While product patents are granted to those who discover new products, process patents are granted to those who discover new methods of making existing products. Under a process patent regime, domestic companies could launch existing drugs as 'new' drugs, so long as they found another method to produce them. Moreover, drugs were approved according to Japan-specific product standards, which made drugs in Japan very different products from those overseas. Most foreign firms were deterred from investing significant time and cost to redevelop a drug in an environment where their products could be easily copied. Japan's pharmaceutical industry therefore evolved as a highly protected domestic industry.

The Korean War between 1950 and 1953 revitalized Japan's pharmaceutical industry. By 1950, many Japanese firms had begun to suffer from falling prices, lack of credit and excess capacity.[22] But special procurements by the United States for civilian and military use bolstered demand and provided solvency to struggling firms. For the Americans, shipments from Japan offered a flexible and low-cost means of providing medicines to American troops in Korea. As in other sectors of the Japanese economy, this strong external demand from the US military resuscitated many domestic firms.[23]

Japanese firms during this period developed production capacities based on technology imports, which increased from $11.9 million in 1955 to $18.4 million in 1960.[24] These technology imports ranged from antibiotics, hormonal preparations, sulfa drugs, antihistamines and anti-tubercular preparations. While most pharmaceutical technology originated from American firms such as Merck and Eli Lilly, Japan also imported technology from firms in other countries, such as Ciba in Switzerland or Behring in Germany.[25]

The industry grew slightly faster than the Japanese economy. Between 1952 and 1961, pharmaceutical production grew more than 1.5 times the rate of GDP growth.[26] Many new firms also entered the sector. The rise in production levels, however, was well in excess of demand.[27]

The excess supply of drugs began to cause strain in the distribution system. To prevent prices from falling and eroding their profits, pharmaceutical wholesalers began to form vertical groupings with manufacturers.[28] Groupings within the pharmaceutical industry were in the form of several wholesalers associated with a manufacturer who held shares in these wholesalers that specialized in the distribution of manufacturers' products in defined regions.[29] Examples included Eisai's *Chokora-kai*, Sankyo's *Sankyo-kai* and Takeda's *Uroko-kai*.[30] These vertical linkages effectively protected Japanese pharmaceutical firms as they created formidable barriers to entry for new entrants. Whether they were domestic or foreign, new entrants often faced difficulty in forming links with wholesalers and establishing distribution networks.

Also, Japan's pharmaceutical industry became more concentrated as larger firms enjoyed greater bargaining power in signing international licensing agreements and achieving economies of scale in production. By the 1960s, 11 firms had more than 1,000 workers. It was true that the Japanese pharmaceutical industry was still comprised of smaller firms than its Western counterparts. After all, more than 75 per cent of Japanese pharmaceutical firms employed fewer than 50 workers.[31] But the larger, pre-war pharmaceutical firms regained their dominance in Japan's pharmaceutical industry.

During the 1950s, both government and firms in Japan's pharmaceutical sector seemed content with the acquisition of technology and disinterested in the development of new, innovative therapies. In particular, the lack of sector-specific industrial policies to encourage R&D – at a time when the American or British governments generously rewarded innovation – severely undermined the development of a research-intensive pharmaceutical industry in Japan.[32]

Volume-based growth under universal healthcare, 1961–1975

Between 1961 and 1975, Japan's pharmaceutical industry grew through the volume production of imitative drugs. After 1961, Japanese firms embarked upon an extraordinary pace of expansion, as the government began to underwrite demand through a universal healthcare system, and continued to nurture firms through import-substitution policies. Japan's intellectual property regime, based on process patents, also protected Japanese firms from foreign firms who would have had to disclose the research results of new drug discoveries without reward to enter the Japanese market. While beneficial in the short term, Japan's intellectual property regime harmed the long-term prospects of Japanese pharmaceutical firms by creating little incentive to invest in R&D.

Thalidomide

The 1960s began with the shock of the thalidomide scandal. Distributed widely between 1957 and 1962 to treat morning sickness, thalidomide acquired notoriety when it caused tens of thousands of birth defects and deaths among babies born to patients taking the drug.[33] The United States had managed to avert a national tragedy when the Food and Drug Administration (FDA) refused to approve the drug in 1960.[34] In Germany, authorities swiftly banned the drug's use in 1961 after thalidomide was linked to the birth defects among babies.[35] But the Japanese government allowed domestic firms to distribute the drug well into 1962.[36] The Japanese government's belated response to the thalidomide tragedy revealed serious lapses in prevailing drug standards and official attitudes towards drug safety.

The creation of a domestic industry

In Japan, physicians both prescribed and dispensed prescription drugs. This practice fuelled demand for prescription drugs, because pharmaceutical firms sold drugs at discounted prices to physicians who profited from reselling their drugs at the official rate. Physicians effectively received a commission for each prescription they wrote. The government's fee-for-service system also created strong incentives for physicians to prescribe new, higher priced drugs that tended to have greater pharmaceutical price differentials. This was not only because physicians could profit from dispensing drugs, but also because the official fees for medical services rewarded physicians more for prescribing drugs than for medical consultations.[37]

The profit incentives created by physicians' dual prescribing and dispensing practice were not insignificant. The MHW revealed that, by 1989, pharmaceutical price differentials averaged around 25 per cent of official drug prices and amounted to 1.3 trillion yen a year.[38] Japanese firms were therefore incentivized to divert resources from R&D spending to marketing.

Most patients passively purchased the many drugs they were prescribed. This was because Japanese patients did not question the authority of physicians; few explanations were made of the medicines prescribed; and consumers were price insensitive.[39] The low reward for innovation and endurance of this dual prescribing and dispensing practice led Japanese firms to launch drugs that were only profitable in the Japanese market. Furthermore, the dissimilarities in regulation and standards between the Japanese and overseas markets generated reluctance among Japanese firms to make the immense investments necessary to expand into America or Europe.

The rapid rate of Japanese economic growth had raised demand for pharmaceuticals among wealthier patients. This, in turn, encouraged companies from other sectors of the economy to enter the pharmaceutical sector. By the mid-1960s, Japan became the world's second largest market.[40] The type and quality of drugs in Japan did seem inferior compared to those available in other developed markets. After all, Japan's pharmaceutical firms were smaller and had less capital compared to other industrialized nations. In 1969, for example, over 80 per cent of firms employed fewer than 50 workers, and the capital–labour ratio was $3,444 in Japan compared to $26,000 in the United States.[41]

As in other Japanese industries, many firms established central research laboratories in the 1960s. The government's new quality standards – such as good clinical practice (GCP) and good post-marketing surveillance practice (GPMSP) – introduced during this time aimed to help Japanese firms develop better quality drugs.[42] But the lack of facilities, equipment and human capital left pharmaceutical firms reliant on academia to pursue R&D.[43] Many Japanese firms lacked incentives to invest in R&D, not only because of capital limitations, but also due to the lack of facilities and equipment, the high cost of raw materials, as well as the lack of export-oriented policies supported by the MITI compared to other industrial sectors.[44]

With its governance by the MHW rather than the MITI, government policies prioritized domestic health agendas over industrial development. The government's developmental health policies were essentially guided by an overarching goal to provide universal access to drugs for Japanese citizens. To do so, the government set drug prices at fixed rate and subsidized patients who purchased prescription drugs. These policies were appropriate in the early post-war period when Japanese consumers were still poor and infectious diseases were rampant. The government was able to afford essential medicines to treat acute, life threatening diseases that required medication for only a short period of time. But these policies persisted into a period when chronic diseases of affluence became the norm.

Japanese firms did increase their R&D spending in the 1960s and 1970s, particularly as the government gradually opened its doors to foreign competition (Figure 2.1). But while R&D expenditures increased 8.5-fold between 1960 and 1975, they were still a third of figures in United States.[45] In 1972, for example, R&D

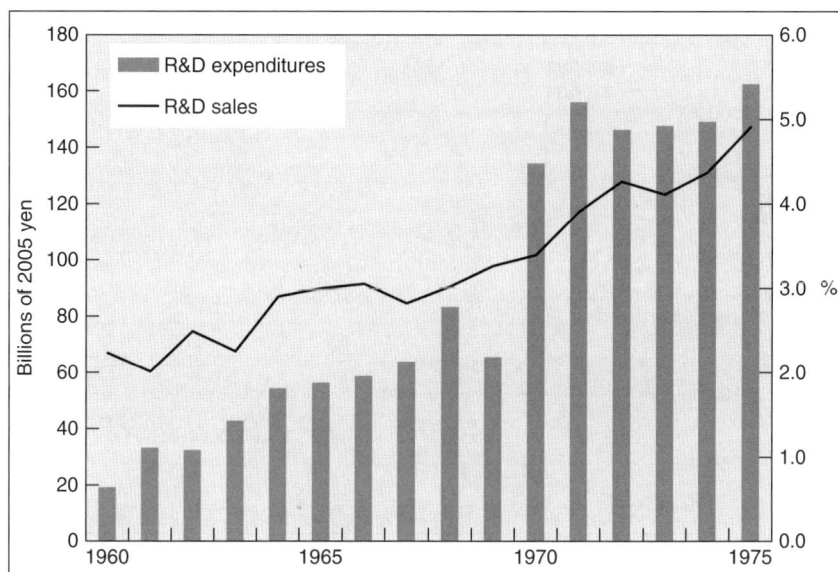

Figure 2.1 R&D expenditures, 1960–1975

Source: Office of the Prime Minister, *Kagaku Gijutsu Kenkyū Chōsa Hōkoku* [Report on the Survey of Research and Development] (various years).

expenditures as a percentage of total sales in Japan were 4.2 per cent compared to 9.2 per cent in the United States and 8.1 per cent in the United Kingdom, respectively.[46] While Japanese trade in pharmaceuticals quadrupled between 1960 and 1975, imports exceeded more than twice the value of exports over the 1960s.[47] In addition, most of Japan's exports were in relatively simple drugs, such as antibiotics and vitamins, that were shipped to the developing – rather than to the developed – world.[48]

Moreover, few Japanese drugs were recognized as drugs in other parts of the developed world. Between 1950 and 1967, less than 2 per cent of drugs introduced in the US, UK or German markets were of Japanese origin. Conversely, of drugs in Japan, 30.6 per cent were from the United States, 12.9 per cent were from Switzerland and 11.8 per cent were from Germany. Japanese drugs comprised just 24.7 per cent of the home market.[49]

Heavily protected, Japanese pharmaceutical firms in the 1960s were able to remain quite profitable without undertaking significant R&D or seeking market expansion. For example, the profitability of Japan's top 12 pharmaceutical firms averaged 5.5 per cent in 1965 and 4.0 per cent in 1975. While these leading Japanese pharmaceutical firms were much less profitable than their Western contemporaries – the profitability of the top 12 Western firms averaged 10.0 per cent in 1975 – they were still more profitable than most other sectors of the Japanese economy (Figure 2.2).[50]

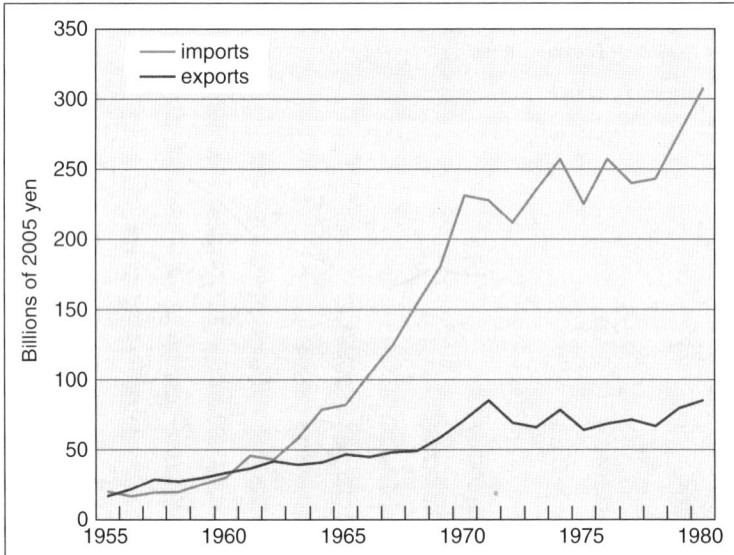

Figure 2.2 Value of pharmaceutical trade, 1955–1980

Source: Ministry of International Trade and Industry, *Tsūshō Hakusho* [White Paper on Trade] (various years).

Economic development and steps towards capital liberalization

Japan's economy grew, and in the 1960s, the international community intensified pressures on Japan to ease its restrictions on foreign direct investment (FDI). Previously, foreign firms were neither able to own a majority share in Japanese firms nor establish a wholly owned subsidiary in Japan. With its accession to the Organization for Economic Cooperation and Development (OECD) and the International Monetary Fund in 1964, Japan agreed to phase in capital liberalization. The imminent introduction of full capital liberalization and product patents incentivized firms to invest more in R&D, modernize facilities and adopt improved quality standards – as they faced greater foreign competition and more stringent criteria to gain drug approval.[51]

While the pharmaceutical industry was not fully open to foreign capital until 1975, the government gave approval for up to 50 per cent investments in 1967.[52] While Japanese firms were still much smaller than leading foreign pharmaceutical firms in terms of capitalization or sales, gaps between the West were narrowing – in profitability, R&D capacity, as well as the number and ability of workers.[53]

Product standards

The government attempted to improve Japan's drug quality standards from the 1960s through administrative guidance.[54] It did so partly in response to recurrent drug tragedies and the need to create safer drugs. In the 'Basic Policies for Drug Manufacturing Approval' in 1967, the government specified product standards for the first time.[55] While these measures improved the quality of drugs available in Japan, they were different from the standards used overseas, and essentially excluded foreign drugs from the Japanese market. Spurred by government-guaranteed demand for prescription pharmaceuticals and sheltered from foreign competition, Japan's pharmaceutical industry embarked upon a remarkable period of expansion. Pharmaceutical production levels in Japan grew 3.4-fold between 1960 and 1975.[56]

This expansion was also fuelled by the relatively low criteria placed on drugs to qualify as a new chemical entity (NCE).[57] This was because Japanese firms could launch and sell numerous new drugs with relative ease. Many of the 'new' drugs launched in Japan during the 1960s and 1970s were approved with modest improvements on existing drugs, such as more suitable doses, convenient forms of administration or fewer side effects.[58] Japanese firms launched numerous new drugs with incremental innovations and marketed these to physicians who could gain from high pharmaceutical price differentials. While Japan's pharmaceutical sector grew steadily during this period, most Japanese drugs could not be translated into overseas markets.

The gradual liberalization of capital controls from the late 1960s prompted a fresh wave of foreign entrants such as SmithKline, Eli Lilly and Wellcome.[59] But unlike other markets, foreign firms had yet to put a dent into Japan's pharmaceutical sector in the 1970s. Not only did Japan's product standards place foreign products out of the Japanese market, foreign firms were reluctant to enter a market where they were less able to recoup large R&D investments on break-through drugs. Also, foreign firms had yet to establish a marketing presence in Japan.[60]

A year of welfare for the people – and for industry: 1973

Despite its struggles in R&D, production and distribution, the government's underwriting of demand continued to help the growth of Japan's pharmaceutical industry. The impact of the government policies was particularly evident in 1973. Dubbed 'the year of welfare', the government greatly expanded health and social welfare provisions in 1973: it reduced the prescription drug cost payable by the consumer to 30 per cent; capped medical fees for high-cost treatments; and provided free healthcare for the elderly.[61] The impact of these reforms on pharmaceutical production was immediate, and while production levels had been increasing since 1961, the 1973 reforms added a fresh surge in momentum. Between 1961 and 1975, production almost tripled to 3.1 trillion yen.[62]

While the market expanded, contemporaries expressed concern about the over-production of similar therapeutic products, which led to intense competition. The lack of a strong intellectual property rights regime had allowed for the entry of many new firms, which intensified the volume-based expansion.[63] Japanese pharmaceutical firms numbered 1,359 in 1975, at a time when American or British firms were far fewer in number.[64] To gain an edge in the market, Japanese firms continued to engage in dumping and excessive bargaining in the form of additional 'samples', bribes or services. Some order was restored in 1970, when the government finally threatened to de-list the drugs of firms engaged in excessive discounting practices.[65]

Transitions to quality-based growth, 1975–1990

By the 1970s, leading Japanese firms had caught up with the leading Western firms in terms of discovery capacity, if not size or sales. Between 1975 and 1979, 4 per cent of new drugs that were launched in the majority of the G7 countries were discovered in Japan. This was a time when 29 per cent of new global products were discovered in the United States; 18 per cent were discovered in Germany; 11 per cent were discovered in Switzerland; and 1 per cent was discovered in the United Kingdom.[66] Japan's pharmaceutical industry reached a turning point, as it began to concentrate on product innovation and on the development of safer, more effective drugs.[67]

Creating a modern market: opening up and protecting intellectual property

In the mid-1970s, the government introduced two measures that aimed to modernize the market. Capital controls were finally liberalized in 1975, and product patents were introduced in 1976.[68] Both changes brought an influx of foreign firms, who could now worry less about the imitation of their products. These measures led Japanese firms to adopt a more research-intensive orientation to compete, and helped protect new discoveries made by Japanese firms.

The cost of an ageing population

By the 1980s, Japan began to feel the pressures of an ageing population. The proportion of the population aged 65 and over reached 9.1 per cent, more than double the level in 1950.[69] There was higher demand for medicines to treat diseases of affluence, and the rising healthcare costs for chronic ailments began to place a burden on Japan's universal healthcare system, which had been based on a population structure characterized by high birth rates and a large population of workers who split the cost of elderly care.[70]

Under financial pressure, the government attempted to contain healthcare costs in two major ways. First, it introduced biennial price reductions in 1981, starting with a steep, across-the-board reduction of 18.6 per cent.[71] In 1982, it ended free healthcare coverage to the elderly and introduced a small co-payment. The response was swift, and production levels peaked in 1982.[72]

The biennial price reductions of prescription pharmaceuticals had a particularly severe impact on Japanese pharmaceutical firms' incentives to invest in R&D. As the graph in Figure 2.3 indicates, while drug prices fell 5.8 per cent between 1976 and 1981, they dropped 46.1 per cent between 1981 and 1986.[73] Unlike the United States or Britain, for example, drug prices in Japan were capped and revised uniformly on a regular basis – regardless of innovative value – throughout the patent protection period. Given the limited profits they could make, Japanese firms were incentivized to launch a stream of new drugs with short product life and little innovative value in order to recoup the costs of R&D, rather than invest in more

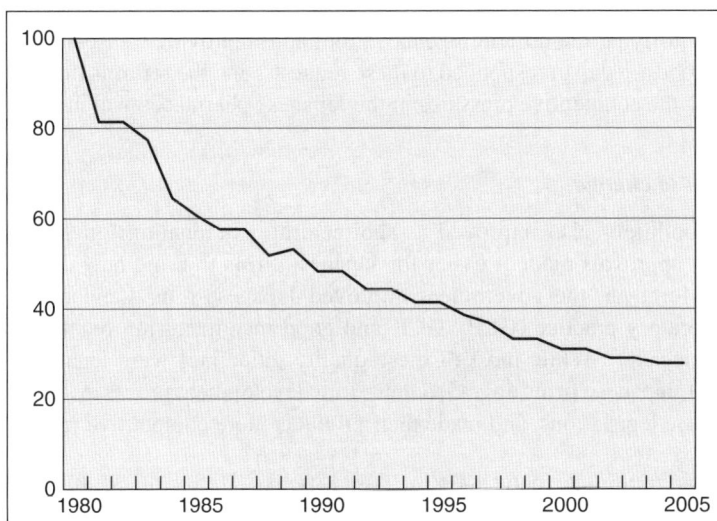

Figure 2.3 Impact of price reductions, 1980–2005 (1980 = 100)

Source: Yakuji Kenkyūkai, *Saikin no Yakumu Gyōsei* [Recent Trends in Pharmaceutical Administration] (2005), 133; Jihō, *Yakuji Handobukku* [Pharmaceutical Affairs Handbook] (various years).

Note: Drug prices in 1980 are indexed to 100.

substantial innovation. These trends hindered the industry's prospects of launching breakthrough drugs that would have been more competitive overseas.

There were several new entrants into the pharmaceutical sector during this period: foreign firms and Japanese firms from other industries. While there were 74 foreign pharmaceutical firms operating in Japan in 1970, there were 239 by 1980.[74] As Japan's various industrial sectors matured, firms from other sectors of the Japanese economy began to diversify into pharmaceuticals. New entrants came from a range of sectors, as evidenced by the textile maker Teijin, milk producers such as Snow Brand Milk Products and breweries such as Kirin Brewery.[75] These new entrants to the industry did not yet pose a serious threat to existing pharmaceutical firms. Some, however, would later become more successful as they launched innovative drugs and established their own distribution networks.

'Gaiatsu' in the Japanese pharmaceutical industry

As frictions grew between Japan and its trading partners in the 1980s, foreign governments began to place pressure on the Japanese government to deregulate and improve access to its market. These foreign pressures, or *Gaiatsu*, were particularly pronounced from the United States. In 1985, American and Japanese officials held market-oriented and sector-selective (MOSS) talks that aimed to remove barriers to market access in four sectors – including pharmaceuticals.[76] Business organizations such as the Pharmaceutical Manufacturers Association (PMA) in the United States and the European Business Council (EBC) in Europe also held regular talks with Japanese officials and requested Japan to reduce barriers by accepting foreign clinical data; clarifying the criteria for innovation; and improving transparency in the pricing process.[77] Japan responded to these requests, and the reforms that followed intensified the competitive pressures in the Japanese pharmaceutical industry.

Responses to change

Market conditions also improved as shorter drug examination times and quarterly drug approvals made it easier for Japanese firms to bring new drugs to the market. Moreover, the government improved Japanese drug standards such as good laboratory practice (GLP), GCP, and good manufacturing practice (GMP) over the decade.[78] While most of these quality guidelines were legally enacted after 1990, Japanese firms upgraded their drug development processes in anticipation of these legislations, and made their products more competitive in the global market.

Between 1975 and 1990, the key change in Japan's pharmaceutical industry was a shift from a manufacturing-based to a knowledge-based industry. A 1987 revision in Japan's patent law further encouraged firms to invest in R&D, as it became possible to extend the effective life of a patent by 5 years and recover the time lost in the drug testing and approval process.[79] In 1970, Japanese firms invested 3.0 per cent of sales in R&D, but by 1990, these figures had increased to 8.0 per cent (Figure 2.4).[80]

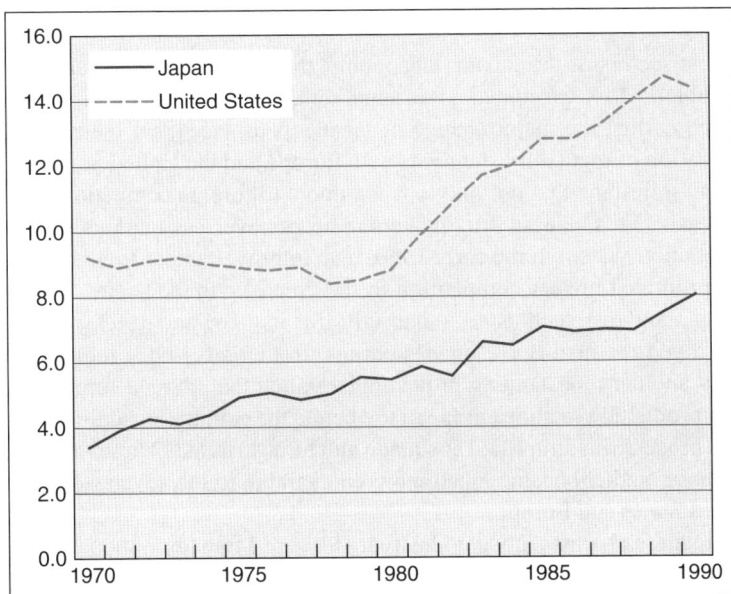

Figure 2.4 R&D as a percentage of sales, 1970–1990

Source: Office of the Prime Minister, *Kagaku Gijutsu Kenkyū Chōsa Hōkoku* [Report on the Survey of Research and Development] (various years); Management and Coordination Agency, *Kagaku Gijutsu Kenkyū Chōsa Hōkoku* [Report on the Survey of Research and Development] (various years); Pharmaceutical Research and Manufacturers of America. *Pharmaceutical Industry Profile 2008* (2008), 53.

Note: It is recognized that there is considerable discrepancy in US R&D statistics produced by the National Science Foundation and the Pharmaceutical Research and Manufacturers of America (PhRMA). This book has used PhRMA data, for which there are more consecutive data. For reasons behind the difference in figures, see Joseph Golec and John Vernon, "Measuring US Pharmaceutical Industry R&D Spending." *Pharmacoeconomics* 26, no. 12 (2008): 1005–1017.

Over the 1980s, Japan had discovered 24.1 per cent of the world's new therapeutic substances, compared to 26.6 per cent in the United States and 48.7 per cent in Western Europe.[81] In the meanwhile, the market continued to expand in terms of production and trade.[82] Japan's export destinations also shifted from the developing to the developed world.[83]

Despite the influx of foreign firms, the majority of Japanese firms had yet to establish a substantial international presence. Japanese firms with overseas operations did triple from 30 to 91 between 1975 and 1990. In 2000, however, less than a quarter of the 1,123 Japanese pharmaceutical firms had expanded abroad.[84] Japanese firms neither developed drugs that would be marketable abroad nor developed the distribution networks that might have allowed them to be more competitive in the global market.[85]

Attempts to build a R&D-intensive, global pharmaceutical industry, 1990–2008

As in most sectors of the Japanese economy, the bursting of the country's asset-price bubble in 1990 prompted a reorientation and modernization of industry. As mentioned earlier, the major change in Japan's pharmaceutical industry was the harmonization of regulatory standards with Europe and the United States. It was a significant milestone that not only opened doors to foreign competition, but also made it easier for Japanese drug makers to access overseas markets. Reforms to the distribution system in the early 1990s also improved transparency in the market and prompted greater competition in the domestic market. The enforcement of quality standards such as GCP and GPMSP in 1990 and 1993, respectively, also improved the quality of Japanese drugs. In the late 1990s, the government discarded another longstanding protectionist policy that obliged foreign firms to establish production facilities in Japan to operate the country. In addition, the drug approval process was simplified and made more transparent.[86] These reforms made the Japanese market became much more comparable to the advanced markets of the United States and Europe.

The Japanese pharmaceutical industry underwent a transformation in the 1990s, as it reorganized, became more global and research-intensive. It was, however, a belated change. The industry continued to expand in terms of production, trade and R&D. But Japan's pharmaceutical industry was still much smaller than global leaders in terms of sales, R&D expenditures or value of exports, and the country remained a net importer of pharmaceuticals.[87] In 2000, less than a quarter of Japanese firms had expanded abroad.[88]

The HIV scandal and an enduring drug lag

A political fallout from an HIV blood scandal made it much more costly for pharmaceutical firms to develop drugs in Japan in the 1990s. This scandal came to light after Japanese haemophiliacs contracted HIV from the circulation of untreated blood products. Despite knowledge over the potential dangers of unheated blood products, the MHW had allowed for their circulation in order to protect Japan's leading provider of blood products. This firm, Green Cross Corp., was not yet prepared to produce heat-treated blood products that were available abroad.[89]

For the Japanese pharmaceutical industry, this scandal was particularly damaging in creating a drug lag, caused by an MHW that was much more cautious and tentative in the drug approval process. By 2000, the average time for drug approval in Japan was 28.5 months compared to 16.5 months in the United States.[90] Between 2000 and 2005, 70 per cent of new drugs approved in Japan were launched 4 years after the United States or Europe.[91] For many firms, R&D in Japan became less attractive, as longer assessment times raised the cost of drug development and undermined the capacity of firms to compete with their rivals abroad.

While the major response to the drug scandal was a delay in the drug approval process, there was a silver lining. The scandal also cut excess demand for unnecessary medicines and contributed to the fall in production levels over the 1990s. The widely publicized scandal produced better-informed patients more sceptical of medicines, increasingly sensitive to out-of-pocket drug expenses, and reluctant to spend on minor medicines – particularly under economic recession.

Distribution reform in 1990: a much needed clean up

In the Japanese pharmaceutical industry, the supply chain linking manufacturers to patients had typically involved two intermediaries: wholesalers and physicians. Since 1951, the retail price of prescription drugs had been set by the government. As a result, dispensing physicians increased their margins by bargaining down the price paid to wholesalers. Until 1992, pharmaceutical manufacturers usually entered into resale price maintenance agreements with wholesalers. These agreements limited the competitive pressure on Japan's many small and inefficient wholesalers and made it difficult for new entrants to sell drugs in Japan.[92] In the 1990s, the distribution of pharmaceuticals changed in ways that promised to increase pharmaceutical innovation. These changes, however, came too late to turn the industry into a global leader.

In 1991, the government introduced several measures to reform the distribution system. These measures were, to a large extent, a response to foreign pressures to reduce barriers to entry into the Japanese market, such as the Structural Impediments Initiative with the United States between 1989 and 1990.[93] As part of the distribution reforms, resale price maintenance in pharmaceuticals was prohibited.[94] This measure basically destroyed the vertical groupings that had long persisted between select wholesalers and manufacturers and lowered barriers to entry.[95] Now able to negotiate the price at which they supplied pharmaceuticals to physicians, wholesalers no longer needed to align themselves with a particular manufacturer. These reforms sparked a wave of consolidation among wholesalers.[96] While there were 403 wholesalers in Japan in 1990, there were only 232 by 2000.[97]

Another part of distribution reform involved a change to the government's method of reviewing drug prices so that the practice of dispensing drugs became less lucrative. Before the 1990s, drug prices in Japan were revised at the ninetieth or eighty-first percentile point of wholesale prices when arranged in an ascending scale.[98] These revisions had facilitated the volume-based expansion of the industry. In order to keep prices from falling, and to expand market share, firms responded by selling 10 or 19 per cent of the total volume of drugs at a higher price while selling the remainder at low prices. In order to reflect market prices more accurately, the new revisions were based on a weighted average of all existing drug prices beyond a specified range of the official price. After this 'reasonable zone method' was introduced, many physicians began to abandon the business of dispensing drugs to patients. In 1990, 87.2 per cent of physicians dispensed drugs; by 2005, only 45.9 per cent of physicians did so.[99]

These changes caused a shift in the strategies of pharmaceutical firms. No longer able to provide generous discounts as a way of inducing physicians to prescribe their drugs, pharmaceutical firms began to invest more in the education of marketing representatives so as to compete on the basis of quality. The distribution reforms reincentivized manufacturers to develop higher priced drugs with greater innovative value that could better compete in the global market.

Sweeping changes in the regulatory environment

Over the 1990s, Japanese drugs increasingly gained approval in other Western markets as the government decided to harmonize its pharmaceutical regulations with the United States and Europe. In 1990, the three regions formed The International Conference on Harmonisation of Technical Requirements for Registration of Pharmaceuticals for Human Use (ICH) to reduce the cost and time involved in duplicating drug development across countries. Japanese drugs could now be more easily approved in the United States and Europe, just as European and American drugs could more easily be approved in Japan. By using resources efficiently, the ICH also aimed to bring quality drugs more quickly to the market.[100]

The adoption of American and European regulations strengthened the criteria for innovation and encouraged Japanese firms to develop drugs that could be approved and successful in world markets.[101] As harmonization made it easier for Japanese firms to access the large markets of Europe and the United States, more firms ventured abroad. In 1990, 91 firms had expanded into overseas markets; by 2005, there were 284.[102] At home, Japanese firms were forced to compete with a greater number of foreign firms as harmonization improved access to the Japanese market.[103] In 1990, no foreign firms were among the top ten Japanese pharmaceutical firms.[104] By 2005, there were two: Pfizer and Novartis.[105]

This momentum for reform continued into the late 1990s. For example, Japanese authorities lowered barriers to foreign entry by dismissing the Japanese language requirement in filing patent applications, disposing of the requirement to conduct clinical trials on Japanese subjects, eliminating the local manufacturing requirement for foreign firms and creating tax incentives for R&D.[106] In 1997, the government also allowed firms to operate more flexibly by recognizing the use of contract research organizations (CROs) to improve efficiency in drug development.[107] Additionally, these CROs further opened the Japanese market, as foreign firms no longer had to acquire drug development expertise specific to the Japanese market.

In many countries, researchers can work for both academia and industry, which facilitates knowledge transfers and the commercialization of academic research. In Japan, academics at national and public universities were considered to be civil servants and were governed by the Civil Service Code.[108] Until 1998, Japanese academics were not allowed to take outside employment. The lack of movement of researchers between academia and industry meant that Japan's pharmaceutical industry was disadvantaged compared to other countries that benefited from the exchange of knowledge between industry and academia. Also, this rule discouraged academics working on pharmaceuticals from commercializing their research.[109] As Hashimoto has noted, informal ties between industrial and academic researchers have been numerous. However, the lack of clear property rights and formal transfer mechanisms impeded the commercialization of Japanese university discoveries.

In 2000, however, the government made it possible for academics to establish companies and made it easier for academics to move between academia and industry.[110] In so doing, the Japanese government hoped that, as in other countries, university start-ups might help translate the fruits of academic research into commercial products.[111]

In addition, the Japanese labour market had become more fluid since the burst of the bubble. An increasing number of firms welcomed mid-career hires and replaced seniority-based pay with meritocratic pay. The improved incentive structure and cross-pollination of ideas across different organizations also strengthened Japan's environment for drug discovery and development.

Enduring barriers in drug development and approval

However, both drug development and approval in Japan remained an extremely costly, inefficient and time-consuming affair compared to other countries.[112] Japan had neither a structured clinical trial system nor an adequate number of qualified reviewers. Japanese trials were, in fact, much less equipped in relation to comparable systems abroad. For example, there has been no system or standards established to conduct clinical trials in Japanese hospitals; in the past, most were conducted through personal connections, on an ad-hoc basis.[113]

In addition, Japanese scientists, physicians and patients, all faced few incentives to participate in clinical trials. For scientists, clinical research in Japan was held in lower regard compared to more fundamental research. Japanese physicians, in the meanwhile, treated the highest number of patients per day among OECD countries and faced little time or financial incentive to participate in trials. Moreover, with most healthcare costs covered under a universal healthcare system, Japanese patients did not face similar financial incentives to undergo clinical trials as their counterparts in private heathcare systems such as the United States.[114]

Furthermore, the Japanese system lacked qualified personnel capable of evaluating drugs. Even in 2004, Japan's Pharmaceuticals and Medical Devices Agency maintained 11 medical reviewers among 71 employees. By comparison, the FDA employed approximately 336 medical reviewers among 2,735 employees.[115] These penalties to investments in innovation deterred firms in Japan from developing therapies and from pursuing drugs that might be globally competitive.

The impact of a greying population and cost containment policies

In the 1990s, Japan's ageing population further intensified the financial pressures on the national health insurance system. The proportion of the population aged 65 and over increased from 12.0 per cent to 17.8 per cent between 1990 and 2000.[116] In response, the government – who subsidized the cost of prescription drugs – continued to legislate reductions in the price of prescription drugs.[117]

The government's policy of containing drug prices reduced the willingness of firms to reinvest their profits in R&D. The potential profits of developing a new drug in Japan were much smaller than the United States, for example, where there were no price restrictions on drugs. They were also smaller than the United Kingdom or Germany, where profit controls or reference pricing systems effectively capped drug prices, but where firms could still set their own drug prices. By 2003, price indices measured in standard units revealed that, when drug prices in the United States were set at 1, prices in Germany, France, UK and Japan compared at 0.52, 0.49, 0.47, and 0.33, respectively.[118] This had a heavy impact on Japanese pharmaceutical firms who, unlike their American counterparts, for example, could not rely on government funding for industrial R&D.[119] It was particularly crucial at a time when R&D processes were becoming increasingly costly and sophisticated.[120] The limited ability to grow also meant that many Japanese firms lacked the capital to acquire foreign firms and expand.

The government's policy of cost containment had another effect: the growth of Japan's generics market. Until very recently, the generics market in Japan was much smaller than its overseas counterparts. The historically low penetration of generics in Japan was due to several reasons. These included: the perception of inferior quality of generic medicines; the preference towards branded drugs among physicians and patients; and the limited profits to be made by physicians from pharmaceutical price differentials by prescribing low-priced generics. Generic medicines also remained less popular in Japan because of the lack of generic substitution rights by Japanese pharmacists; slower review times in the drug approval process, and difficulties in working with Japanese pharmaceutical distributors – many of whom were closely tied to established branded manufacturers.[121]

However, with the government's continued promotion of generics since the millennium – from raising physicians' prescription services fee for generics to slashing the prices of branded drugs where generic versions were available – the market had grown to 306.2 billion yen by 2007.[122] Generics accounted for 17.2 per cent of prescriptions dispensed in volume terms by 2008, although this remained much lower than generic penetration rates in the United States, Britain or Germany – where generics accounted for over 60 per cent of prescriptions dispensed.[123] Yet many firms view the Japanese generics market to have significant growth potential, as may be evident from high profile mergers and acquisitions (M&A) such as Daiichi-Sankyo's acquisition of the Indian generics firm Rambaxy and Kowa's joint venture with the Israeli generics firm Teva in 2008.[124]

Effects of globalization

Facing more rigorous standards and sophisticated technologies in R&D and greater competition from foreign firms, Japanese firms continued to intensify their R&D orientation after 1990. Between 1990 and 2005, R&D expenditures almost doubled while R&D expenditures as a percentage of sales rose from 8.0 per cent to 10.0 per cent. Japanese firms also became net exporters of pharmaceutical technology after 1997.[125] But in global context, these figures remained much smaller than the leading pharmaceutical markets. For example, the average R&D budgets of the top ten Japanese firms were still about one-fifth of the average of the top Western companies in 2000.[126]

Japan's pharmaceutical industry remained a net importer of pharmaceuticals (Figure 2.5). In 2007, Japan still imported 3.4 times more drugs than it exported, with a deficit of 5.8 billion dollars.[127] While these figures were smaller than the US trade deficit in pharmaceuticals of around $20 billion, far fewer Japanese drugs were recognized globally compared to those produced by American or European firms. In 1999, only one eighth of NCEs launched by Japanese firms became international, compared to more than one-third among US and European firms. In addition, although foreign sales among Japanese firms increased, they still accounted for only around a fifth of those among US and European firms.[128] Also, in 2007, Japan's top three pharmaceutical firms Takeda, Astellas and Daiichi Sankyo derived 50.5 per cent, 50.3 per cent and 40.8 per cent of their sales from overseas markets, respectively. These figures were comparable to those of the top three global firms, Pfizer, GlaxoSmithKline and Sanofi-Aventis who derived 52.2 per cent, 68.1 per cent and 56.6 per cent of sales from overseas markets, respectively.[129] While the gap in R&D expenditures widened between Japanese firms and leading Western firms in the 1990s, figures for the proportion of foreign sales to total sales did narrow.

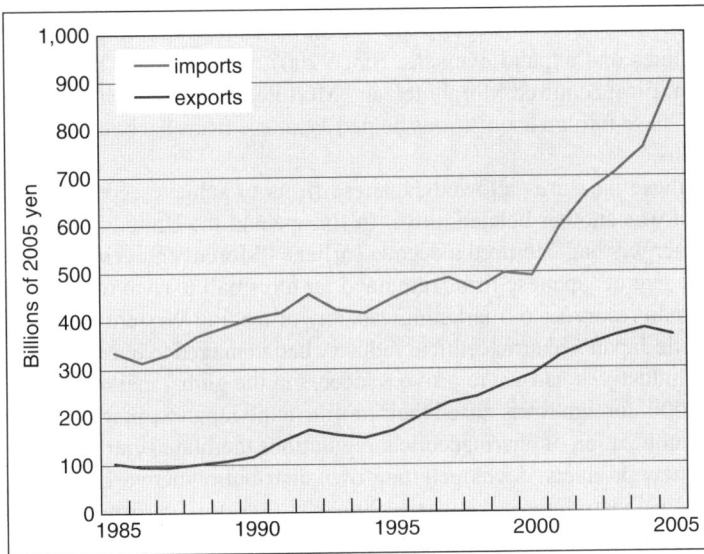

Figure 2.5 Value of pharmaceutical trade, 1985–2005

Source: Ministry of International Trade and Industry, *Tsūshō Hakusho* [White Paper on Trade] (various years); Ministry of Economy Trade and Industry. *Bōeki Dōkō Dētabēsu* [Database on Trends in Trade] (various years).

As Japanese firms reorganized and expanded into overseas markets in the 1990s, the performance gap widened between Japanese firms that were globally competitive and those that were domestically oriented.[130] Leading Japanese firms such as Takeda increasingly transferred their core operations abroad where there were both larger markets and greater reward for innovation – such as the United States. The nationality of these globally oriented Japanese firms become increasingly questionable, as while management was located in Japan, both the sources of innovation and potential for growth were located overseas.

These trends are reflected in the decline of clinical trials conducted in Japan versus the rise of clinical trials conducted abroad.[131] This was because of the higher cost and longer duration of clinical trials conducted in Japan in comparison to the United States or Europe.[132] Drug approval times also took longer, not only because of the reluctance to approve new drugs after the HIV blood tragedy, but also because of the dispersion of clinical trials across many hospitals, the adoption of more rigorous clinical trial standards and severe lack of qualified personnel to evaluate new drugs relative to the United States or Europe.[133]

From the late 1990s, a wave of mergers swept the Japanese pharmaceutical industry as firms aimed to achieve scale economies and strengthen R&D operations to survive global competition. The first mergers in Japan began with Mitsubishi Chemicals merging with Tokyo Tanabe into Tokyo Mitsubishi Pharmaceutical in 1999, and its merger with Welfide in 2001.[134] Several other mergers followed, such as Yamanouchi and Fujisawa merging into Astellas, and Daiichi and Sankyo merging into Daiichi Sankyo in 2005.[135]

Japanese firms have also begun to pursue the acquisition of foreign firms to boost their pipelines and expand overseas. Since 2007, for example, Takeda acquired Millenium, Eisai acquired Morphotek and MGI Pharma, while Shionogi acquired Sciele.[136] These foreign acquisitions helped Japanese firms become stronger, more global firms.

While these measures allowed Japanese firms to achieve economies of scale in R&D, it was another belated move. In Europe and the United States, a similar wave of mergers had occurred a decade earlier.[137] Moreover, even with the M&A boom, the size of Japanese firms remained far too small to rival the sales, profits, R&D, human resources or marketing capacity of leading Western pharmaceutical firms. While Japan's pharmaceutical industry had managed to become a profitable domestic industry, it had yet to prove a success in the global market.

After 2000, foreign firms raised their profile in the Japanese market, particularly as the harmonization of pharmaceutical regulations facilitated entry. Foreign firms launched new products, developed their own distribution networks and increased their sales in Japan. Indeed, between 1996 and 2005, foreign firms accounted for more than 70 per cent of Japan's new drug approvals and were a major source of growth in Japan's pharmaceutical industry.[138] Several foreign firms even made high-profile acquisitions, such as Roche's purchase of Chugai in 2002.[139]

Japan's pharmaceutical industry at the turn of the twenty-first century presented a mixed picture. Japanese firms after the 1990s were stronger and dynamic, more R&D-intensive and global. The industry continued to grow in terms of production,

R&D investments, sales and overseas operations. But economic recession, combined with rigid and outdated institutional structures, also dampened growth prospects. The number of NCEs discovered in Japan declined relative to other countries in the 1990s, and Japan no longer led NCE launches after 1995.[140] Biennial price reductions also discouraged new entries into the Japanese market.[141] Even with the M&A boom, the size of Japanese firms remained far too small to rival the sales, profits, R&D, human resources or marketing capacity of leading Western pharmaceutical firms. For decades, Japan's pharmaceutical industry had been a highly successful domestic industry. But it had yet to become a global leader.

The relative weakness of Japan's pharmaceutical industry: a restatement

There are several reasons why Japan did not develop a strong, globally competitive pharmaceutical industry. The major reasons for this include: the weak incentives for pharmaceutical firms to invest in R&D; the government's protectionist policies; and the smaller size of Japanese pharmaceutical firms compared to leading global firms. The underperformance of Japan's pharmaceutical industry can also be explained by: the historical origins of Japanese pharmaceutical firms; barriers to entrepreneurship among university academics; as well as the lack of initiative taken by Japanese firms to expand into overseas markets.

3   Developing a modern industry

The antibiotics sector

This book argues that Japanese pharmaceutical firms were historically much smaller, less R&D-intensive and more domestically oriented in comparison with other developed countries such as the United States, the United Kingdom and Switzerland. Japan's pharmaceutical industry also remained relatively weak in comparison with the country's leading industries such as automobiles and electronics. But some sectors of the Japanese pharmaceutical industry were much stronger than others. This was particularly true of Japan's antibiotics sector. Antibiotics have been Japan's leading pharmaceutical export and have, at times, recorded a trade surplus.[1]

This chapter examines the history of the Japanese antibiotics sector and provides several explanations for its strong performance. The antibiotics sector emerged in the late 1940s under the guidance of the American Occupation forces. By the early 1980s, Japanese firms had become global leaders in antibiotics.[2] In the mid-1980s, for example, antibiotics developed in Japan and produced under licence by American firms accounted for 20 per cent of the US antibiotics market.[3]

From the early post-war period, Japanese pharmaceutical firms were able to discover innovative antibiotics. In fact, some of the antibiotics discovered and developed by Japanese firms in the 1950s remain in worldwide use to date. In the 1990s, the majority of firms involved in antibiotic research in the world were still Japanese or American.[4] Japanese firms also dominated the domestic market with their own products – even after the government's protectionist policies were lifted in the mid-1970s.[5]

This chapter examines the development of the antibiotics sector over five phases. In the first phase between 1945 and 1949, the antibiotics sector emerged under the American Occupation. This was followed by the rise of Japanese antibiotic discoveries and the acquisition of production capacities in a protected market via technology imports between 1950 and 1961. During the third phase between 1961 and 1975, the antibiotics sector experienced volume-based expansion under universal healthcare while developing R&D capacities through process innovation. This was followed by a phase of government deregulation, which encouraged the development of R&D capacities in product innovation via capital liberalization and a new product patent regime between 1975 and 1990. Since the burst of the bubble in 1990 to 2005, the industry matured alongside efforts to harmonize regulatory guidelines with international standards under ICH.[6] The chapter concludes by providing an explanation for the strong performance of the Japanese antibiotics sector.

Japan's antibiotics sector during the Allied Occupation period

The creation of the antibiotics sector after 1945 was important for several reasons. First, antibiotics dramatically improved public health conditions in Japan, where many were suffering from infectious diseases. Second, antibiotics were the foundation of the modern Japanese pharmaceutical industry.[7] This section follows the experience of Japanese firms in establishing the antibiotics sector through the first antibiotic, penicillin – and later, streptomycin. It considers the reasons behind the remarkable rise of Japan's antibiotics sector over the late 1940s.

Early efforts to produce antibiotics

Antibiotics are substances that kill or inhibit the growth of other microbes. The age of antibiotics began with the discovery of penicillin by Alexander Fleming in 1929. Fleming, a bacteriologist at the University of London, accidentally discovered penicillin when he noticed that a mould that had contaminated one of his bacterial cultures had caused the bacteria to deteriorate.[8] With its remarkable efficacy in treating infectious diseases, penicillin revolutionized the practice of medicine.[9] While scientists had developed other antibacterials such as alkaloids and sulfa drugs in the first half of the twentieth century, it was penicillin that gave birth to the modern antibiotics era.

Although British scientists had discovered penicillin, it was the US firms such as Merck, Squibb, Lederle and Pfizer that were able to commercialize penicillin during the Second World War.[10] Fleming had abandoned research on penicillin in 1929 after he found it difficult to isolate the substance and grew increasingly sceptical of its viability as an actual drug.[11] While Oxford scientists led by Howard Florey, Ernest Chain and Normal Heatley took up penicillin research in the late 1930s, they could not interest British firms such as ICI or Boots in commercializing the drug. It was only after Florey and Heatley brought penicillin to the attention of the United States in 1941 that the US government and the leading American firms, working together, were able to mass-produce penicillin in 1943.[12]

The Japanese Army learned of penicillin in late 1943. Since 1942, the Ministry of Foreign Affairs and the Ministry of Education had operated an information service that dispatched recent Western medical journals from Germany via submarine. These publications heightened the Army's interest in penicillin production.[13] One article in the *Klinische Wochenschrift* was of particular interest, as it contained abstracts of penicillin related papers published by the Oxford Group between 1940 and 1943.[14]

Upon reading these articles, Katsuhiko Inagaki of the Army Medical School established a small research group in January 1944 to explore penicillin production in Japan. Inagaki called upon leading scientists at his Alma Mater, the

University of Tokyo – such as Yūsuke Sumiki and Hamao Umezawa – to collaborate on this project.[15] But what truly jumpstarted penicillin production in Japan was a newspaper article published on 28 January 1944. A national daily, *Asahi Shimbun*, erroneously reported that Winston Churchill had been cured of pneumonia with a new drug called penicillin.[16] While later reports clarified that the British premier had actually been cured by sulfa drugs, the Japanese Army immediately requested its medical school to organize a production committee within two to three days, and to supply the Army with penicillin by August of that year.[17] At the first Penicillin Committee held on 1 February 1944, members of the Army Military School and scientists at Japanese universities decided upon how to produce penicillin.[18]

The Army Medical School ran Japan's wartime penicillin project. The Army organized several research groups comprised of Japanese academic scientists and requested them to inform the Army of their research results through detailed reports.[19] By international standards, it was a small-scale project: a mere 1.9 billion yen project compared to the 63.5 billion yen spent to develop penicillin by the United States.[20] Nevertheless, Japanese scientists began to produce penicillin by the end of 1944.[21]

The two facilities used to produce penicillin were selected by members of the Penicillin Committee. Inagaki, who found striking similarities between milk production plants and images of penicillin production plants abroad, contacted Morinaga president Hanzsaburō Matsuzaki, and requested that the confectioner and milk producer cooperate in penicillin production. Accordingly, Morinaga produced its first batch of penicillin at its Mishima plant with the help of Penicillin Committee scientists in December 1944. The sulfa drug maker Banyu Pharmaceuticals followed shortly thereafter, producing its first batch of penicillin at its Okazaki plant in February 1945.[22] The penicillin produced during this time was still low in volume, of limited efficacy and reached few patients. But Japanese firms – still operating during the war – were able to produce some penicillin under the guidance of the Army and university scientists for military purposes.[23]

The first year of the Occupation

The rise of Japan's post-war antibiotics sector – and its post-war pharmaceutical industry – began with the rebuilding of penicillin production capacities that began during the Second World War.[24] With its wartime experience, Japan was equipped with a network of scientists in universities and firms to re-engage in penicillin production. To a certain extent, the rapid rise of Japan's penicillin industry was also possible because Japan's antibiotics makers had sustained relatively little damage during the war.[25]

In the immediate post-war period, Japanese firms faced high demand for therapies that might cure infectious disease. The lack of foodstuffs and unsanitary conditions heightened morbidity and mortality levels for a range of infectious diseases, including tuberculosis, dysentery and diphtheria.[26] Repatriated soldiers also brought a fresh surge in morbidity levels as they carried infectious diseases from foreign lands.[27]

As a growing number of firms began to produce penicillin, the Occupation authorities were confronted with the need to control the quality and prices of penicillin in Japan. Unapproved, counterfeit or mislabelled products were rife, and a large volume of penicillin of dubious quality was traded on the black market.[28] In 1946, the GHQ banned sales of penicillin produced in Japan because of its limited efficacy and heavy side effects.[29] The Occupation authorities decided to improve penicillin production in Japan – both for the Japanese and the American Army stationed in Japan.

The Allies' decision to improve penicillin production in Japan was not entirely based on altruistic motives. For the GHQ, enabling Japanese firms to mass-produce antibiotics offered a more cost-effective means of public health administration and of providing antibiotics to American troops in Japan.[30] In fact, approximately 60 per cent of the first penicillin ration was distributed to treat syphilis in the American Army at the Recreation and Amusement Association and Yoshiwara hospitals, while another 30 per cent was used to treat bronchitis among Japanese civilians.[31]

Given the costs involved in communication, transport and time, it was much cheaper and convenient to produce antibiotics in Japan using improved domestic facilities, rather than import antibiotics from the United States. Additional supplies were imported from the American Red Cross, UNICEF, LARA and CARE, but these could not fully satisfy domestic demand.[32] Production in Japan could also be more easily monitored and adjusted to fluctuations in demand. Also, improving public health conditions in Japan was expected to win the loyalty of the Japanese, and help the Occupation authorities achieve their broader agendas to democratize and demilitarize Japan – and prevent the country from becoming Communist.[33]

As an occupied nation, Japan was in a unique situation where the GHQ had absolute authority. The Occupation forces were able to build an antibiotics sector in Japan without heavy opposition from vested interests. The early Japanese antibiotics sector therefore caught up quickly with other advanced nations, equipped with modern technology, regulatory standards and the expertise necessary for subsequent development.

The GHQ introduced several measures to improve the conditions of Japan's penicillin market during the first year of the Occupation. In January 1946, the Occupation authorities requested scientists at the University of Tokyo to evaluate the quality of penicillin submitted by potential manufacturers to the government for manufacturing approval.[34] A Penicillin Ration Committee comprised of university professors was formed in June 1946 to help coordinate the distribution of scarce penicillin supplies.[35] The distribution routes were based on Japan's wartime rationing organizations, such as the Medicines Control Company (*Iyakuhin Tōsei Kabushiki Kaisha*).[36] The creation of these routes helped restore some order to the chaos of pharmaceutical distribution in the immediate post-war period.

The GHQ also requested the formation of a forum to exchange information on penicillin production between government, industry and academia.[37] The Japan Penicillin Association (*Nihon Penishirin Kyōkai*) as was established on 15 August

1946, and was led by the early penicillin makers Banyu, Morinaga, Wakamoto and Yaesu. An academic organization, the Japan Penicillin Research Association (*Nihon Penishirin Gakujutsu Kyōgikai*) was established soon thereafter – a successor to the wartime Japan Antibiotic Penicillin Research Committee that was dissolved in 1945.[38] But what truly transformed penicillin production in Japan were a series of technology transfers provided through Jackson Foster, a scientific consultant appointed by the GHQ.

Crawford Sams and Jackson Foster

> I have sent back for a technician who will show your manufacturers how to make high potency penicillin and we and we are working with both your manufacturers and the Ministry to produce good penicillin, which will be sold in adequate doses.
> (Crawford F. Sams, 'Address to Tokyo Pharmacists', 7 March 1946)[39]

During the Occupation, Japan's pharmaceutical industry was regulated by the Public Health and Welfare Section led by Colonel Crawford F. Sams.[40] A physician by training, Sams was Brigadier General of the US Army and in charge of reforms in public health and welfare. Under Sams' administration, the Occupation played a crucial role in the building of Japan's antibiotics industry by orchestrating the direct transfer of penicillin technology. The most important technology transfers occurred in 1946 and 1947, when Jackson Foster visited Japan.[41] Foster was an industrial scientist who had been involved in the commercialization of penicillin at Merck in the United States during the Second World War.[42] The American scientist's direct transfer of penicillin technology was essential to the eventual mass production of penicillin in Japan.

Foster not only imparted his knowledge of penicillin to the Japanese, but also offered the strains of bacteria found to be effective in producing penicillin in the United States. Perhaps the most significant event was a three-day symposium on penicillin production held in November 1946.[43] The event was attended by 380 leading figures in Japan, representing government, industry and academia.[44] After the lectures, Foster provided the University of Tokyo with the right strains for both surface culture production and for deep-tank production, as well as a petroleum can full of corn steep liquor – which were then distributed to researchers throughout Japan. During his five-month stay, Foster also provided direct guidance at various production plants across Japan.[45]

The Occupation authorities further nurtured the development of penicillin production in Japan by establishing research laboratories, which promoted the diffusion of penicillin technology across government, industry and academia, in various regions of Japan.[46] The GHQ's decision to enable Japanese firms to produce penicillin was a windfall for the Japanese. After all, the United States had invested six years and 20 million dollars in research to develop penicillin technology.[47] The direct transfer of this technology enabled Japan to leapfrog over investments and accomplishments that would have been impossible for a war-torn economy.

Putting Foster's gift to work

Helped by the interventions of the Occupation forces, Japan's antibiotics sector grew quickly. By 1951, Japanese firms produced 147 million units.[48] Penicillin production rose, both as existing firms acquired mass-production capacities, and as new firms began to produce penicillin. While 'shortages of critical raw materials, fuel, and power' remained a problem, in 1948, Japan became the third country after the United States and the United Kingdom to become self-sufficient in penicillin.[49]

A major turning point occurred in 1948, when Japanese firms acquired mass production capacities.[50] Until that time, Japanese firms produced penicillin from surface grown cultures in thousands of glass bottles. While Japanese scientists did manage to increase yields by improving culture media and penicillin strains, this did not lead to a substantial rise in production levels.[51] It was only after milk bottles were replaced with fermentation tanks that Japanese firms were to mass-produce penicillin and satisfy domestic demand.[52] Indeed, between 1947 and 1948, penicillin production increased 21-fold.[53]

The mass production of penicillin led to a dramatic fall in prices – and expanded access to penicillin for Japanese citizens.[54] Despite general inflation, penicillin prices plummeted 62 per cent from 1,333 yen in 1947 to 500 yen in 1948 (Figure 3.1). In fact, penicillin prices fell by 70 per cent in both 1949 and 1950, and by 56 per cent in 1951.[55]

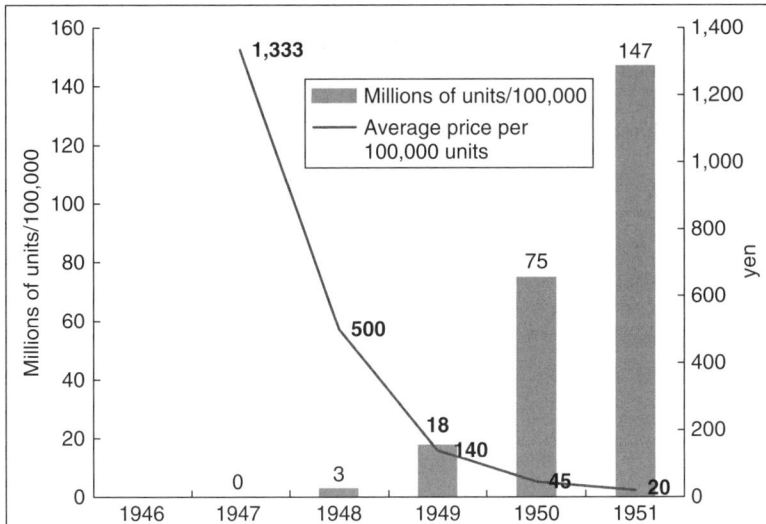

Figure 3.1 Penicillin production and prices, 1946–1951 (nominal)

Source: General Headquarters, Supreme Commander for the Allied Powers, Public Health and Welfare Section, *Public Health and Welfare in Japan* (1949), 123.

The growth of Japan's nascent penicillin industry was also supported by several other measures. In January 1947, for example, the government introduced a rule to secure production materials for specific products, such as medicines.[56] The Occupation forces also imported equipment and machinery necessary 'to aid in indigenous pharmaceutical production and to provide high standard testing equipment' for Japan's National Institute of Health.[57]

Thinning out

Attracted to the low-risk, yet high-profit potentials of penicillin manufacture, many Japanese firms began to produce antibiotics in the late 1940s. In fact, the entry of so many firms made Japan's antibiotics sector intensely competitive. Top penicillin makers also changed rapidly. In 1946, the top five penicillin makers were Banyu, Meiji Seika, Yashima Kagaku, Daito Shokusan and Showa Yakuhin. In 1951, the top five were Nippon Kayaku, Takeda, Meiji Dairies, Meiji Seika and Banyu.[58] By the end of the Occupation, firms such as Banyu, Meiji Seika and Takeda had survived the clear out (Table 3.1) and had established their position in the market.[59] A similar clear out of industry was observed in the United States, where in 1950, 12 of the 20 firms engaged in penicillin production during the Second World War remained.[60]

From the end of the war until 1949, almost all FDI was banned from Japan.[61] The Occupation authorities restricted FDI because foreign capital was viewed as an unnecessary complication that might set back the administration of the Occupation as well as undermine Japan's economic recovery.[62] Japan experienced dramatic inflation after the war. It was believed that, if FDI were permitted, foreign firms could take over undervalued Japanese firms and dominate the domestic market and deplete Japan's foreign reserves. The GHQ's strict capital controls protected Japan's antibiotic sector from foreign competition. Had the GHQ allowed foreign antibiotics firms into Japan during the Occupation period, Japan's budding industry might have been destroyed.

Table 3.1 Members of the Japan Penicillin Research Association, 1946–1956

Year	Number of firms
Start	39
1946	55
1947	72
1948	54
1949	34
1950	21
1951	19
1952	19
1953	19
1954	18
1955	16
1956	15

Source: Nihon Penishirin Kyōkai [Japan Penicillin Association], *Penishirin no Ayumi: 1946–1961* [The History of Penicillin: 1946–1961] (1961), 170.

Diversification and Streptomycin: branching out

In the late 1940s, a second antibiotic, streptomycin, began to interest authorities in Japan. The mass production of streptomycin in the United States had begun in 1946, three years after its discovery by Selman Waksman at Rutgers University.[63] As a therapy that could cure tuberculosis, the leading cause of death in Japan, several firms developed an interest in producing streptomycin.

As a stopgap measure to reduce demand pressures, the Occupation authorities imported streptomycin via the Government and Relief in Occupied Areas (GARIOA) programme and commercial funds from 1949.[64] But the very high incidence of tuberculosis in Japan meant that sufficient dollar funds were not available for the level of imports necessary to meet demand.[65] Because of this, the Occupation authorities were keen to enable Japanese firms to achieve self-sufficiency.

To assist in making streptomycin, the Occupation authorities helped provide supplies of raw materials. The Public Health and Welfare Section requested and received the bacterial strain that would enable commercial streptomycin production from Selman Waksman via the Department of the Army.[66] These cultures were transferred to the Japanese government and distributed by the National Institute of Health to researchers interested in commercial production.[67] The Occupation forces also encouraged Japanese firms to produce streptomycin by: emphasizing its therapeutic value, outlining the preparations required for domestic production and guaranteeing the procurement of any streptomycin produced.

The Central Streptomycin Research Council helped coordinate technology transfers between firms in Japan and the United States.[68] Comprised of members of the Occupation forces, Japanese government officials and university professors, the council orchestrated two contractual agreements made between Merck and Meiji Seika and Kyowa Hakko. In exchange for royalty payments, Merck supplied its patent rights, technical data, strains and plant design.[69] In 1949, the American firm also sent two scientists to provide technological guidance to the Japanese firms.[70] Whereas penicillin technology had been transferred to many firms, universities and research organizations throughout Japan, streptomycin was initially transferred to only a handful of firms.[71]

The first commercial batch of streptomycin was made available in July 1951.[72] Meiji Seika, Kyowa Hakko, the Institute of Science, Shimane Chemical and Japan Seibutsu Kagaku became its first licensed producers.[73] As with penicillin, the first manufacturers of streptomycin were new entrants such as confectioners, brewers and chemical firms rather than Japan's traditional pharmaceutical firms. Placed on the ration control list until 1952, the Occupation ensured streptomycin producers of profits. With the aid of supplies, technology transfers, protectionist policies and distribution routes secured by the government, production levels surpassed 400 kg in December 1951.[74]

Meiji and Kyowa's streptomycin alliance with Merck marked the first of numerous alliances with foreign firms to import antibiotic technology. As one of the most novel therapeutic discoveries of the times, antibiotics comprised the majority of the technology imports in the 1950s – although imports ranged from sulfa drugs, antihistamines, to hormonal preparations. Other alliances formed during this period included Sankyo's alliance with Parke Davis in 1951 for chloramphenicol, Banyu's alliance with Bristol Laboratories in 1953 for procaine penicillin and 1955 for tetracycline, and Yamanouchi's alliance with Boehringer in 1954 for chloramphenicol.[75] As the end of the Occupation neared, the Allied forces transferred more responsibilities to the Japanese. Technology transfers were increasingly arranged between Japanese and foreign firms without mediation by the authorities.[76]

Summary of the Occupation period

Japanese firms managed to develop, produce and distribute quality antibiotics within an extraordinarily short period of time. This was largely due to the guidance provided by the Occupation authorities. The Occupation forces supplied the necessary raw materials, provided technical assistance in antibiotic production and stimulated demand by purchasing antibiotics for the use of American forces stationed in Japan. The Occupation authorities also introduced protectionist policies that eliminated foreign competition in Japan. The very existence of Japan's antibiotics sector owes itself to the policies of the Allied forces.

The technology transfers arranged by the American authorities were able to create a modern pharmaceutical industry because Japanese firms were capable of adopting the knowledge provided. The human capital and connections with universities that had survived the war helped to rebuild the pharmaceutical industry. Two types of firms produced antibiotics in Occupied Japan: new entrants such as confectioners or brewers and the traditional pharmaceutical firms.[77] Neither had been heavily damaged from the bombings during the Second World War. Brewers and confectioners were particularly well positioned to use their idle facilities to produce antibiotics, as there was little demand for non-essential foodstuffs after the war. As such, the rebuilding of Japan's pharmaceutical industry in the Occupation period was not as difficult as in other sectors that had been devastated by the war. Towards the end of the Occupation, technology transfers took place between individual firms, with less intervention by government.

Building production capacities and discovering new antibiotics, 1951–1961

The 1950s evolved as an era of antibiotic discovery. While the government became less interventionist than it had been during the Occupation, it extended a strong degree of protection to enable Japanese firms to catch up with those in the West. As with other sectors of the Japanese economy, strong demand from the American Army during the Korean War (1951–1953) fuelled the growth of the antibiotics sector. In addition to the foreign capital restrictions, the government also fostered the development of the antibiotic sector through research funding. This section shows how Japan's antibiotics sector evolved after the Occupation era.

Japan's first antibiotic discovery

Japanese scientists began to search for new types of antibiotics in the late 1940s. Both in Japan and worldwide, the discovery of new antibiotics during this period involved the large-scale screening of soil samples to locate bacteria that might produce antibacterial substances. As a labour-intensive process that required little expensive equipment, antibiotics R&D was suited to a developing economy.

The first Japanese-origin antibiotic was discovered by a team of researchers led by Yasuo Koyama and Akio Kurosawa of the Kobayashi Bacteriological Laboratory.[78] After four years of research, colistin was discovered out of a soil sample in 1950. The drug was valued for its potential application against dysentery and whooping cough, for which no effective therapies existed.[79]

Colistin was commercialized through the collaboration of scientists in academia and industry. The drug was developed through collaborations with Lion Pharmaceutical, Tohoku University and Tohoku Pharmaceutical University.[80] Following clinical trials carried out at Keio University, Tokyo University and Teishin Hospital, initial attempts at mass production were conducted at Snow Brand Milk Products.

Colistin was approved for use in 1951.[81] The drug's therapeutic effects were recognized internationally, and it became the first Japanese-origin antibiotic to be licensed overseas. While colistin was not approved in the United States until 1962, it was approved in Europe by Laboratories Roger Bellon (France) in 1959.[82] For Lion Pharmaceutical, colistin proved commercially successful.[83]

Import substitution and growth

While Japanese scientists began to discover and develop antibiotics, the Japanese antibiotics market in the 1950s was mostly comprised of antibiotics imported in finished form. These were then replaced by domestically produced antibiotics based on imported technology. As in the Occupation era, the major players in the early 1950s remained the non-traditional pharmaceutical firms equipped with fermentation facilities.

But the traditional pharmaceutical firms – wholesalers of Western medicines – began to regain their footing in the market in the mid-1950s, as they began to produce antibiotics under foreign licences.[84] Following the discovery of streptomycin, American firms continued to make important antibiotic discoveries in the 1950s, such as chlortetracycline/Aueromycin (Lederle), oxytetracycline/Terracycline (Pfizer) and terracycline/Tetracyn, Achromycin (Pfizer). Larger firms had greater capital to license-in these technologies. In addition, Japan's larger, traditional pharmaceutical manufacturers began to form vertical *keiretsu* groupings with wholesalers in the 1950s. These alliances helped the traditional pharmaceutical firms to strengthen their marketing capacities and deter the entry of new firms.

Sankyo, for example, shifted its focus from dealing in anthelmintics, DDT and BHC to dealing in antibiotics. By 1960, antibiotics comprised almost a quarter of Sankyo's total pharmaceutical sales of 18.1 billion yen, mainly via licences from Parke Davis, Løvens Kemiske, Sando and Squibb.[85] Shionogi also formed alliances with Eli Lilly to launch antibiotics such as erythromycin. By 1960, antibiotics comprised 12.7 per cent of production at Shionogi.[86] Even Takeda, primarily a vitamins producer, launched antibiotics such as tetracycline and kanamycin in the late 1950s.[87] Many of the antibiotics marketed in Japan originated from large American firms such as Parke Davis, Bristol, Squibb, Beecham, Pfizer, Upjohn and Eli Lilly.

During the 1950s, technology imports of antibiotics far outweighed any other therapeutic sector, accounting for 21 of the 70 technology imports for pharmaceuticals between 1951 and 1960 (Table 3.2).[88] In addition to the restrictions to foreign capital, by limiting imports to products that remained unavailable in Japan or production processes that remained undeveloped in the domestic market, Japanese firms were protected from foreign competition. Japan's process patent regime lowered barriers to entry and promoted the diffusion of new technologies across many firms.

While firms such as Roche and Taito-Pfizer had established operations in Japan, the few foreign firms in Japan did not pose a threat to domestic antibiotics firms.[89] This was because foreign firms were few in number, affiliated with Japanese firms, and had yet to establish their own distribution routes. The government's protectionist measures also encouraged the growth of an imitation – rather than innovation – industry during the 1950s. Yet the government's import-substitution policies in the 1950s were crucial to offering Japanese firms a chance to catch up with the West.

While its market share relative to Japan's overall pharmaceutical industry may have declined, the antibiotics sector experienced stable growth over the 1950s

Table 3.2 Significant imports of antibiotic technology after the Occupation

Product	Length of contract	Companies
Procaine penicillin	1953 (15 years)	Banyu–Bristol Laboratories
Streptomycin	1951 (15 years)	Merck–Kyowa Hakko, Meiji
Chloramphenicol	1951 (15 years)	Sankyo–Parke Davis
	1954 (10 years)	Yamanouchi–Boehringer
Chlortetracycline	1953 (15 years)	Japan Lederle–American Cyanamid
Oxytetracycline	1953 (15 years)	Taito Pfizer–Pfizer
Tetracycline	1953 (15 years)	Japan Lederle–American Cyanamid
	1954 (15 years)	Taito Pfizer–Pfizer
	1955 (14 years 4 months)	Banyu–Bristol Laboratories
Penicillin Aminoesthyl	1954 (5 years)	Sankyo–Løvens Kemiske
Dypenicillin	1953 (15 years)	Banyu–Wyeth International

Source: Yakugyō Keizai Kenkyūjo, *Yakuji Nenkan* [Pharmaceutical Annual] (1957), 59–60.

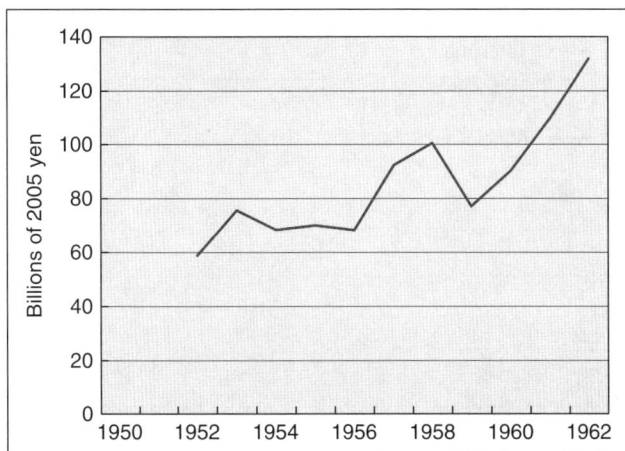

Figure 3.2 Value of antibiotic production, 1952–1962 (in billions of 2005 yen)

Source: Yakugyō Keizai Kenkyūjo, *Yakuji Nenkan* [Pharmaceutical Affairs Annual] (1957); Ministry of Health and Welfare, *Yakuji Kōgyō Seisan Dōtai Chōsa Tōkei* [Annual Survey on Production in the Pharmaceutical Industry] (various years).

(Figure 3.2).[90] Antibiotics were the leading therapy in 1952, comprising almost 16 per cent of total production. A decade later, antibiotics comprised less than 10 per cent of total production, and vitamins overtook antibiotics as the leading therapeutic sector between 1958 and 1969.

Japan's imports of antibiotics declined during the 1950s both as special procurements by the US Army came to an end and as imports were replaced by antibiotics produced in Japan (Figure 3.3). Antibiotic trade also declined in significance relative to total pharmaceutical trade.[91] While antibiotics had comprised almost half of total pharmaceutical trade at the beginning of the decade, figures dropped to only 6 per cent by the end of the decade. Antibiotics had comprised a significant proportion of both imports and exports of total pharmaceuticals in the early 1950s. In 1951, imports and exports of antibiotics comprised 72.7 per cent and 25.8 per cent of imports and exports of total pharmaceuticals, respectively.[92] But by the end of the decade, imports and exports of antibiotics had dropped to 8.0 per cent and 4.8 per cent of total pharmaceuticals, respectively.[93] Antibiotic exports did increase as Japanese firms became capable of producing antibiotics, particularly as leading firms began to recapture some of the South East and East Asian markets that it had lost during the war.[94] The rise in exports, however, was much smaller than the fall in imports.[95]

In terms of trading partners, Japan exported older antibiotics to the developing world while the country imported newer antibiotics from the developed world. In the late 1950s, antibiotics comprised approximately 17 per cent of pharmaceutical exports and 15 per cent of pharmaceutical imports in Japan.[96] Japan exported older

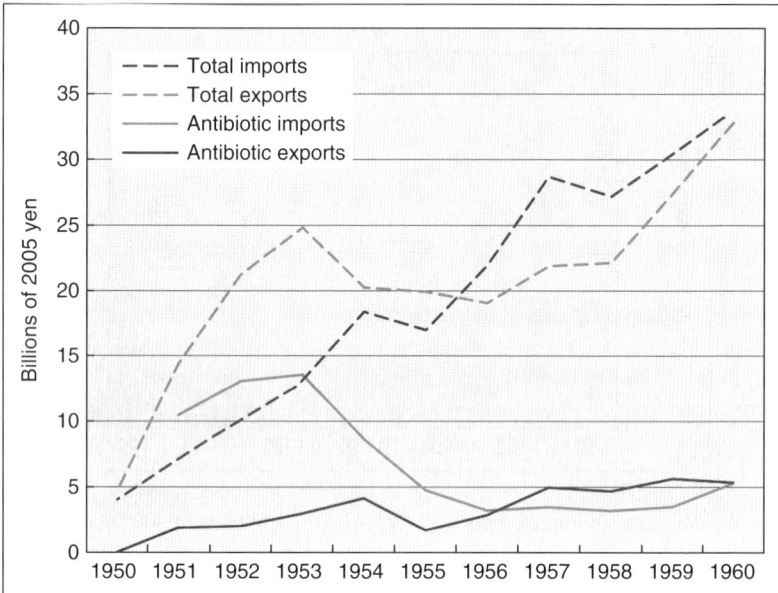

Figure 3.3 Value of antibiotic trade, 1950–1960 (in billions of 2005 yen)

Source: Yakugyō Keizai Kenkyūjo, *Yakuji Nenkan* [Pharmaceutical Affairs Annual] (1957); Yakugyō Keizai Kenkyūjo, *Yakuji Nenkan* [Pharmaceutical Affairs Annual] (1961).

antibiotics such as streptomycin and penicillin to India, Taiwan, Okinawa and Italy, while the country imported newer antibiotics such as chloramphenicol and viomycin, from the United States, the United Kingdom and Germany.[97]

Kanamycin and internationalization

As Japanese firms acquired the capacity to produce leading antibiotics, and competed to develop better drugs, more firms attempted to discover their own original drugs. Between 1950 and 1960, Japanese firms discovered five of the 22 antibiotics (23 per cent) marketed in Japan. These included colistin by Lion Kinyaku in 1951, sarkomycin by Meiji Seika in 1954, kitasamycin by Toyo Jozo in 1956, kanamycin by Meiji Seika in 1958 and mitomycin by Kyowa Hakko in 1959.[98] Four of the five antibiotics originated out of small-scale confectionery or brewery firms, reflecting the importance of non-traditional pharmaceutical firms in the antibiotics sector.

It is worth noting that government funding of antibiotic R&D also played an important role in the discovery and development of Japanese antibiotics. As mentioned earlier, the Ministry of Health and the Ministry of Education had supported research on antibiotics since 1946. The Ministry of Health, for example, provided funding through the Japan Antibiotic Research Association (JARA), which not only supported academic research but also promoted its dissemination through the publication of the *Journal of Antibiotics* – which remains the leading journal on antibiotic research in Japan to date.[99] Partly because government funding was given to academic institutions, antibiotic discoveries in Japan evolved out of the academic laboratory. While a few industrial laboratories were established by firms such as Takeda, Fujisawa and Daiichi in the 1950s, industrial laboratories in most of Japanese pharmaceutical firms until the 1960s.[100] Where they did exist, industrial research concentrated primarily on process innovation rather than product innovation. Government funding for antibiotic R&D provided the impetus for the discovery of antibiotics through academic laboratories in Japan. These discoveries were then commercialized through informal collaborations with various firms.

The increasing cases of antibiotic resistance also encouraged firms to invest in R&D. Before the 1950s, the purpose of antibiotic R&D was to locate any naturally occurring substance effective towards bacterial infections. But the rise of antibiotic resistance and realization of significant side effects renewed demand for antibiotics where similar therapies were already available.

Meiji Seika

One of the major antibiotic discoveries in the mid-1950s was Meiji Seika's kanamycin. Kanamycin had been discovered by a scientific team led by one of Japan's leading scientists, Hamao Umezawa, who had led antibiotics research in Japan since the Second World War.[101] Since 1952, Umezawa had developed a systematic approach to antibiotic R&D, and studied antibiotic agents that: derived from a particular strain of bacteria; halted bacterial growth; were water-soluble; were basic; and had low toxicity.[102] After collecting soil samples from schools, community health centres and regional offices throughout Japan, scientists isolated kanamycin in 1955.[103]

Umezawa developed kanamycin in collaboration with Meiji Seika. The company had been established in 1916 as one of the first Western-style confectionery firms in Japan. Faced with a limited market for sweets after the war, however, Meiji Seika diversified its operations. In 1946, the firm decided to build upon its fermentation capacities and produce penicillin, as profits were ensured through government procurements.[104] By 1958, Meiji Seika had become one of the leading penicillin makers in Japan, and one of 13 firms to survive the intense competition in the penicillin market.[105] Meiji Seika's involvement in developing kanamycin was an extension of its business in antibiotics.[106]

Much like colistin, kanamycin's development was a joint project between academia and industry. The drug was developed in collaboration with Tokyo University, Meiji Seika, Bristol Laboratories and Merck. Clinical trials were carried out at Tokyo University, where the drug was found effective towards tuberculosis, dysentery and other infectious diseases.[107]

Kanamycin was launched by Meiji Seika in May 1958.[108] The drug was valued for its low toxicity and its effectiveness against strains of bacteria that had become resistant to earlier antibiotics.[109] Kanamycin also proved effective in relatively low doses, and was found suitable to mass production in tank cultures.[110] For Meiji

Seika, kanamycin proved to be a tremendously successful drug that became one of Japan's top antibiotics exports and remains in use to date.[111]

Kanamycin, however, also showed how Japan's process patent regime penalized innovative drug discoveries. Process patents allowed firms to reverse engineer drugs and did not protect the discoveries of innovative firms. Meiji Seika had risked 200 million yen to pursue R&D of kanamycin at a time when the firm had a capital of 840 million yen.[112] Yet after official approval in April 1958, Meiji Seika had a monopoly in the Japanese market for less than five months, as Banyu, Yamanouchi and Tanabe launched their own versions of kanamycin in September 1958.[113] For many firms, the lack of government protection or support for product innovation undermined incentives to discover new drugs.

Summary of the period between 1950 and 1961

As in the Occupation period, the major reason for the development of the antibiotics sector between 1950 and 1961 was government policies. As foreign firms were prevented from entering the Japanese market, Japanese antibiotics makers were protected from foreign competition. In addition, Japan's process patent regime encouraged firms to reverse engineer drugs discovered abroad, find another method to manufacture the drug, and launch this drug as a 'new' product in Japan. This discouraged investments in R&D.[114] Still, some Japanese drug companies did begin to invest in antibiotic R&D and discover new therapies that were licensed overseas. The search for new antibiotics involved little equipment and was a labour-intensive and serendipitous process – a form of pharmaceutical R&D conducive to firms in a developing economy. The discovery of antibiotics was also facilitated by the informal collaborations between academia, government and industry.

But unlike the United States, for example, where most research had been transferred to pharmaceutical firms by 1950, antibiotic research in Japan remained in universities and public research institutes.[115] Antibiotic research in the industrial laboratory would gradually take root over the following decades, as Japanese firms strengthened their capacity to produce and discover global antibiotics.[116]

Nurturing industry through process innovations and domestic demand, 1961–1975

Between 1961 and 1975, Japan's antibiotics sector saw a phenomenal expansion in terms of production, trade and R&D. In 1961, antibiotics accounted for 10 per cent of total drug production and increased to more than 20 per cent by 1975.[117] Antibiotics were the largest therapeutic sector in Japan between 1970 and 1988.[118] While the dominance of antibiotics in the pharmaceutical market was echoed in most other developed countries around the globe, the rate and extent of expansion in Japan was distinct.[119] Confectioners and brewers such as Meiji Seika and Toyo

Jozo continued to compete alongside the more traditional pharmaceutical firms such as Takeda, Yamanouchi and Fujisawa into the mid-1970s.[120]

Building a domestically oriented antibiotics sector

While Japan did export some antibiotics to countries in East Asia, Europe and North America, Japan's antibiotics sector evolved as a domestic oriented industry over the 1960s.[121] This was mainly because the government introduced universal healthcare, created distinct product standards, allowed physicians to dispense medicines and set modest criteria for drug approval. Japan's antibiotics sector began to expand rapidly within this highly protected environment – where the government also sponsored demand.

In addition, Japanese physicians both prescribed and dispensed antibiotics.[122] Japanese physicians were particularly incentivized to over-prescribe these drugs because official prices were high, and they could negotiate a steeper discount for wholesale prices. In addition, antibiotics could be prescribed to a large patient population. Infections were common complaints, antibiotics had relatively few side effects, and as a short-term therapy, the total cost of medicines was much lower than in chronic diseases. Furthermore, the 1967 legislation established modest criteria for a substance to qualify as a new drug in Japan. The Japanese antibiotics sector expanded rapidly in an environment with strong demand for high-priced antibiotics, and where incremental innovations easily qualified as new drugs. At the same time, however, the antibiotics sector became heavily domestically oriented, as both the demand structure and drug approval criteria were specific only to Japan.

A shift in antibiotic R&D

There was a major transition in antibiotic R&D over the 1960s, in terms of both the approaches used and the ability demonstrated by Japanese firms to discover new antibiotics. Antibiotics were no longer discovered out of serendipity from naturally occurring substances, but from chemical compounds of known structure and potential therapeutic value. The quality of antibiotics also improved during this time, as the newer drugs offered greater potency, wider antibacterial spectra and lower toxicity. R&D methods also became more sophisticated, and entailed greater risk, cost, scale and complexity.[123]

While it is true that many Japanese firms continued to produce new antibiotics based on foreign technologies in a highly protected environment, Japanese firms proved increasingly successful in the discovery and launch of globally competitive antibiotics as they acquired the capacity to pursue advanced methods of R&D. The central research laboratories and new quality standards – such as GCP and GPMSP – established during this time, also helped Japanese firms strengthen their development capacities.[124] Indeed, a total of 22 Japanese-origin antibiotics, or 22 per cent of post-war discoveries, were discovered between 1961 and 1975.[125] Of these, approximately a third were eventually distributed worldwide.

These transitions in antibiotic R&D in Japan are well illustrated in the experiences at Yamanouchi and Fujisawa.

Yamanouchi

In 1970, Yamanouchi Pharmaceutical launched a new antibiotic, josamycin, that was recognized around the world. Founded by Kenji Yamanouchi in 1923, Yamanouchi prospered in the pre-war era as Japan's first manufacturer of sulfa drugs. By the 1940s, the firm had captured 30 per cent of Japan's sulfa drug market.[126] While Yamanouchi did license-in antibiotics after the war, sulfa drugs remained a more important part of its business.[127] In 1960, Yamanouchi still derived over a quarter of its sales from sulfa drugs, followed by antibiotics and diuretics. While the proportion of antibiotic sales did not change markedly over the 1960s, antibiotic sales almost quadrupled over the decade.[128]

Josamycin was discovered in 1967 out of numerous soil samples collected across Japan.[129] The drug was developed by Takashi Osono at Yamanouchi's central research laboratory in collaboration with Yoshiro Okami and Hamao Umezawa at the Institute of Microbial Chemistry. Clinical trials were conducted at the School of Medicine at Juntendo University.[130] While the drug's development was less rigorous compared to contemporary standards overseas, the government's new guidelines had prompted firms to modernize facilities, revise procedures and write more comprehensive reports. Compared to earlier antibiotics, josamycin was less toxic, more easily absorbed and more effective for a wider range of infections – including several strains of bacteria found to be resistant towards existing antibiotics.[131]

Josamycin recorded strong domestic sales following its launch in February 1970.[132] For Yamanouchi, josamycin also prompted the firm's expansion into overseas markets. The drug also gained patent approval for countries ranging from the United States, Britain, West Germany to Switzerland.[133] The drug's first global launch was through E.I. du Pont de Nemours in 1974.[134] For Yamanouchi, the drug was a success, as antibiotic sales increased from 15.2 billion yen in 1970 to 19.8 billion yen in 1980.[135]

Fujisawa

Around the same time, Fujisawa also launched a new antibiotic that proved successful in both domestic and international markets. Cefazolin belonged to a new category of antibiotics called cephalosporins, which were stronger and more effective towards a wider variety of infections. Whereas scientists had previously discovered antibiotics by screening countless soil samples, cefazolin was developed out of a known chemical structure. This marked a transition from previous methods of antibiotic R&D.

While Fujisawa had been engaged in antibiotics in the past, its decision to invest heavily in antibiotic R&D was something new. Founded by Tomokichi

Fujisawa in 1894, Fujisawa grew quickly in the pre-war period through tonics and anthelmintics such as camphor and santonin. In the post-war period, Fujisawa developed by importing foreign technologies from firms such as Geigy of Switzerland and Astra of Sweden. A 1953 alliance with the Italian firm Carlo Erba enabled the firm to channel its growth in the antibiotics sector by launching chloramphenicol/Kemicetine in Japan.[136] By the early 1960s, Fujisawa had become known as one of Japan's leading antibiotics makers, and derived around 15 per cent of sales from antibiotics.[137]

In 1961, Fujisawa signed a licensing agreement with the National Research and Development Corporation (NRDC) in the United Kingdom to develop a substance called cephalosporin C.[138] Cephalosporin C had been identified by the bacteriologist Giuseppe Brotsu of the University of Cagliari in 1945. Research at the NRDC had led to the discovery that part of cephalosporin C, a chemical structure called 7-ACA, could be isolated and chemically manipulated to locate new antibiotic substances. Compared to existing antibiotics, the cephalosporins held the promise of greater potency, a wider effective spectrum, less toxicity, greater stability and fewer side effects.[139]

Fujisawa spent approximately 7.7 per cent of its annual research costs to import cephalosporin C technology.[140] Scientists at Takeda and Toho University then worked together to develop this substance into a drug. Using the university laboratory to substitute for the firm's lack of facilities, the scientists developed cefazolin in 1967.[141] Fujisawa – along with Glaxo and Lilly – was one of three firms who were ultimately able to develop a viable therapeutic from the licences obtained from the NRDC.

Fujisawa's decade-long investment of over 150 million yen to develop cefazolin was, at the time, unprecedented for a Japanese firm. But the firm's entrepreneurial venture began to pay off. Following its launch in 1971, cefazolin was eventually marketed in more than 100 countries in Europe, North America and Asia. Thanks to cefazolin, antibiotic sales at Fujisawa doubled within five years of its launch to 64.6 billion yen in 1976.[142]

Still, for many firms, Japan did not offer an attractive environment for innovation. Products of domestic origin often competed against products that were discovered overseas, licensed-in or reverse engineered. By the time Fujisawa had launched cefazolin, for example, Eli Lilly and Glaxo's cephalosporin drugs, cefalothin and cefaloridine, respectively, were already marketed in Japan. Eli Lilly, the first to develop cefalothin from cephalosporin C in 1962, provided an import/sale licence to Shionogi in 1966, while Glaxo, who had developed cefaloridine in 1964 exported its drug to Shin Nihon Jitsugyo, which was distributed by Torii Yakuhin in 1965.[143] As the first cephalosporin drugs, Shionogi's Keflin and Torii's Ceporan showed strong sales in the domestic market. Many Japanese firms were long content to pursue import-substitution policies because it proved profitable, and the domestic market remained dominated by antibiotics discovered outside of Japan. Between 1961 and 1975, only 14 of the 43 antibiotics (33 per cent) introduced into the Japanese market were of Japanese origin.[144] Only a third of the antibiotics market was comprised of drugs from Japan.

Nevertheless, Fujisawa's success in cefazolin spearheaded an era in which Japanese pharmaceutical firms would invest heavily in antibiotic R&D.[145] Japanese firms improved their capacity to discover, develop and launch innovative antibiotics over the 1960s and 1970s. While government policies did help non-innovating firms survive, it did seem to offer sufficient incentive for some firms to pursue innovative discoveries in antibiotics.

A year of welfare for the people – and for antibiotics makers: 1973

Between 1961 and 1975, the antibiotics sector expanded rapidly in terms of production, trade and new drug discoveries.[146] The high rate of growth in the antibiotics market coincided with the launch of a universal health insurance system in 1961 and an era of high-speed economic growth. As Figure 3.4 indicates, production levels rose almost sixfold between 1961 and 1975 from approximately 109.5 billion yen to 633.1 billion yen.[147] Growth in the antibiotics sector was particularly pronounced, as the size of the overall pharmaceutical market grew less than threefold during the same period.

The 1973 welfare reforms – which expanded coverage for family dependants, capped the cost of high cost treatments and introduced free health care for the elderly – appeared particularly instrumental in raising production levels.[148] In response, growth rates jumped with 19 per cent year-on-year growth in 1973. In fact, production growth in the five years after 1973 was 27 per cent higher than the previous 5 years. Japan's rapid economic growth, too, had propelled the rise of the antibiotics sector, as more patients could afford antibiotic treatments. Supported

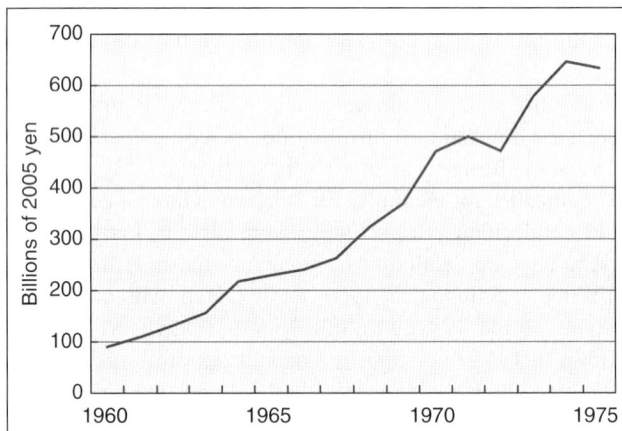

Figure 3.4 Value of antibiotic production, 1960–1975 (in billions of 2005 yen)

Source: Ministry of Health and Welfare, *Yakuji Kōgyō Seisan Dōtai Chōsa Tōkei* [Annual Survey on Production in the Pharmaceutical Industry] (various years).

by policy measures and economic conditions, the Japanese antibiotics sector experienced phenomenal growth in the 1960s and 1970s.[149]

Opening up

Despite the steps taken towards capital liberalization, the product standards introduced in 1967 still limited the entry of foreign firms in Japan. This was because foreign drugs that did not meet Japanese specifications were not considered drugs in Japan. Also, foreign firms had yet to establish a marketing presence in Japan. But the gradual opening of the market did bring a fresh wave of foreign investment in Japan's pharmaceutical industry.

Antibiotic trade also grew during this period and trade values soared 8.3-fold from 10.7 billion yen to 88.0 billion yen between 1960 and 1975.[150] The growth of antibiotic imports was particularly remarkable, as it grew 14.7-fold from a mere 5.28 billion yen to 77.7 billion yen between 1960 and 1975. By comparison, the average growth of imports in other therapeutic sectors was 6.9-fold – large, but less than half the figure for antibiotics. But the growth of antibiotic exports was much slower, as it grew only 1.9-fold from 5.38 billion yen to 10.3 billion yen. This was because many Japanese products were not approved in other markets, and because Japanese firms had yet to establish distribution networks overseas.[151]

As with most OECD countries, Japan relied on the United States for most of its pharmaceutical imports. In 1975, for example, 46.3 billion yen of antibiotic imports came from the United States, followed by 16.5 billion yen from Singapore and 10.8 billion yen from the United Kingdom.[152] While exports did grow (Figure 3.5), the massive trade deficit – both in antibiotics and in other therapeutic sectors – suggested that Japanese drugs were of inferior quality to those in other developed countries.

Transitions in the export destinations of antibiotics did suggest that the quality of Japan origin antibiotics was improving. In 1961, for example, the leading export destinations for Japanese antibiotics were East Asian neighbours such as Okinawa and Taiwan, followed by exports destined for Germany and other European countries.[153] But by the mid-1970s, the majority of antibiotic exports were destined for more developed countries; in 1975, for example, antibiotic exports were destined for South Korea, West Germany, Belgium and the United States, in descending order.[154] As the quality of Japan origin antibiotics improved, the country's export destinations shifted from the developing to the developed world.

Summary of the period between 1961 and 1975

There were several reasons for the strong performance of Japan's antibiotics sector in this period. All of these reasons lay in government policies that were highly favourable to the industry. The strongest stimulus was the introduction of

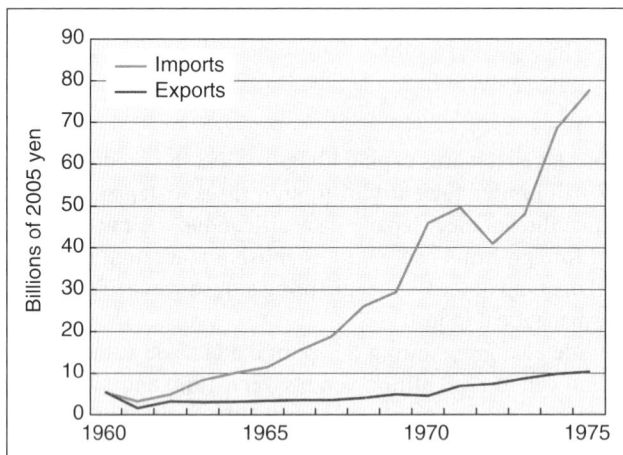

Figure 3.5 Value of antibiotic trade, 1960–1975 (in millions of 2005 yen)

Source: Ministry of International Trade and Industry, *Tsūshō Hakusho* [White Paper on Trade] (various years).

universal healthcare in 1961. Universal healthcare spurred demand for antibiotics as the government covered most of the costs of patients' prescription drugs. This made it much easier for firms to sell drugs.

Japanese antibiotics makers also benefited from the practice permitted among Japanese physicians to both prescribe and dispense medicines. This practice created strong incentives among physicians to prescribe the newest and most expensive antibiotics, which tended to have the greatest price differentials. Given the government's modest criteria for drug approval, the antibiotics sector flourished. Both firms and physicians were incentivized to expand the domestic market for financial gain.[155] While many antibiotics would not have been approved elsewhere, Japanese firms could prosper in an environment that remained heavily protected. In addition, FDI was restricted until 1975. Furthermore, Japan's distinct drug standards provided additional protection from foreign competition.

Perhaps because the government subsidized the cost of prescription drugs, Japanese patients were price insensitive, and purchased unnecessary antibiotics. Indeed, the over consumption of antibiotics became an oft-debated topic during the 1970s and 1980s. But other factors also accounted for this over consumption. Some scholars have attributed patient deference towards physicians in Japan to a Confucian heritage of respect for authority, while others have noted the lack of professional information available to patients.[156] Prescribing antibiotics also allowed physicians to preserve their reputation with patients who often expected a prescription drug upon a visit to the doctor.[157]

While many Japanese pharmaceutical firms established corporate research laboratories over the 1960s, most research laboratories specialized in reverse engineering Western products rather than in pursuing product innovations. The government's drug pricing policy, whereby the government set the prices for prescription drugs, effectively capped the potential profits that could be made from drug discoveries, reducing incentives to invest heavily in R&D. But the prices of antibiotics were relatively higher than in other therapeutic sectors. This encouraged some drug companies to invest in antibiotic R&D – and develop internationally competitive antibiotics.

The maturation of the market and transition to product innovation, 1975–1990

> The Japanese have proved themselves master soil searchers. In the last decade, many of the cephalosporins have come from Japan. Antibiotics are important there because it is the biggest user, per capita, of the wonder drugs, ahead even of the United States.
>
> N.R. Kleinfeld, 'Intense Battle for Antibiotics', *The New York Times*,
> 13 June 1983.

The antibiotics sector continued to expand in the 1970s. After 1975, government measures to liberalize foreign capital and strengthen intellectual property rights protection supported the growth of a number of Japanese pharmaceutical firms that had acquired the financial, scientific and technological capacity to assume higher risks and pursue more substantial innovations. Firms from other industries seeking new business opportunities entered the pharmaceutical sector during this period, as did foreign firms that had previously been alienated from the Japanese market.

While the government's decision to contain healthcare costs through biennial price reductions dealt a swift and intense blow to production levels after 1981, it also helped the transition from volume- to value-based production. Facing rising competition and falling profits in the home market, Japanese firms expanded their operations abroad. While Japan's expertise in antibiotic science and research networks were certainly important in sustaining the growth of Japan's antibiotic sector, it was the timely implementation of government policies that ultimately dictated its fortunes between 1975 and 1990.

Cutting excess demand

Following from the previous decade, antibiotic production continued to grow rapidly after 1975 (Figure 3.6). Between 1975 and 1980, production levels grew from 633.1 billion yen to 1.0 trillion yen.[158] The antibiotics sector was particularly hard hit by the biennial price reductions, as the government began to impose

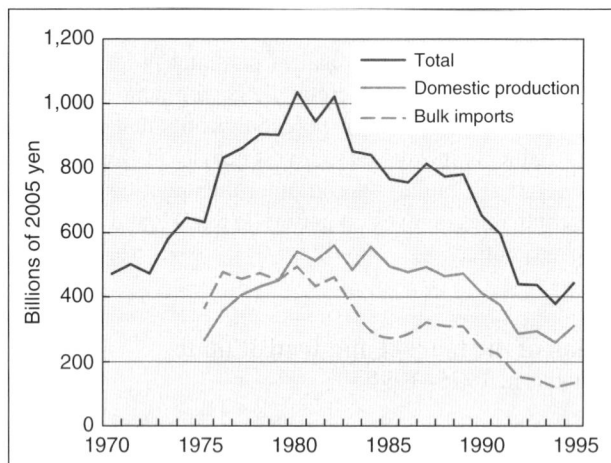

Figure 3.6 Value of antibiotic production, 1975–1995 (in billions of 2005 yen)

Source: Ministry of Health and Welfare, *Yakuji Kōgyō Seisan Dōtai Chōsa Tōkei* [Annual Survey on Production in the Pharmaceutical Industry] (various years).

steeper reductions on older drugs with less innovative value.[159] Combined with the reforms to end free healthcare for the elderly in 1983, antibiotics production peaked in 1982 and began to contract over the decade. In 1990, antibiotics production stood at 652.8 billion yen, a 47 per cent fall from its peak, and only a 3 per cent increase compared to 1975.[160]

Despite this decline, however, the size of Japan's antibiotics market was unparalleled in the global market. Japanese antibiotics makers produced drugs worth well over 600 billion yen throughout the decade – at times reaching 1 trillion yen.[161] In 1988, for example, the Japanese antibiotics market was valued at $4.8 billion, compared to $3.4 billion in the United States and $360 million in the United Kingdom. This translated into a per capita consumption of $39.1 in Japan, compared to $13.8 in the United States and $6.4 in the United Kingdom.[162] Bulk imports also declined from 336.3 billion yen in 1975 to 240.8 billion yen in 1990.[163]

While antibiotic R&D involved less cost or risk compared to other therapeutic sectors, the biennial price reductions still deterred Japanese firms from pursuing R&D. Yet, to a certain extent, the price reductions were actually useful in nudging firms away from the overproduction of antibiotics towards newer categories of drugs that were less subject to heavy reductions. It also helped end an era of volume-based expansion, as the minimal pharmaceutical price differentials lowered physician demand for antibiotics. In fact, it also encouraged the more innovative firms to pursue more favourable market opportunities abroad.

An increasing emphasis on R&D

Quinolones

The greater emphasis on R&D was well observed in the firms that developed quinolone antibiotics. With the many antibiotic programmes launched after the discovery of cefazolin in the 1970s, Japanese firms spearheaded the discovery of new antibiotics. One of these belonged a group of drugs called fluoroquinolones, a subset of the quinolone family of antibiotic drugs discovered in the 1960s. The discovery of these drugs were particularly timely, as by the 1970s, many strains of bacteria had grown resistant to sulfa drugs – the first synthetic antibacterials discovered in the 1940s.[164]

The first quinolone antibiotic was introduced by the American firm Sterling Winthrop, which launched nalidixic acid in 1962. In subsequent years, scientists discovered that the addition of a fluorine atom to the quinolone structure significantly improved the drug's properties. The new quinolone antibiotics were valued for their superior potency, absorption, distribution and effectiveness against a wide range of bacteria – particularly with antibiotic resistant strains. These drugs made outpatient therapy possible among patients where hospitalization had previously been required.[165] Perhaps one of the most well-known, best-selling quinolones worldwide has been Bayer's Cipro (ciprofloxacin, 1987).[166]

Kyorin

In Japan, Kyorin discovered the fluoroquinolone antibiotic norflaxacin. Founded as a manufacturer and distributor of new medicines in 1923, Kyorin was known more for its cardiovascular agents such as Behyd/benzylhydrochlorothiazide, Cholexamin/nicomol and Hespander/hydroxyethyl starch that it had offered since the 1960s. While the firm established a central research laboratory in 1977, its R&D capacities remained limited.[167] Kyorin's R&D collaborations with university researchers were particularly crucial to norflaxacin's discovery. Forming close alliances with researchers at the Gunma University School of Medicine, Kyorin's researchers conducted experiments to develop the drug by manipulating the quinolone structure.[168]

Kyorin's development of norfloxacin reflected considerable advances in antibiotic R&D among Japanese firms. Not only had drug development evolved from the sifting of numerous soil samples, but the quality, safety and effectiveness guidelines had also become more rigorous. Laboratory tests spanned longer durations with complex tests conducted on larger sample sizes. Clinical trials also became more sophisticated, with double-blind testing and greater attention paid to safety as well as efficacy. Norfloxacin was a product of these developments.[169]

Norflaxacin, with its wider antibacterial spectrum and greater potency compared to existing antibiotics, not only proved highly profitable, but also brought Kyorin global recognition that helped the firm expand its business beyond Japan. Approved in 1984, norflaxacin was distributed domestically by Kyorin and Torii

Pharmaceutical as Baccidal.[170] Shortly thereafter, norfloxacin was approved in the United States in 1986, and marketed by Merck Sharpe and Dohme in over 20 countries as Noroxin.[171] The drug brought substantial sales to Kyorin, as Noroxin sales amounted to $41 million in 1988.[172]

Daiichi

Around the same time, a research team at Daiichi Pharmaceutical was also searching for new quinolones with Gunma University's School of Medicine.[173] It was not surprising that Daiichi entered the antibiotic sector with the discovery of quinolone drugs. Daiichi was Japan's leading sulfa drug maker. Both sulfa drugs and quinolones are synthetic antibacterial compounds, and Daiichi could build upon its existing expertise. Moreover, demand for sulfa drugs had declined. Not only were existing sulfa drugs becoming less effective towards multiple bacterial strains, but also they were being replaced by antibiotics with greater efficacy and fewer side effects.

Daiichi was formed in 1915 as German imports came to a halt during the First World War. Daiichi was one of several new firms that launched salvarsan during this period as Japanese scientists succeeded in producing the drug. In the interwar period, Daiichi flourished as the leading provider of antisyphilitic remedies. In the post-war period, Daiichi remained a leading provider of sulfa drugs, and became a producer of vitamins and cardiovascular drugs. Thanks to its long history and prominent standing, Daiichi had also developed considerable marketing strengths in pharmaceuticals.[174]

Daiichi's ofloxacin was developed out of Wintomylon/nalidixic acid, which was licensed-in from Winthrop in 1964, and remained a popular quinolone drug until the early 1980s.[175] The new drug was a product of 20 years of research, through collaboration with researchers at Gunma University. Like norflaxacin, ofloxacin was valued for its potency, wide antibacterial spectrum and effectiveness towards bacteria that had developed antibacterial resistance.

Much like Kyorin's norfloxacin, Daiichi's launch of ofloxacin as Taravid in 1985 fuelled the firm's growth and internationalization.[176] A decade after its launch, antibiotics sales at Daiichi had grown almost threefold to 69.2 billion yen, and the firm's share of antibiotics to total pharmaceutical sales doubled to 30 per cent. Largely a domestic firm until the mid-1980s, in five years, exports had also nearly doubled to 15.4 billion yen in 1990.[177]

While Daiichi discovered norfloxacin a year after Kyorin, Daiichi's superior marketing strategies, larger size and previous alliances with foreign firms helped its drug achieve much greater success in the domestic and global markets. Daiichi licensed ofloxacin to foreign firms such as to Hoechst (Germany), Johnson & Johnson (United States), Sigma Dow, Glaxo Italy (Italy) in 1983 and to Roussel-Uclaf (France) in 1984.[178] Eventually reaching more than 120 countries, ofloxacin's worldwide sales reached $500 million in 1990.[179] By 1994, ofloxacin was the sixth top selling antibiotic with global sales of $538 million.[180] Daiichi's greater success relative to Kyorin embodied some of the changes in the pharmaceutical industry more generally, where marketing was becoming as important as R&D in securing sales.[181]

Other antibiotics

There were other antibiotics firms that invested in R&D and expanded overseas. This included Sumitomo Pharmaceutical, which launched meropenem.[182] Sumitomo's meropenem belonged to the carbapenem family of antibiotics, and was developed by altering the chemical structure of Merck's imipenem, which had been launched in 1985. Compared to imipenem, Sumitomo's new antibiotic proved to be more effective and easy to use. Research collaborations were essential to the drug's development.[183] Test results reflected higher criteria in the drug approval process and greater internationalization in the research process.

Sumitomo's drug quickly gained global recognition. In fact, meropenem was first launched in Italy in 1994 before it was launched in Japan as Meropen in 1995. Sumitomo licensed meropenem to ICI to develop the drug for most major markets outside of Japan. After FDA approval in June 1996, meropenem was launched in September by Zeneca Pharmaceuticals as Merrem in the United States.[184] With sales of 13.3 billion yen in 2000, or 10.8 per cent of total sales, meropenem proved a blockbuster discovery. For Sumitomo, meropenem not only allowed it to gain footage in the domestic market, but also helped its internationalization.[185]

Led by successes like these, Japan's antibiotics sector experienced its height of antibiotic discovery during this period. Indeed, Japan discovered more than 40 per cent of its antibiotics in the decade after 1975.[186] As the figures in parentheses in Table 3.3 show, the increase in the proportion of globally recognized Japanese-origin antibiotics recognized globally after 1975 reflects the shift from volume- to value-based growth.[187]

From a global perspective, too, the number of antibiotics discovered by Japanese firms at this time was significant. A study of new drugs discovered worldwide between 1969 and 1980 revealed that a total of 113 antibiotics were discovered during this period. Of these, 22.5 substances, or almost 20 per cent, originated from Japan, while 37 (or 33 per cent) were discovered in the United States, 11.5 (or 10 per cent) in Italy and 9.5 (or 8 per cent) in the United Kingdom.[188] It was true that the innovative value among these substances likely varied, and that

Table 3.3 Worldwide antibiotic discoveries originating from Japan, 1946–1995

Number of products discovered					Total
1946–1955	*1956–1965*	*1966–1975*	*1976–1985*	*1986–1995*	
11	12	23	40	13	99
(4 = 36.4%)	(4 = 33.3%)	(5 = 21.7%)	(18 = 45%)	(7 = 53.8%)	(38 = 38.4%)

Source: Joichi Kumazawa and Morimasa Yagisawa, "The History of Antibiotics: The Japanese Story," *Journal of Infection and Chemotherapy* 8, no. 2 (2002): 127; Morimasa Yagisawa, "Antibiotics, Chemotherapeutics and Other Microbial Products Originated from Japan," unpublished document.

Note: Figures in parentheses represent the number of Japanese discoveries that were licensed abroad.

Japanese antibiotics may have been more incremental than breakthrough discoveries. Nevertheless, the figures provide insight into the fruition of Japanese efforts in antibiotic research during this time.

Expanding abroad

The liberalization of foreign capital and the increase of new entrants into the pharmaceutical industry prompted many Japanese firms to seek opportunities abroad from the 1970s, as they faced limited growth prospects at home (Figure 3.7). The introduction of product patents in 1976 encouraged Japanese firms to intensify their R&D efforts to develop innovative drugs. Foreign pressures to deregulate the domestic market in the 1980s further opened the market to foreign competition, while the introduction of better quality standards improved the quality of domestic drugs. Japanese firms expanded their overseas ventures as government policies shifted from protection to liberalization, imitation to innovation, volume- to quality-based, domestic- to export-oriented growth.

Antibiotic exports continued to grow after 1975. Between 1975 and 1990, antibiotic trade grew 50% from 88.0 billion yen to 128.0 billion yen.[189] Antibiotic imports, appeared to be heavily influenced by government reforms. The decline of imports after 1981, for example, corresponds to the government's introduction of biennial price reductions that reduced both physician demand for antibiotics as well as firm's incentives to produce antibiotics. The growth of exports, in the mean time, reflected the rising competitiveness of Japanese antibiotics, as government policies to introduce product patents or liberalize foreign capital incentivized

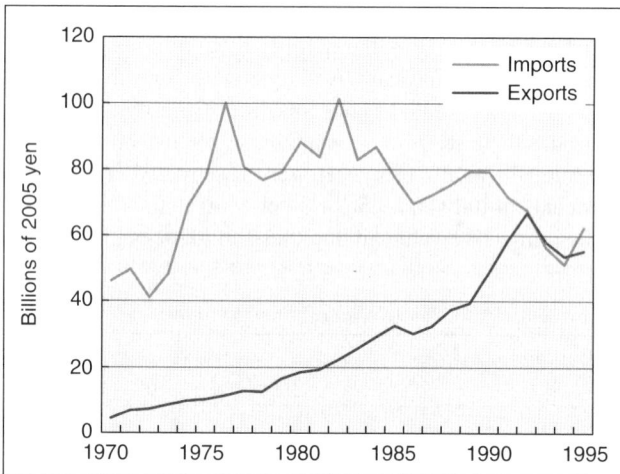

Figure 3.7 Value of antibiotic trade, 1970–1995 (in billions of 2005 yen)

Source: Ministry of International Trade and Industry, *Tsūshō Hakusho* [White Paper on Trade] (various years).

Japanese firms to adopt a more R&D-intensive orientation. Antibiotic imports rose only slightly from 77.7 billion yen in 1975 to 79.3 billion yen in 1990 while exports more than quadrupled from 10.3 billion yen to 48.7 billion yen.[190] While import growth was somewhat stunted by the regular price cuts, export growth reflected the rising capacity of Japanese firms to launch globally competitive antibiotics.

While production levels began to contract in the early 1980s, the Japanese anti-biotics sector experienced solid growth in international trade and R&D between 1975 and 1990. The growth in trade was largely due to the government's steps to lift the protective barriers that secured profits for Japanese firms and opened up the market. This was done first through the liberalization of capital controls, and later through the harmonization of Japan's pharmaceutical regulations with those in foreign countries. While these measures made it easier for foreign drugs to penetrate the Japanese market, it also made it easier for Japanese drugs to access overseas markets.

The strong performance of the antibiotic sector was also fuelled by advances in antibiotic R&D. With advances in science and technology, and health and indus-trial policies to promote volume-based production, discoveries of semisynthetic and synthetic antibiotics were made during this period.[191] As more became known of the therapeutic benefits and disadvantages of antibiotics – as well as outcomes of their use over the long term and in specific populations – better antibiotics were developed.[192] To counter resistant bacterial strains, firms continuously modified and developed new products.[193]

The introduction of product patents and capital liberalization marked a shift, as Japanese industry was incentivized to develop novel drugs that could compete against non-Japanese products and was prepared to do so. Antibiotic R&D under the process patent regime had centred on the development of new methods of production or new types of formulations to the extent it did not infringe upon patent law. Given the lower threshold for innovation that merited government rec-ognition of NCEs, however, many Japanese firms pursued incremental product innovations after the introduction of the product patent law. The Japanese antibiot-ics market grew mostly through the proliferation of similar products, rather than the discovery of original drugs.[194] Still, Japanese strengths in drug development evolved in step with advances in safety, quality and efficacy standards and were recognized internationally. By the mid-1980s, antibiotics developed in Japan and licensed to American companies accounted for about 20 per cent of the $5 billion US antibiotics market.[195]

Maturation and international standards: 1990–2005

By the 1990s, the Japanese antibiotics sector had matured as a strong, domestically oriented industry. But the antibiotics market continued to evolve over the 1990s. Facing increasing competition in a saturated home market, many firms diversified out of antibiotics while other firms stepped up efforts to strengthen their over-seas presence. These antibiotics makers intensified their R&D efforts to develop globally competitive products. The antibiotics market contracted during this period, as firms suspended sales of imitative antibiotics and innovative antibiotics makers began to concentrate on developing their overseas operations.

A shrinking domestic market

With regular price reductions, rising co-payment levels and the re-evaluation of existing prescription drugs aimed to reduce healthcare costs, the Japanese anti-biotics market contracted rapidly in the 1990s.[196] As the government's policies provided symptomatic relief to its finances, the policies also reduced the size of the antibiotics market. In 1994, Japan still had the largest market for antibiotics, with 31 per cent of the global market. Yet by 1997, it had fallen behind the US and European markets.[197]

The biennial price reductions, combined with the lower launch prices of anti-biotics, placed an enormous dent in physician prescribing incentives. Artificial demand fell as pharmaceutical price differentials became minimal.[198] The gov-ernment's decision to raise co-payment levels from the late 1990s also lowered patient demand for antibiotics. Many firms no longer viewed antibiotics as a profitable business, as physician demand for antibiotics fell and an increasing number of better-informed patients were more wary of purchasing unnecessary antibiotics.[199]

In addition, fewer antibiotics came onto the market.[200] Part of this was due to low levels of discovery during this period. Indeed, manufacturing and import approvals for new antibiotics also tapered off after the 1990s.[201] The number of antibiotics approved for manufacture or import averaged 1.9 per year in the 1990s compared to 4.9 per year in the 1980s. With the continual need to develop new drugs for antibiotic resistant infections, firms invested in new, advanced meth-ods of drug discovery such as genomic science, high throughput screening, rapid DNA sequencing, combinatorial chemistry and cell based assays to launch inno-vative antibiotics.[202] Daiichi Pharmaceutical, for example, had entered a collabo-rative agreement with the US firm Pharmacopoeia to use combinatorial chemistry and high throughput screening for new drug discovery.[203] Yet in Japan, as else-where, fewer new antibiotics were discovered in the 1990s compared to previous decades.[204]

Moreover, the antibiotics market became smaller as the few antibiotics that were discovered encountered longer drug approval times. Politically, exposure of the HIV blood scandal in the 1980s slowed the drug approval process and discouraged many firms from investing in antibiotics. For many firms, invest-ment in antibiotics became less attractive, as longer assessment times raised the cost of drug development for a now relatively low-priced drug. Also, the drug scandal had produced better-informed patients reluctant to spend on unneces-sary antibiotics.

The decline in actual therapeutic demand, too, reduced size of the antibiot-ics market. By the 1990s, with improvements in healthcare and public health, demand for antibiotics had become minimal. While it was true that the incidence of infectious disease in Japan remained higher than countries such as the United States, United Kingdom or Germany, mortality and morbidity rates for infectious diseases were remarkably lower that they were half a century ago – and continued to decline.[205]

For the first time since the 1940s, antibiotics production fell to almost half the level a decade earlier (Figure 3.8). While antibiotic production levels averaged 858 billion yen during the 1980s, for example, these figures almost halved to an average of 456 billion yen during the 1990s, before steadying near 400 billion yen.[206] In the end, few firms found it attractive to invest in what were now relatively low-priced drugs that were reduced every two years – particularly given the rising cost of drug development and declining physician dispensing rates. Facing saturated markets at home, many firms began to suspend their antibiotics business or seek new opportunities abroad.[207]

Stepping up efforts at globalization

While the biennial price reductions dented innovative incentives, the government's new policies to harmonize regulations and encourage rigorous innovation encouraged Japanese firms to develop globally competitive products. While antibiotic discoveries were not numerous, new antibiotics such as quinolones were launched by Daiichi, Dainippon and Toyoma Kagaku, while several cephalosporin drugs were launched by Shionogi, Takeda and Fujisawa.[208] The major dilemma for

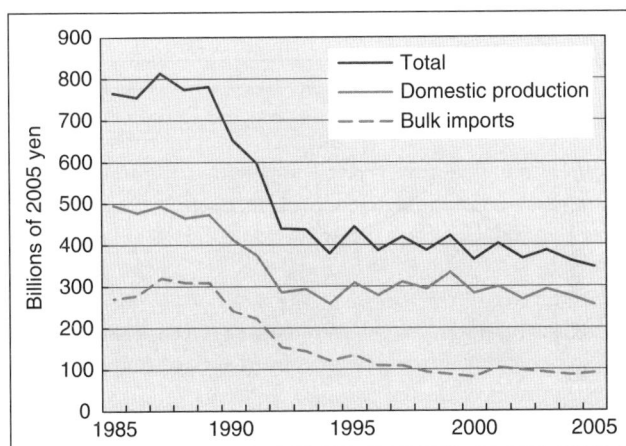

Figure 3.8 Value of antibiotic production, 1985–2005 (in billions of 2005 yen)

Source: Ministry of Health and Welfare, *Yakuji Kōgyō Seisan Dōtai Chōsa Tōkei* [Annual Survey on Production in the Pharmaceutical Industry] (various years); Ministry of Health, Labour and Welfare, *Yakuji Kōgyō Seisan Dōtai Chōsa Tōkei* [Annual Survey on Production in the Pharmaceutical Industry] (various years).

Japanese antibiotics makers was not so much to strengthen their R&D capacities but to develop the capacity to commercialize their discoveries abroad. Japanese antibiotics firms were latecomers to the global market. While they had previously gained profits from licensing agreements, they failed to reap the gains from a direct marketing presence abroad.

Trade figures demonstrate that Japan's antibiotic sector was gaining the capacity to compete in the global market. Over the 1990s, antibiotic exports rose from 48.7 billion yen to 57.3 billion yen while imports declined slightly from 79.3 billion yen to 57.3 billion yen (Figure 3.9). Japan's imports of antibiotics originated from Britain, Germany and Switzerland while its exports were destined for China, Thailand and Italy.[209]

But these data need to be interpreted with caution, as they do not fully capture Japan's performance in antibiotics. For example, the export destinations of Japanese antibiotics have mostly been to the developing world rather than to the developed world.[210] Import figures also do not include the rise in the number of overseas products directly distributed by foreign firms. Import figures may also be lower due to downward price pressures in the domestic market. Japanese drug prices have been roughly comparable with other countries, but the biennial price reductions have led to a more rapid decline in prices over the patent protection period.[211] At the same time, export figures also do not capture the availability of Japanese antibiotics abroad, as most firms licensed out their technologies rather than directly distributing their products abroad.[212] Antibiotics makers struggled to expand in the midst of increasing competition with lower cost, quality antibiotics from the developing world – and from high barriers to entry in most markets. Historical data on antibiotic trade, technology trade and NCE discoveries well

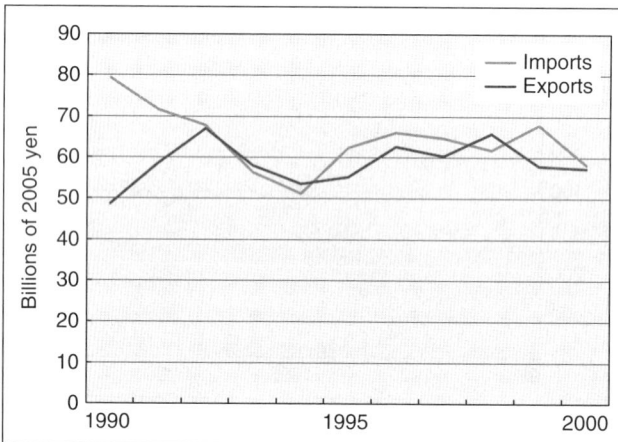

Figure 3.9 Value of antibiotic trade, 1990–2000 (in billions of 2005 yen)

Source: Ministry of International Trade and Industry, *Tsūshō Hakusho* [White Paper on Trade] (various years).

demonstrate the strengths of Japan's antibiotics sector, as do qualitative data from academic and popular press.[213]

In the Japanese antibiotics market, foreign firms remained conspicuously absent. By the new millennia, large multinational firms such as GlaxoSmithKline, Abbott, Bayer and Roche topped global antibiotics rankings and dominated most antibiotics markets in world, ranging from United States, the United Kingdom and Germany.[214] But these firms were largely absent in Japan. Instead, domestic firms such as Shionogi, Fujisawa and Daiichi dominated the Japanese market (Table 3.4).[215]

To be fair, antibiotic usage varied across countries. Countries such as Britain, for example, favoured older treatments while Italy, for example, favoured newer, parenteral drugs. Also, countries have supported their national antibiotics makers. In the 1990s, for example, prescribers in Britain remained loyal to SmithKline, while those in Germany and France remained loyal to Bayer and Rhône-Poulenc Rorer, respectively.[216]

In addition, the Japanese market still posed barriers to entry. Antibiotics were a mature sector comprised of many substitutable, high-quality drugs that were marketed by numerous firms with extensive distributional networks. Japan was not an attractive market for most foreign firms, as local partnerships were essential for distribution, just as the reverse was true for Japanese firms. Yet Japanese firms were also globally competitive. Indeed, during the mid-1990s, four of the top 15 global antibiotics firms were Japanese, while six were American.[217] While the strengths of these firms were better known to the domestic – rather than global – market, the government's earlier policies had succeeded in establishing a strong Japanese antibiotics industry.

Summary of the period between 1990 and 2005

The value of antibiotics produced declined substantially over the 1990s. It did so for several reasons. Antibiotics were a now a mature drug with relatively low prices. Rather than invest in developing antibiotics, many firms opted to invest in launching more profitable types of drugs. In addition, the 1992 reforms to Japan's distribution system eliminated the artificially high demand for antibiotics and lowered production levels. Moreover, in the 1990s, the government

Table 3.4 Leading antibiotics in the Japanese and global markets

Japan (1997, $ million) Total: $5,804			Global (1997, $ million) Total: $23,414		
Drug	Company	Sales	Drug	Company	Sales
1 Cravit/levoflaxacin	Daiichi	352	Cipro/ciprofloxacin	Bayer	1,529
2 Cefzon/cefdinir	Fujisawa	273	Augmentin/amoxycillin + clavulanate	SmithKline Beecham	1,517
3 Banan/cefpodoxime	Sankyo	203	Rocephin/ceftriaxone	Roche	1,035

Source: G. Philip White, *Antibiotics: Market Review and Development Trends* (1999), 24, 27, 32.

began to harmonize Japan's pharmaceutical regulations with those in America and Europe. As drugs approved in foreign countries were recognized in Japan, domestic firms faced greater competition from foreign firms in their home market. Antibiotics of minimal innovative value were no longer able to compete in the Japanese market. In addition, as drugs approved in Japan were recognized in the United States and Europe, more Japanese firms began to channel their efforts on expanding abroad.

Chapter summary

This section considers several possible explanations as to why the Japanese antibiotics sector flourished in comparison with the rest of the industry. One hypothesis is that Japan's strong foundations in science supported the development of a strong antibiotics sector. The historical strengths of Japan's medical research, in particular, have been cited by scholars such as James Bartholomew.[218] Contributions to the international scientific community made by Meiji era scientists such as Sahachirō Hata, Shibasaburō Kitasato, and Hidyeyo Noguchi, who led scientific research both inside and outside of Japan attest not only to the calibre of scientists in Japanese universities, but also to the academic infrastructure that supported scientific research since the Meiji period.

Some scholars have argued that while the Japanese have been very competitive in the applied sciences, the country's comparative weakness in the basic sciences may have undermined the development of a stronger pharmaceutical industry.[219] The Meiji era achievements of Japanese academic science, particularly in bacteriology, suggest that this is untrue.[220] But even if the claims made by these scholars held some validity, Japan's relative strengths in applied science in fact, would not have hampered the discovery or development of antibiotics, which are based more on the linear, incremental and evolutionary learning rather than breakthrough discoveries. While Japan's historical foundations in science demonstrate how the country provided a favourable environment for antibiotic development, it does not fully explain why Japanese firms were actually able to develop a strong antibiotic sector.

A more plausible explanation for the strength of Japan's antibiotics sector stems from firm size. Japan's pharmaceutical industry was dominated by many small firms compared to the pharmaceutical industries of other countries. While Japanese pharmaceutical firms were smaller than their foreign counterparts, antibiotic R&D required fewer resources compared to other types of drugs, such as anticancer drugs. As Japanese firms used their comparative advantage to invest in antibiotic R&D, they were able to develop a strong antibiotics sector.

With a large number of firms engaged in antibiotic production, Japan's antibiotics sector was also intensely competitive. Moreover, the barriers to entry were relatively low, and food, beverages and textiles firms were able to enter the industry. In order to survive intense competition, Japanese firms developed antibiotics with better quality, safety and efficacy profiles. While the competitive domestic environment may have contributed to the strong performance of Japan's antibiotics sector, it does not ultimately account for its strengths. The United States, for example, developed a world-class antibiotics sector in a market dominated by a few large firms. Firm size alone does not provide a sufficient reason for the strengths of Japan's antibiotics sector.

The research links formed between Japanese academia and the pharmaceutical industry also help explain why the antibiotics sector became internationally competitive. During the Second World War, for example, government, academic and industry scientists collaborated in their attempts to commercialize penicillin. These collaborative links were often based on longstanding personal connections developed during university, and persisted well into the post-war era. The government supported antibiotic research since the immediate post-war period, and these connections were invaluable in helping to translate the fruits of academic research into leading commercial discoveries such as kanamycin, josamycin or ofloxacin in later years. Japanese academics were not restricted from collaborating with firms in the formative years of Japan's antibiotics sector.

While restrictions on formal collaborations with industry were put in place after the student protests of the late 1960s, this rule had a limited impact on the formation of the antibiotics sector. In addition, the restrictions were lifted in 1998.[221] Louis Galambos and Jane Eliot Sewell have argued that networks of collaboration were essential to the building of a competitive pharmaceutical industry in the United States.[222] The same was true in Japan. But smaller firms without links to academia such as Kyorin and Toyama Chemical were also able to build a strong foothold in the Japanese antibiotics market. The strength of Japan's antibiotics sector cannot be sufficiently explained by the existence of collaborative networks.

Another explanation for the development of a strong antibiotics sector in Japan relates to the strong demand for antibiotics created under the country's medical system. Japanese physicians both prescribed and dispensed drugs. Under Japan's fee-for-service system, Japanese physicians were compensated not only for each service, but also more generously for prescribing rather than consultation services. Physicians were particularly incentivized to prescribe drugs that could be easily administered to a wide patient population, and had a greater difference between wholesale and retail prices. Japan's antibiotics sector grew, as both physicians and patients were insensitive to actual drug prices under the universal healthcare system. After all, the government reimbursed physicians for drug sales and subsidized patients for drug expenses.

Finally, it was the effectiveness of government policy that helped develop a strong, globally competitive antibiotics sector. From the early post-war period, the government funded antibiotic R&D. Until the 1970s, Japan's government concentrated on enabling Japanese firms to acquire foreign technologies. As Japanese firms caught up with Western firms, the government gradually opened the market.

The most important turning point occurred when the government liberalized capital controls in 1975 and introduced product patents in 1976. The shift from a process patent regime to a product patent regime encouraged Japanese pharmaceutical firms to pursue product innovations. To compete against foreign firms, Japanese antibiotic firms began to strengthen their R&D capacities and launch more competitive products.

The government's introduction of product and quality standards since the 1970s also helped improve the quality, safety and efficacy of Japanese pharmaceutical products, but it is worthwhile noting that country-specific standards also protected firms from foreign competition, and eased Japan's transition to a more R&D intensive and global industry. This was because foreign firms found it overly costly and risky to adapt their products for the Japanese market. Government policies helped nurture Japan's pharmaceutical industry within a heavily protected environment.

The harmonization of Japanese pharmaceutical regulations with Europe and the United States in the 1990s further pressed Japanese firms to invest in substantial innovations to survive the rising competition from foreign firms. The Japanese government changed its policies towards the antibiotics sector in a timely fashion, encouraging Japanese firms to pursue breakthrough innovations after Japan had caught up with the West. The timely implementation of these policies was key to the strong performance of Japan's antibiotics sector.

Government intervention was more effective in developing the antibiotics sector than in other therapeutic sectors because of certain features specific to antibiotics. Antibiotics can be prescribed for a wide variety of infections. As a remedy for an acute ailment, its cost burden was relatively low, yet its effects were quickly observable and patient demand was high.

Other features of antibiotics facilitated Japan's entry into global markets. Antibiotics are medicines that are used for a short period of time for a wide range of infectious ailments, and have few side effects. Patients and physicians can evaluate the safety and efficacy of antibiotics within a short period of time. These features are particularly important when translating drugs into overseas markets. Obtaining approval in foreign drug regimes is difficult for drugs that require long-term administration or have heavy side effects – such as anticancer drugs. Japanese firms have been much more successful in exporting or licensing antibiotics because their safety and efficacy are relatively easy to establish for drug authorities.

In addition to its industrial policies, the government's health policies also helped strengthen Japan's antibiotics sector. In introducing universal healthcare in 1961, the government guaranteed demand for prescription pharmaceuticals and supported the growth of Japan's pharmaceutical industry. The government further expanded this market by reducing co-payment levels and introducing free healthcare for the elderly. By setting high prices on antibiotics, the government also provided strong incentives for firms to launch antibiotics, while the greater price differentials in high-priced drugs incentivized physicians to prescribe more new antibiotics. As a drug prescribed to a wide population, these government policies were particularly helpful in expanding the size of Japan's antibiotics market.

The Japanese antibiotics sector was built upon a long history of expertise in fermentation technology, strong academic science and informal networks between government, industry and academia. By a stroke of luck, antibiotics proved relatively easy to discover, produce and export in a developing economy. Helped by the Occupation regime and the government's developmental health and industrial policies, Japanese firms were able to develop a globally competitive antibiotics sector.

4　What went wrong?
The anticancer drug sector

In the early 1980s, many Western observers speculated that the Japanese pharmaceutical industry might become a global leader. In fact, *The Economist* reported in 1983 that Japan rivalled America as a place of discovery for new drugs, and that Western pharmaceutical companies were increasingly turning to Japan as a source of new discoveries. In particular, it emphasized the strengths of the Japanese antibiotics sector, and the potentials of the anticancer drug sector.[1] *The Economist* was suggesting that Japanese pharmaceutical firms were about to penetrate overseas markets and achieve successes similar to those of Toyota and Sony in the automobile and electronics sectors. Other Western publications in the 1980s discussed the potential threat posed by Japanese firms who might – with their traditional strengths in fermentation technology – be better positioned to take advantage of new advances in biotechnology to develop innovative therapies, including anticancer drugs.[2]

Japanese pharmaceutical firms have largely failed to live up to these predictions. The weakness of Japan's pharmaceutical industry is especially visible in the realm of anticancer drugs. Japan has had a massive trade deficit in anticancer drugs; most anticancer drugs in the country are either imports or foreign-discovered drugs produced under licence.[3] It is true that Japanese pharmaceutical firms have launched several anticancer drugs that have been used in other countries. But the successes have been few and far between, and contradict the general trend depicted in the trade data. In addition, the more successful Japanese drug companies that have developed global drugs, such as Takeda, have expanded abroad by transferring their R&D, production and marketing operations overseas. These firms have sought to benefit from overseas environments more favourable to pharmaceutical innovation. The experience of firms such as Takeda suggests at why Japan's anticancer drug sector as a whole has underperformed.

The previous chapter demonstrated why Japan's antibiotics sector flourished. In contrast, this chapter surveys the development of the anticancer drug sector in Japan and considers why it failed to live up to the optimistic predictions made by foreign observers in the 1980s. It concludes by providing several possible explanations for the failure of Japan to develop a globally competitive anticancer drug sector.

This chapter follows the development of the anticancer drug sector across four phases of development. The first phase refers to the historical foundations of anticancer drug development before the Second World War. In the next phase from 1945 to 1975, Japanese firms launched anticancer antibiotics and produced small-scale batches of foreign anticancer drugs under licence. Between 1975 and 1990, there was a volume-based expansion of drugs for the domestic market. During this phase, anticancer drugs of limited efficacy proliferated in a market protected by universal health insurance, unique product standards, a distinct medical system – and links between government, industry and academia. The Japanese pharmaceutical industry, in fact, lost more than a decade in developing a globally competitive anticancer drug sector, as it misdirected investments into developing largely ineffective drugs rather than breakthrough drugs.

After the early 1990s, regulatory reforms opened the market to foreign firms and drugs, and the government improved incentives for firms to adopt a more research-intensive orientation. But with more favourable regimes for innovation abroad, leading Japanese firms began to move some of their core R&D operations abroad. While the more outward oriented Japanese firms became stronger, launched blockbuster drugs and expanded their global reach, the more domestically oriented firms began to suffer as they faced stiff competition from foreign firms in the domestic market.

On anticancer drugs

Anticancer drugs refer to a substance, other than food, that is used to prevent, diagnose, treat or relieve symptoms of cancer, a disease in which abnormal cells divide without control.[4] Cancer treatments range from surgery, radiation, chemotherapy, immunotherapy, hormone therapy and bone marrow transplantation.[5] The specific drugs used to treat cancer differ according to the afflicted body region, type and stage of cancer.

As in other therapeutic sectors, the product attributes of anticancer drugs shape its market dynamics. As newer drugs, the safety and effectiveness profile of anticancer drugs remain unknown and require improvement. The most effective anticancer drugs are also the most poisonous.[6] To balance the effectiveness of anticancer drugs against the high levels of toxicity, the amount and type of drug prescribed is carefully adjusted according to patients' needs in a hospital setting.

A single anticancer drug is generally used as part of a therapy with other anticancer drugs for a particular type and stage of cancer over a prolonged period of time. Given that the number of cancer patients that can be treated by a single anticancer drug is generally relatively small, anticancer drugs are produced on a more limited scale compared to other therapeutic sectors, such as antibiotics – in which a single drug can treat a variety of ailments. This means that the costs of developing the drug must be recovered from a small number of patients. As treatment for a life threatening disease, therapeutic demand for anticancer drugs is strong and price insensitive. Switching costs are also high due to the long-term and individualized nature of cancer therapy, and because changing to another therapy carries additional risk. Anticancer drugs therefore tend to be highly profitable, with significant first-mover advantages. This is particularly so in Japan, where the government sets initial prices of anticancer drugs at a high level and does not lower them as quickly as in other therapeutic sectors.[7] Sales in the anticancer drug market tend to be determined by a drug's therapeutic quality and the marketing efforts of medical representatives, rather than price – as patients pay generously to survive.[8]

Before 1945

In Japan or elsewhere, there were no anticancer drugs available before the Second World War. But while they did not discover drugs to treat cancer, Japanese scientists were actively engaged in cancer research well before the war. Japanese efforts in cancer research, in fact had merited the formation of national research institutes such as the Japan Foundation for Cancer Research (*Gankenkyūkai*) in 1908 and the Japanese Cancer Association (*Gangakkai*) in 1935.[9] In fact, Japan was among the first countries to establish national cancer research institutes. While Britain's Imperial Cancer Research Fund was established in 1902, the American National Cancer Institute was established in 1937, and the German Cancer Research Center (*Deutsches Krebs Forschungs Zentrum*) was established in 1964.[10]

Despite these early developments, however, Japanese cancer research remained relatively small, unorganized and lacked coordination between fundamental and applied research. This poorly integrated approach to research often lacked the momentum to translate academic research into a final product. After 1945, cancer research in the United States was backed by the American government, who helped coordinate and organize large-scale, interdisciplinary and results-oriented industrial research at the National Cancer Institute.[11] By the time of the Second World War, Germany and the United States had managed to integrate academic science in pharmaceuticals with industrial research through active collaboration among researchers, whereas academic pharmaceutical research in Japan remained relatively detached from the industrial laboratory well after the war.[12]

Japan was unable to develop a strong anticancer drug sector despite its early efforts in cancer research. Most of Japan's small pharmaceutical firms lacked the capital or equipment necessary to develop anticancer drugs. While research institutes, such as Riken, were established to promote university–industry collaboration in scientific research, there remained a relative disconnection between university scientists who pursued research for purely academic purposes and industrial scientists who pursued research for commercial ends.[13] The government also showed little commitment to encourage collaboration between academic and industrial researchers to help translate the fruits of academic research into commercial products.

Beginnings, from 1945 to 1975

Japan's anticancer drug sector emerged during the 1950s when the first chemotherapy drugs began to be sold in Japan. As elsewhere, the only cancer treatments available prior to this time were surgery and radiation. Despite its later weakness, Japan's anticancer drug sector was relatively successful in its early years. Japanese firms launched improved versions of foreign discovered drugs and developed original anticancer drugs that were distributed worldwide and continue to be used today. In a heavily protected environment, Japanese firms were able to profit from launching domestic versions of foreign-discovered drugs. Japanese firms were also able to discover several anticancer drugs that were basically a type of antibiotic effective towards cancer. For Japanese firms operating in a still emerging economy, the low-cost, labour-intensive and serendipitous method of developing these drugs suited their comparative advantage.

Yet in terms of size, Japan's anticancer drug sector remained small and undeveloped until the early 1970s. As Figure 4.1 shows, anticancer drug production rose dramatically after the mid-1970s. This was because the therapeutic demand for anticancer drugs was less than for other types of therapies, such as antibiotics. Moreover, the anticancer drugs developed during this time had limited efficacy despite their heavy side effects. While the introduction of national health insurance in 1961 and launches of several new anticancer drugs such as mitomycin, bleomycin and ftorafur did increase production levels in the 1960s, they did not prompt a substantial expansion of the anticancer drug market.

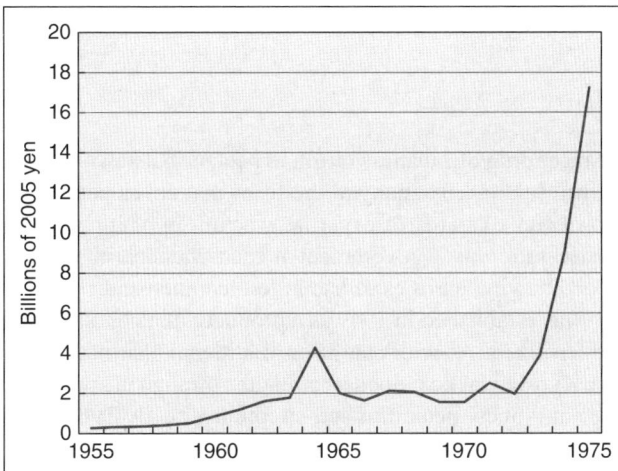

Figure 4.1 Value of anticancer drug production, 1955–1975

Source: Ministry of Health and Welfare, *Yakuji Kōgyō Seisan Dōtai Chōsa Tōkei* [Annual Survey on Production in the Pharmaceutical Industry] (various years).

Note: When the Japanese government began to collect statistics on anticancer drugs after the mid-1950s, these figures were aggregated into the category of anti-tumour drugs. As the vast majority of anti-tumour drugs are comprised of anticancer drugs, this book has used anti-tumour drugs as a proxy for anticancer drugs over the post-war period.

Yoshitomi

The discovery of one of Japan's early anticancer drugs, nitromin, originated out of academia. During the Second World War, US scientists had found the chemical weapon, nitrogen mustard, to be effective in fighting cancer.[14] Soon after the war, Morizō Ishidate and Tomizō Yoshida, two leading cancer scientists based at the University of Tokyo and Tohoku University, respectively, succeeded in reducing its toxicity.[15] The scientists then collaborated with Yoshitomi Pharmaceutical Industries to commercialize the drug, whereby the scientists guided the firm through the screening and manufacturing process.[16]

Yoshitomi was a small pharmaceutical firm that had been established in 1940 as a joint venture between Takeda Pharmaceuticals – Japan's leading pharmaceutical firm – and Mitsubishi Chemicals. Yoshitomi developed quickly after the war, and by 1950, employed over 1,000 workers and produced 2.3 per cent of the nation's pharmaceuticals. From its inception, Yoshitomi had particularly strong ties with Takeda, which distributed most of its products.[17]

Despite its success in developing a new anticancer drug, launching nitromin in 1952 did not lead to substantial sales for Yoshitomi.[18] While nitromin marked a milestone as one of the first anticancer drugs developed in Japan, demand for the drug remained limited – due to the still small number of cancer patients and the drug's heavy side effects. In fact, nitromin accounted for only 0.5 per cent of Yoshitomi's total sales in 1960.[19] Despite the ability of some academic scientists to develop and launch drugs through informal collaboration with private firms, the anticancer drug market grew slowly.

Kyowa Hakko

The first anticancer drug of Japanese origin to be distributed worldwide was mitomycin by Kyowa Hakko. Like many of the firms that developed anticancer drugs in Japan, Kyowa Hakko's area of expertise was not in pharmaceuticals. In fact, the firm's predecessor was a government-funded chemical manufacturer established in 1933.[20] Drawing on its expertise in fermentation and chemical synthesis, Kyowa Hakko was established in 1949 as a producer of alcohol, pharmaceuticals, chemicals and fertilizers. As with many non-traditional pharmaceutical firms during this period, Kyowa Hakko gained its strengths through the production and sale of the leading antibiotics: penicillin and streptomycin. By 1960, Kyowa Hakko had developed into a fairly large firm, which was capitalized at 12.9 billion yen and employed over 2,700 workers.[21]

Kyowa Hakko entered the anticancer drug sector in 1955, when the firm gained approval to sell eight anticancer drugs. The firm obtained licences to market these drugs through alliances formed with research organizations such as the Kitasato Research Institute or foreign firms such as Roche.[22] In terms of its own R&D, Kyowa Hakko concentrated on the development of anticancer antibiotics, which were essentially a category of antibiotics that were effective towards cancer.[23]

Kyowa Hakko's development of mitomycin was motivated by university researchers who contacted the firm to jointly develop its discovery. In 1955, the Kitasato Institute for Infectious Diseases formed an alliance with Kyowa Hakko to capitalize on the firm's expertise in fermentation.[24] Japan's first anticancer antibiotic, carzinophilin, had actually been discovered by the Institute in 1954 and developed by Kyowa Hakko.[25] Similar to many antibiotics of its time, mitomycin had been isolated from a soil sample, but was found to be effective in destroying cancer cells.[26] This collaboration resulted in the isolation of mitomycin C, which was developed into a drug.[27]

The development of this drug was a product of government funding for academic research in antibiotics, and of informal collaborations between academic and company scientists.[28] Research on mitomycin was also conducted abroad, and favourable results by prominent scientists such as Kanematsu Sugiura of the Memorial Sloan–Kettering Institute for Cancer Research in the United States helped the drug gain international recognition.[29]

But while the Japanese government approved mitomycin C in 1959, differences in drug approval standards meant that the drug was not available in some major markets for a considerable time. The United States, for example, initially rejected mitomycin as a potential cure for cancer.[30] When the FDA later granted approval in 1974, mitomycin was distributed by Bristol–Myers Squibb.[31] By the mid-1980s, the drug was available in more than 60 countries.[32]

While mitomycin became one of Kyowa Hakko's core products, its sales records suggested why many firms could not justify the heavy investments necessary for innovation. Japan's process patent regime meant that the fruits of R&D could easily be shared by a rival firm. While Kyowa Hakko's mitomycin, for example, was launched in October 1959, another firm, Sankyo, was able to launch mitomycin in the same month. Also, although mitomycin was one of Kyowa Hakko's key products, the firm's production of the drug was less than a fifth than the value for streptomycin – which was produced under licence.[33]

With its success in mitomycin, Kyowa Hakko carved out a prominent position in the anticancer drug sector – initially through anticancer antibiotics. After all, the government offered funding for antibiotic research, set relatively high prices for both antibiotics and anticancer drugs, and provided rewards for incremental innovations. Kyowa Hakko invested heavily in its human resources, and concentrated its investments on drugs that utilized the firm's expertise in fermentation technology to strengthen R&D capacity.[34] Kyowa Hakko also formed alliances with academic and industry research laboratories both inside and outside of Japan to build upon its limited technological expertise.[35] Since the mid-1960s, the company had also sent its key researchers to study at leading cancer research centres in the United States. These efforts helped Kyowa Hakko to learn of cutting-edge research and strengthen its research capacities.[36]

Nippon Kayaku

Nippon Kayaku, another firm that launched an anticancer antibiotic, was also a firm with core interests outside of pharmaceuticals. The firm was established in

1916 to produce explosives for the construction sector as German imports became unavailable during the First World War. The firm then diversified into chemical dyes and pharmaceuticals in the interwar period. By 1950, Nippon Kayaku had established itself as the ninth leading pharmaceutical firm in Japan.[37] The launch of its anticancer drug, bleomycin, strengthened the firm's pharmaceutical business.[38]

Nippon Kayaku's entry into the anticancer drug sector was motivated by the firm's contacts with university researchers who worked at the Institute of Microbial Chemistry.[39] In 1962, Hamao Umezawa of the Institute discovered bleomycin in a soil sample and asked Nippon Kayaku for assistance in its development.[40] The drug was developed through collaborations with the First Tokyo National Hospital.[41] Bleomycin's launch in 1969 solidified the firm's position in the anticancer drug market. The drug was recognized globally, with overseas approval in Denmark, Norway, France and Taiwan before it was approved in the United States in 1973.[42]

These successes in drug discovery, however, were brief. While Kyowa Hakko and Nippon Kayaku had introduced globally recognized anticancer drugs, Japanese firms had yet to discover therapies unrelated to antibiotics. Cancer research in Japan received limited government funding and was poorly coordinated.[43] At any rate, the firms involved in this sector did not prioritize the sale of anticancer drugs at this time.

Evolving disease patterns

Part of the reason that the anticancer drug market remained undeveloped over the 1950s and 1960s, stemmed from the smaller therapeutic demand for anticancer drugs in Japan compared to drugs such as antibiotics. As indicated in Figure 4.2, cancer deaths rose gradually after the Second World War. But it was not until the mid-1950s that figures for cancer overtook those for tuberculosis, which was only one type of infectious disease. On the other hand, cancer deaths in the United States and Britain, for example, had overtaken deaths from infectious disease much earlier.[44] Moreover, while deaths from cancer became more common than deaths from infectious diseases in Japan, the number of cancer patients remained significantly lower than the numbers with infectious diseases such as tuberculosis well into the 1970s.[45]

Changes in government policy

To a certain extent, the undeveloped status of Japan's anticancer drug sector during the 1950s and 1960s might be explained by the lack of government guidance. At a time when the therapeutic demand for anticancer drugs remained low but antibiotics remained high, the government was much more active in supporting antibiotic research.[46] While the MHW and the Ministry of Education did launch cancer research subsidies from 1963, these did not immediately translate into sub-

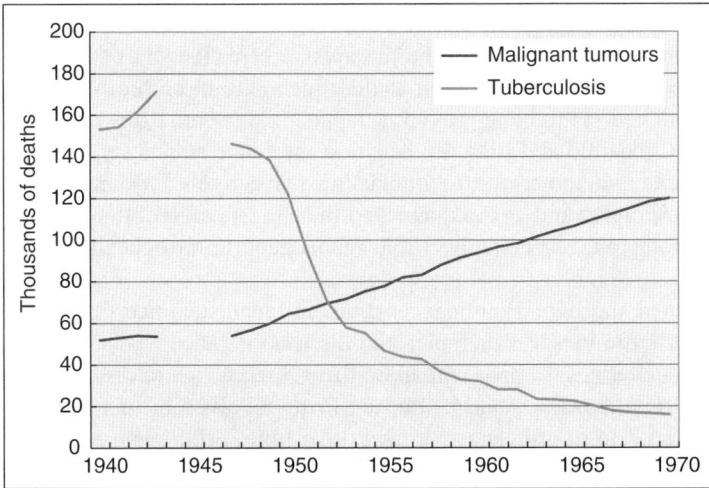

Figure 4.2 Deaths from tuberculosis and malignant tumours, 1940–1970

Source: Ministry of Health, Labour and Welfare, "Deaths by Leading Cause of Death, Population and Households" (various years).

stantial drug launches.[47] By 1970, however, much more attention was paid to the development of anticancer drugs as the death toll from cancer had more than doubled since the immediate post-war years.

Summary of period between 1945 and 1975

Despite the small size of the domestic anticancer drug market, Japanese firms were able to launch globally competitive anticancer drugs. Japan's emergence in this field might be explained by the same reasons for the strengths of its antibiotics sector. After all, the development of these drugs involved the same scientists, universities and firms involved in the development of antibiotics.[48] As mentioned earlier, the anticancer antibiotics launched by the Japanese were essentially antibiotics effective against cancer rather than bacteria. Anticancer antibiotics were suited to a developing economy as it did not require high levels of R&D investment or human capital. Similar to antibiotics, anticancer antibiotics were discovered out of serendipity, screening thousands of soil samples to locate bacteria that produced substances that would harm cancer growth – and could be done by scientists from a range of disciplines. It was relatively easy for Japanese scientists to learn, adapt and build upon these techniques and develop anticancer antibiotics. In addition, the limited reward for undertaking significant risk in the Japanese pharmaceutical market disincentivized many firms from developing other types of anticancer drugs.

While some firms developed new anticancer drugs and others obtained approval to sell imports of new anticancer drugs, Japan's anticancer drug market remained small. Not only were the therapeutic effectiveness of the few drugs available counterbalanced by their toxic effects, the more recent drugs developed abroad had yet to be approved in Japan.[49] Overseas, firms such as Roche, American Cyanamid and Eli Lilly began to introduce anticancer drugs ranging from fluouracil, methotrexate, to vinblastine, respectively.[50] Domestically, firms such as Meiji Seika and Takeda launched the anticancer antibiotics sarkomycin and chromomycin, respectively, while Japan Lederle introduced methotrexate (Table 4.1).[51]

The belated approval of anticancer drugs in Japan stemmed from the lack of demand for more invasive therapies and the lack of cancer specialists to examine or use such drugs in Japan. Japanese firms also had yet to discover therapies unrelated to antibiotics. At any rate, the firms involved in this sector did not prioritize the sale of anticancer drugs at this time. Still, some Japanese firms were able to launch globally competitive anticancer drugs that remain in use to date.

A period of volume-based growth, 1975–1990

In the 1970s and 1980s, most pharmaceutical firms around the world were still uninvolved in anticancer drugs. Even in 1987, less than 2.6 per cent of global pharmaceutical sales came from anticancer drugs.[52] While Japanese firms such as Kyowa Hakko, Sumitomo and Takeda did license in drugs such as fluoracil, tamoxifen and methotrexate, respectively, these were not their strategic products and did not comprise a major part of their business.[53] After all, anticancer drugs at this time – whether in Japan or worldwide – did not cure the disease. At best, they contained metastases. Despite heavy side effects, most anticancer drugs tended only to extend life by a few months.[54]

However, while the anticancer drug markets in Europe and the United States grew gradually through the introduction of numerous different products,

Table 4.1 Anticancer antibiotics discovered in Japan

Anthracyclines (2)	Aclarubicin (1975)	Pirarubicin (1979)
Bleomycin Group (2)	* Bleomycin (1965)	Peplomycin (1974)
Miscellaneous (5)	* Sarkomycin (1953)	Crazinophilin (1954)
	* Mitomycin C (1955)	Chromomycin A_3 (1956)
	* Zinostatin (1965, previously Neocarzinostatin)	

Source: Compiled from Joichi Kumazawa and Morimasa Yagisawa, "The History of Antibiotics: The Japanese Story," *Journal of Infection and Chemotherapy* 8, no. 2 (2002): 125–133; Morimasa Yagisawa, "Antibiotics, Chemotherapeutics and Other Microbial Products Originated from Japan," unpublished document.

Note: Nine substances. * indicates those that have also been used outside of Japan.

the Japanese market expanded rapidly through only a few products – which were not approved in other pharmaceutical markets. At a time when FarmItalia, ICI and Bristol introduced drugs such as Adriamycin (doxorubicin, 1974) Nolvadex (tamoxifen, 1977) and Platinol (cisplatin, 1978), respectively, Chugai's Picibanil (1975) and Kureha's Krestin (1976) dominated the Japanese market.[55]

By the 1980s, more anticancer drugs were being sold in Japan than in any other country, including the United States.[56] In fact, Japan's anticancer drug market in 1985 was 2.5 times larger than that of the United States.[57] For nearly 15 years, Chugai's Picibanil, along with Kureha and Sankyo's Krestin comprised approximately half of Japan's anticancer drug market and accumulated over 1 trillion yen in sales (Figure 4.3).[58]

In the short-term, Japanese pharmaceutical firms derived large profits from the sale of these anticancer drugs. The problem was that the anticancer sector of the industry was built on standards that were not recognized in other developed markets. Japanese firms lost more than a decade by diverting their energies into the development of largely ineffective therapies.

The formation of a distinctly domestic anticancer drug market

It should be remembered that Japan's anticancer drug sector grew through a particular category of new anticancer drugs. The phenomenal expansion of Japan's anticancer drug market had begun soon after the launch of the cancer

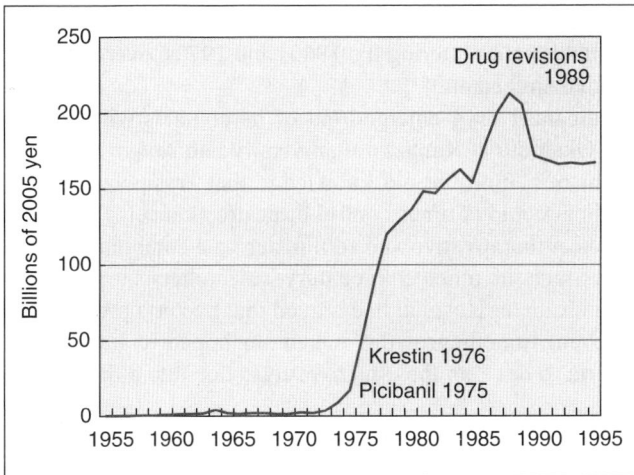

Figure 4.3 Value of anticancer drug production, 1955–1995

Source: Ministry of Health and Welfare, *Yakuji Kōgyō Seisan Dōtai Chōsa Tōkei* [Annual Survey on Production in the Pharmaceutical Industry] (various years).

immunotherapy drugs, Krestin and Picibanil.[59] A third drug of the same category, SSM (Specific Substance Maruyama), was not officially approved, but was also used widely. Rather than attacking the tumour directly, cancer immunotherapy drugs aimed to boost the immune system to destroy or control cancer – providing an alternative or a complement to existing cancer therapies. Unlike existing anti-cancer drugs, these drugs were approved for a wide range of cancers, in various stages and locations of the body. These drugs offered remedies with significantly fewer side effects compared to radiation or chemotherapy, which, for physicians, made them relatively easy to prescribe. The new drugs also gave hope to patients for whom surgery was not an option.[60]

Given that other developed countries used numerous drugs to treat different types of cancer, it seemed rather peculiar that so few drugs were used to treat cancer in Japan. After all, cancer is comprised of over 100 types of complex diseases.[61] In addition, the gradual increase in cancer morbidity and mortality levels did not explain the 88-fold jump in anticancer drug production between 1970 and 1980.[62] Cancer immunotherapy drugs were popular with doctors in Japan because they were easy to prescribe, not because they were particularly effective at fighting cancer.

Chugai – Picibanil

Chugai, a mid-ranking pharmaceutical firm, launched the first of these immuno-therapy drugs. Picibanil became a blockbuster drug that changed both the firm's fortunes and altered the dynamics of the anticancer drug sector. Chugai sold no anticancer drugs before 1975. The entrepreneur Jūzo Ueno had founded the firm in 1925 as an import distributor of drugs from the German pharmaceutical firm, Gehe & Co.[63] The company had developed expertise in substances such as disinfectants and anthelmintics. During the 1960s and 1970s, over a third of Chugai's sales came from disinfectants.[64]

Chugai's anticancer drug emerged out of its contacts with academia. Since 1954, Hajime Okamoto at Kanazawa University had sought to identify the scientific mechanism behind the old knowledge that erysipelas, a type of bacterial skin infection, could at times control or destroy cancer. This bacteriological approach to cancer therapy involved administering a combination of dead bacteria to patients. Since the nineteenth century, researchers such as William Coley of the New York Cancer Hospital had argued that bacteria produced a substance that could prevent tumour growth.[65] Okamoto hoped to identify the relevant strain of bacteria to develop the effective substance into a drug – with the help of Chugai.[66]

Launched in October 1975 as the first officially recognized cancer immu-notherapy drug in the world, Picibanil was popular because of its claimed applicability to a wide range of cancers and remarkably minor side effects compared to existing cancer therapies.[67] During the 1980s, Picibanil sales ranged from 10 per cent to 15 per cent of the anticancer drug market, and generated approximately 25 billion yen in annual revenues.[68] Chugai, which had previously been struggling from falling sales, was able to recover its financial health. But the drug did not meet approval criteria in Europe or the United States, and remained a domestic drug. Japanese critics also began to question whether approval standards had been particularly ambiguous or lenient, as strong sales were not followed by widespread evidence of efficacy.[69]

Kureha – Krestin

It was somewhat surprising not only that Kureha discovered a new anticancer drug, but also that this would become a blockbuster drug. Kureha, established in 1944, specialized in plastics, agrochemicals and other industrial chemicals. The mid-ranking chemical firm had no experience in pharmaceuticals, let alone anti-cancer drugs. In the 1970s, the firm was best known for its popular plastic food wrap 'Kurerappu'.[70]

Kureha entered the anticancer drug sector by accident. In 1965, Chikao Yoshi-kumi, a company researcher began to investigate the antitumour properties of Kawaratake mushrooms, following on rumours that the traditional remedy could cure stomach cancer.[71] In 1968, Kureha formed an academic alliance with the Kyoto Institute of Technology to identify the effective agent.[72] The company then consulted researchers at the Japan Foundation for Cancer Research and the University of Tokyo to develop the drug, and received guidance from government officials in the drug application process.[73]

To substitute for its lack of experience in pharmaceutical distribution, Kureha chose Sankyo as a marketing partner. After its launch in October 1976, Krestin sales rose from approximately 15 billion yen in 1977 to a peak in 1984 with 31.1 per cent of the Japanese anticancer drug market at approximately 52 billion yen.[74] In fact, in 1986, it was the top selling drug in Japan – and twelfth worldwide.[75] Among the world's best-selling anticancer drugs in 1988, Krestin ranked first followed by Zeneca's Nolvadex (tamoxifen) and Erbamont's Adriamycin (doxorubicin hydrochloride) (Table 4.2).[76]

As in Picibanil, Krestin was marketed as a drug that could cure many types of cancer, had limited side effects and was easy to take. Krestin sold well, but its therapeutic effects were not matched by its extraordinary sales performance.[77] Critics began to voice scepticism over drug approval standards, particularly as

Table 4.2 Leading anticancer drugs in Japan vs. United States and Europe

Japan (1989, $ million)			United States and Europe (1988, $ million)		
Drug	Company	Sales	Drug	Company	Sales
1 Krestin	Sankyo	399	Adriamycin/doxorubicin	Erbamont	330
2 Picibanil	Chugai	234	Nolvadex/tamoxifen	Zeneca	271
3 Fluoracil/5FU	Kyowa Hakko	148	Methotrexate	American Cyanamid	160

Source: Christopher Dunn, *Scrip's 1994 Review of Cancer Chemotherapy* (1994), 355–356.

it was revealed, for example, that much of the research had been published in non-refereed company-sponsored journals and that efficacy had been measured in terms of tumour size rather than survival.[78]

Zeria – SSM

In the late 1970s, a small Tokyo-based pharmaceutical firm filed an application for SSM, another cancer immunotherapy drug. Unlike Picibanil and Krestin, however, SSM never gained official approval. This decision was extremely controversial and prompted intense public debate over Japan's drug approval process. Critics charged that the drug was denied approval due to the influence of competing pharmaceutical firms.[79] SSM's rejection suggested that the success of a drug was determined more by a firm's political clout rather than the intrinsic merits of a drug. More specifically, it implied that scientists and firms needed to develop strong connections to key individuals in the regulatory bureaucracy to facilitate a drug's success.

Like Chugai and Kureha, Zeria had accidentally entered the anticancer drug sector when SSM's discoverer proposed to co-develop the drug. SSM was discovered by Chisato Maruyama, a physician at a small private university in Tokyo, the Nippon Medical School. Maruyama, who followed the bacteriological approach to cancer therapy, developed SSM from human tuberculosis bacilli in the 1940s.[80]

Established in 1955, Zeria was known mostly for its dietary supplement chondroitin, and was engaged in the import distribution or manufacture of pharmaceuticals.[81] The Tokyo-based firm was neither heavily engaged in R&D nor prescription drugs until the mid-1980s.[82] Zeria resembled Chugai, Kureha or Sankyo as a new entrant to the anticancer drug sector, but was a much smaller firm, with limited links to individuals in academia or government.

Without the political connections of larger firms, however, Zeria was placed in a more disadvantaged position compared to Chugai or Sankyo. For example, four of the 12 examiners on SSM's approval committee had direct conflicts of interests with its approval, because they had been involved in the development of its rival drugs, Picibanil and Krestin.[83] These drugs were highly profitable and the approval of SSM, which made with similar therapeutic claims, would likely have taken sales away from the two leading drugs. In 1979, Picibanil and Krestin comprised 15.8 per cent and 33.4 per cent of the anticancer drug market, respectively.[84] At a time when Krestin and Picibanil charged 3,254 yen and 5,313 yen for treatment per day, respectively, Maruyama had been prescribing SSM for just 125 yen per day.[85] The popular press and Diet proceedings stated that ready opponents and the lack of strong supporters undermined the drug's potential for success.

SSM's rejection had revealed that Japan's drug approval process was not transparent – and that its decisions were not entirely binding, either.[86] After all, Maruyama had opened a clinic and sold the drug without official approval.[87] Moreover, while the approval of Krestin and Picibanil was swiftly decided in one year and two and a half years, respectively, the decision on SSM was not made for almost five years.[88] Moreover, while the government eventually rejected the drug, it allowed SSM to be supplied to patients who were willing to pay to participate in so-called clinical trials for the drug's development.[89] Since, 1981, the period of clinical testing has been extended for almost three decades.[90]

As public scepticism about the efficacy of Picibanil and Krestin grew, the MHW began to re-evaluate these and a number of other drugs that it had approved earlier.[91] After a reappraisal in December 1989 banned Picibanil and Krestin from being prescribed as the main drug in an anticancer regimen, both drugs' production levels plummeted by two-thirds within a year.[92] Japan's anticancer drug sector began to shrink as suddenly as it had grown two and a half decades earlier. The bubble in Japan's anticancer drug market had burst.

Reasons for Japan's lost decade in anticancer drugs

Japan's anticancer drug sector of the 1970s and 1980s differed from those of other developed countries in two major ways: the size of its market and the drugs widely used. Additionally, while Picibanil, Krestin and SSM were remarkably similar in their manner of discovery, therapeutic attributes and mechanisms of action, they experienced different levels of success in the Japanese market. It is worth examining more closely why the demand for anticancer drugs in Japan grew so rapidly with drugs not approved beyond Japan – and why the three immunotherapy drugs experienced very different fortunes in the domestic market.

The impact of medical culture

Japanese medical culture had a significant impact on the expansion of Japan's anticancer drug market during the 1970s and 1980s. Different approaches to cancer therapy in Japanese medical practice help explain why many anticancer drugs of questionable efficacy were prescribed and sold in Japan. The key differences in Japanese approaches were the non-disclosure of cancer diagnoses and preference towards safer, even if less effective, drugs. As Julia Yongue has noted, this preference for safety over efficacy in Japan was not only limited to anticancer drugs, but also applied to drugs more generally.[93]

As noted earlier, anticancer drugs of the time could not cure cancer patients, but could only extend life by a few months while creating severe side effects.[94] Given the minimal benefits to be gained from an arduous therapy, many Japanese physicians preferred not to tell patients they had cancer.[95] Doctors typically prescribed anticancer drugs with the fewest side effects so as to prevent patients from discovering that they had an almost fatal disease. As prescriptions given to patients were not labelled, many patients remained ignorant of both the nature of the drugs prescribed and their diagnosis. Japanese physicians' aversion to side effects may also have stemmed from the widely publicized drug tragedies such as thalidomide that resurfaced over the 1960s and 1970s.[96] Effective but highly toxic anticancer drugs such as adriamycin and vincristine were available for use in Japan at this time, but had lower sales in comparison to those in Western markets.[97]

Physician demand for a particular drug translated easily into patient demand in a hierarchical society where patients did not question the authority of physicians, where few explanations were made of the medicines prescribed.[98] While the recent diffusion of cancer information on the Internet has empowered patients, who have become more informed and assertive in demanding particular treatments by researching options online, this technology was not available in the 1970s or 1980s. Japanese medical practice therefore played an important role in generating demand for safe yet largely ineffective therapies.

R&D incentives under universal healthcare

Another reason why Japan's anticancer drug sector developed rapidly through ineffective drugs lay in R&D incentives, whereby firms were forgiven for a lack of innovation but stood to benefit from launching drugs with limited side effects that could be prescribed to a wide population.[99] By comparison, policies in countries such as the United States, Germany and Britain were designed to penalize imitations and encourage pioneering innovations that would be accepted worldwide.

Before the product patent system was introduced in 1976 – and even after – the criteria for innovation in Japan were lower than in other advanced markets. As mentioned earlier, the national health insurance system essentially guaranteed that the government would underwrite demand. Japanese physicians also continued to adhere to the traditional practice of both prescribing and dispensing drugs. To profit from the difference between wholesale and retail drug prices, physicians were incentivized to prescribe newer and higher priced drugs that tended to have the steepest price differential.[100]

Newer drugs, such as anticancer drugs, had higher prices compared to older drugs such as antibiotics.[101] The cancer immunotherapy drugs also offered the promise of a remedy that existing anticancer drugs could not achieve. Anticancer drugs such as Picibanil and Krestin experienced tremendous success, not only because of their high prices and large pharmaceutical price differentials, but also because they could be prescribed to many patients.

The impact of rudimentary infrastructure

To a certain extent, the proliferation of ineffective drugs also had to do with Japan's undeveloped research environment that neither produced innovative drugs nor seriously condemned the largely ineffective drugs in circulation. Japanese firms had fewer skilled researchers, received little government funding and spent a lower proportion of sales on R&D compared to leading global counterparts.[102] But the problem with Japanese research lay not simply in the scarcity of resources but also in how these resources were used.

For example, rather than seeking breakthrough discoveries, Japanese industrial researchers mostly continued to focus on incremental product innovation, while Japanese academic researchers focused on applied over basic research.[103] Also, in a rigid labour market, Japanese industry research lacked fluidity of knowledge transfers from academic research. While collaborations between academia and industry did exist, the informal and ad-hoc nature of these led to duplicative work and an absence of large-scale projects with long-term vision. Neither equipped with the strategy to pursue breakthrough discoveries nor able to exploit synergies from industrial and academic research, Japanese firms were unlikely to develop innovative drugs. Indeed, cancer immunotherapy drugs, such as antibiotics, were characterized by a serendipitous, low-cost and labour-intensive method of drug discovery. They were very different products from the innovative drugs developed using exceptional skills and cutting-edge technologies – from a deep understanding of the mechanisms of the disease and the drugs.

Moreover, the infrastructure for developing and testing anticancer drugs remained underdeveloped in Japan. In the early 1980s, for example, there were 5,000 cancer specialists in the United States and just 100 in Japan – which had half the population of the United States.[104] The absence of cancer specialists amidst a diverse assortment of public and private hospitals and clinics meant not only that Japanese pharmaceutical firms found it extremely difficult to conduct clinical trials, but it also meant that Japanese physicians were also unable to administer effective yet often highly toxic cancer therapies to Japanese cancer patients.[105] Physicians who administered too little of the drug found the expense to be wasteful, as the drug was ineffective. Those who administered too much of the drug found the serious harm done to patients too devastating to use the drug again.

Links between government, industry and academia

Another reason for the volume-based expansion of the anticancer drug sector lay in Japan's opaque drug approval system, where the criteria for drug approval remained unclear. A drug approval system that is transparent, stable and based on scientific criteria incentivizes firms to invest in developing quality drugs that can also be approved in other markets.[106] But a more opaque or politically charged drug approval system incentivizes firms to invest in political rent-seeking at the expense of R&D.[107] The governance of the Japanese pharmaceutical industry by a set of administrative guidance, ministerial orders and quality standards created room for ambiguous interpretation. In particular, the blurring of the boundaries between government, industry and academia created conflicts of interest. In this environment, firms benefited from forming strategic alliances with key individuals in government and academia to facilitate drug approval.[108]

The volume-based expansion of Picibanil and Krestin was supported by their links to powerful individuals with overlapping roles in government, industry and academia – by excluding competition from drugs such as SSM that did not have similar links.[109] Officials explained that such conflicts of interests were to some extent inevitable due to the lack of qualified experts. But these conflicts of interests, including the continued use of company-sponsored journals as evidence of efficacy, undermined both the quality and credibility of drugs from Japan.[110] This was particularly true as approvals were granted not only to ineffective drugs but also to unsafe drugs, resulting in tragedies involving drugs such as thalidomide, chloroquine and sorivudine.[111] The opaque criteria for drug approval disincentivized firms from undertaking riskier, innovative R&D projects, as they could not assess the risks involved in drug development.

The main reasons for rapid growth with drugs of limited efficacy

There were other explanations for the abundance of largely ineffective drugs in Japan during this period. Part of Krestin's dramatic sales record, for example, was attributed to Sankyo's marketing strategy and sales network.[112] However, the main reasons for the idiosyncratic growth of Japan's anticancer drug sector lay in Japanese medical culture, its healthcare system and undeveloped infrastructure. These were the same reasons why Japan did not develop a world-leading pharmaceutical industry.

Summary of the period between 1975 and 1990

There are several reasons why the Japanese anticancer sector experienced a phenomenal expansion through anticancer drugs that did not exist in leading Western markets during this period. One of the major reasons lay in Japan's opaque drug approval process and the lack of government funding for research in anticancer drugs. It is important to note, however, that even if innovative drugs had been developed and approved, the Japanese medical system was not prepared to take advantage of such drugs. The delivery of anticancer drugs is dependent on physicians and technicians with expertise in cancer and anticancer drugs to administer the drug, as well as hospitals equipped with the relevant equipment to deliver the drug. The lack of such infrastructure not only disincentivized innovation, but they also maintained invisible yet significant barriers to entry to foreign firms despite formal attempts at deregulation – and provided life support for non-innovating firms. The absence of R&D incentives, lack of regulatory transparency and distinct medical culture helped encourage the development of high-priced, safe yet largely ineffective drugs that would not have survived in other advanced markets. These factors were the source of Japan's weakness in anticancer drugs.

Hollowing out, 1990 onwards

Japan's anticancer drug sector changed markedly after 1990. As the decade progressed, the Japanese market increasingly resembled those of other advanced Western markets. By 1998, Japan's anticancer drug market was 60 per cent of its size a decade earlier.[113] The commonly used drugs in Japan became similar to those in the United States and Europe. Well into the millennium, Japan still had the only anticancer market among developed countries that was dominated by domestic, rather than multinational firms. However, the Japanese market now offered a greater variety of drugs that were developed overseas, many of which were launched by foreign firms.

Whereas Japan's leading pharmaceutical firms had previously little to do with anticancer drugs, this changed in the 1990s.[114] A handful of leading firms such as Takeda and Yakult also discovered and developed globally competitive anticancer drugs. Yet Japan's anticancer drug sector remained weak compared to countries such as the United States, the United Kingdom and Germany. This was demonstrated clearly in Japan's large trade deficit and trading partners. In 2005, for example, Japan imported more than 17 times as many anticancer drugs as it exported. While imports of anticancer drugs originated from developed countries, led by the United States, the United Kingdom and France, its exports were primarily destined to developing countries, led by China, Taiwan and Middle Eastern countries such as Egypt, Syria and Jordan.[115] Japan remained reliant on Western imports, and its anticancer drug sector was not able to compete in advanced Western markets.

Part of this could be explained by an environment that was not entirely hospitable to pharmaceutical innovation. Japanese university professors, for example, faced barriers in commercializing their research; venture capital was less available to support biotechnology start-ups; and the smaller sized Japanese firms had less to invest in R&D compared to the leading American and European firms. But a much more compelling reason for the weakness of Japan's anticancer drug sector was the comparative lack of research incentives; the lack of specialized experts or facilities for drug development; and the distinct medical practices that restricted demand for highly innovative anticancer drugs.

What was notable, however, was the hollowing out of R&D in Japan. To circumvent inferior incentives in the home market, Japan's leading pharmaceutical firms began to prioritize drug development in American or European regimes that were more favourable to pharmaceutical innovation. Companies such as Takeda and Yakult shifted their core R&D operations to the United States or Europe, where they developed and launched their anticancer drugs – leuprorelin and oxaliplatin, respectively – before they did so in Japan.[116] These firms were increasingly rootless, as the sources of innovation and potential for future growth were now based overseas.

Lagging drug approvals and problems in infrastructure

In the 1990s, fewer anticancer drugs were approved in Japan compared to other advanced markets. Despite having the second largest cancer market in the world after the United States, 30 cancer therapies approved in the United States had not been approved in Japan.[117] This drug lag was a new phenomenon that had not been observed in previous decades.[118]

Some argued that Japan's delayed approval of innovative drugs was a result of administrative failure. The government had been reluctant to consult foreign test data or quicken its pace of examination following criticism over the approval of

Krestin and Picibanil in the 1980s and the HIV blood scandal in the early 1990s. While this was true to some extent, the issue was more complex: the Japanese government lacked the resources, funds and capacity – in terms of human capital, facilities and organization – to support drug R&D and review drugs efficiently compared to overseas competitors in the United States and Europe.[119] For one, the Japanese clinical trial system was less equipped in relation to comparable systems abroad. Japan's Pharmaceuticals and Medical Devices Agency in 2005 maintained approximately 250 staff, including ten clinical examiners, of whom three were biological statisticians. By comparison, the FDA employed approximately 2,300 staff, with 300 clinical examiners, including 100 biostaticians.[120] Moreover, there has been no system or standards established to conduct clinical trials in Japanese hospitals; in the past, most were conducted through personal connections, on an ad-hoc basis.[121]

A number of studies have discussed how private health insurance in the United States expanded the demand for pharmaceuticals.[122] Yet the impact of private insurance on expanding demand for anticancer drugs in Japan – and incentivizing firms to develop innovative drugs – was likely minimal. Despite a universal healthcare system, many Japanese have taken out private, supplemental medical insurance and cancer insurance. Both have worked alongside Japan's public healthcare system by offering fixed-rate daily cash benefits that fill the gap between public medical coverage and actual expenses.

By 2004, the market for supplemental medical insurance reached 5.7 trillion yen while the market for cancer insurance reached 2.6 trillion yen.[123] Meanwhile, average out-of-pocket spending per patient on cancer treatments exceeded 931,000 yen a year.[124] By 2006, over half of Japanese households had taken out some form of cancer insurance, over half of whom were insured for at least 10,000 yen a day.[125]

Yet, it is unlikely that private insurance in Japan has increased demand for anticancer drugs. First, the extent to which private medical insurance is used for cancer treatments is unclear. Second, the lack of cancer diagnoses limited demand for cancer related products until the 1990s.[126] Third, while the cancer insurance market was expanding rapidly, Japan's leading pharmaceutical companies still prioritized overseas R&D over domestic R&D, suggesting that the popularity of cancer insurance did not make the Japanese market particularly more attractive to firms.[127] Moreover, major insurers in Japan have not offered a specific category of benefits to cover pharmaceuticals, although patients have been able to use some of their cash benefits towards this.[128] Given the variations in patient preference and limited coverage for pharmaceuticals, suggesting that private insurance raised demand for anticancer drugs would be speculative at best.

Private insurance in Japan might have had a greater impact on firm incentives to develop innovative drugs had mixed billing been allowed.[129] Even amidst a drug lag, firms could have expected a larger domestic market for new drugs had Japanese patients been allowed to pay for drugs covered under public health insurance at the discounted rate alongside non-covered drugs through private health insurance. However, Japanese patients who have opted to purchase non-covered drugs have had to pay for their entire medical expenses out of their own pocket. With little demand for non-covered drugs, Japanese firms did not prioritize the domestic market to develop breakthrough therapies, including anticancer drugs.

In addition, there were fewer cancer specialists and facilities compared to many other countries. Oncologists, for example, were only certified in 2007, more than 35 years after the United States.[130] In 2008, Japan still had only 1.6 oncologists per million population, compared to 42.3 in the United States or 34.5 in the United Kingdom.[131] The lack of infrastructure long limited the demand for anticancer drugs, as it meant that fewer Japanese physicians were capable of prescribing the drugs, and fewer facilities were equipped to administer the drug to cancer patients. These inadequacies in infrastructure meant that even if potentially effective therapies were discovered, they could not easily be translated into commercially viable products.

A shift in Japan's anticancer drug market

Following the revisions of the two cancer immunotherapy drugs, the composition of Japan's anticancer drug market changed (Figure 4.4). Compounded with the biennial price reductions, the anticancer drug market became smaller. The size of the market also reflected delays in the approval process, which limited the availability of anticancer drugs in Japan – despite their availability overseas. Still, the demand for these drugs remained strong. More anticancer drugs of foreign origin were available in the market. As a disease that mostly affects the elderly, Japan's ageing society also contributed to a rising cancer population.[132]

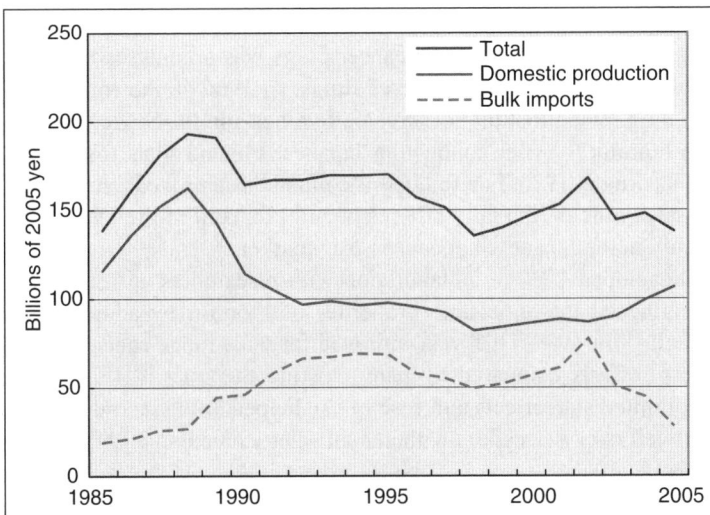

Figure 4.4 Value of anticancer drug production, 1985–2005

Source: Ministry of Health and Welfare, *Yakuji Kōgyō Seisan Dōtai Chōsa Tōkei* [Annual Survey on Production in the Pharmaceutical Industry] (various years).

Table 4.3 Changes in best-selling medicines in Japan's anticancer drug market

	1995 (total: ¥ 502 billion)			2005 (total: ¥ 535 billion)		
	Drug	*Company*	*Sales ¥ billion*	*Drug*	*Company*	*Sales ¥ billion*
1	UFT/tegafur-uracil Furtulon/	Taiho Japan	70	Leuplin/ leuprolide acetate	Takeda	63
2	doxyfluridine	Roche	30	Taxol/paclitaxel Casodex/	Taiho	33
3	Zoviraex/Acyclovir	Wellcome	29	Bicalutamide	AstraZeneca	32

Source: Yakugyō Jihōsha, *Yakuji Handobukku* [Pharmaceutical Affairs Handbook] (1996); Jihō, *Yakuji Handobukku* [Pharmaceutical Affairs Handbook] (2007).

Whereas the top three anticancer drugs in 1985 were domestic drugs not approved in the United States or Europe, a decade later, the top three anticancer drugs – Taiho's UFT, Roche's Fruturon and Takeda's Leuplin – were all therapies recognized beyond Japan (Table 4.3).[133] Although Japan's anticancer drug market remained undeveloped, it was becoming less backward relative to its Western counterparts.

Taiho

One of the leading anticancer drug makers since the 1980s began as a small import distributor of Western medicines. Established in 1963 as a subsidiary of a leading OTC drug maker, Otsuka, Taiho offered numerous therapies ranging from anti-allergy to digestive medicines.[134]

Taiho's decision to invest in anticancer drugs was an outgrowth of its past in reverse engineering foreign-discovered drugs. In 1969, Taiho formed a partnership with the Latvian Institute of Organic Synthesis in the Soviet Union in 1969 to launch Ftorafur.[135] After conducting Japanese clinical trials from 1970, Taiho launched its drug in 1973. For Taiho, this collaboration proved a strategic success. Ftorafur sales rode on the tails of Krestin and Picibanil in the 1980s and placed Taiho firmly in the Japanese anticancer drug market.[136]

Taiho developed UFT in collaboration with researchers at Osaka University, who strengthened the anticancer properties of Ftorafur by adding a substance called uracil.[137] In 1984, UFT was approved for wide range cancers and featured few adverse effects compared to many existing therapies.[138] Its wide range of approval, limited side effects and ease of use helped Taiho record robust sales in Japan for well over a decade – with annual sales exceeding 80 billion yen in the mid-1990s.[139]

However, UFT was met with mixed reception abroad. The drug was approved in more than 15 countries, and was marketed by Merck in countries such as the UK, France and Germany by 2005.[140] It was, however rejected in the United States in 2001.[141] Admittedly, UFT was not an entirely new therapy, but rather an improvement on an existing anticancer drug. While it was more effective compared to Japan's previous anticancer drugs, it had yet to be fully recognized internationally.

To counter the government's periodic price reductions of existing therapies, Taiho continued to invest in R&D and launch new drugs. These efforts resulted in the launch of another anticancer drug TS-1, in 1999. In step with improvements in Japanese approval standards, TS-1 was recognized with a licence for worldwide distribution by Sanofi-Aventis in 2006.[142]

Yakult Honsha

It was during these times that Yakult Honsha launched its successful anticancer drugs, irinotecan and oxaliplatin. Yakult Honsha is a food company known for its probiotic drink, 'Yakult', that entered pharmaceuticals and cosmetics in the 1970s. 'Yakult' was first launched in 1935 by the bacteriologist Minoru Shirota as a nutritional supplement. The company had been established in 1955 in order to manufacture and sell the drink. Yakult Honsha expanded over the decades through its international operations – mostly in food and beverages.[143]

Facing saturation in these markets, however, Yakult Honsha decided to take advantage of new developments in biotechnology, and develop a pharmaceutical business. The entry of Yakult Honsha into pharmaceuticals represented a wider phenomenon in the 1970s and 1980s, when Japanese firms from a range of maturing sectors began to diversify into this industry.[144] The firm invested heavily to develop its research capacity by hiring new scientists and forming alliances with universities and other firms.[145]

The research that led to Yakult's anticancer drug, irinotecan, had actually begun in America. In 1966, researchers led by M.E. Wall at the Research Triangle Institute in North Carolina isolated camptothecin, an extract from a Chinese tree that was found to be effective against certain mouse cancers.[146] While clinical trials at the US National Cancer Institute during the 1970s were unsuccessful and withdrawn, elsewhere, research continued on camptothecin.[147]

During the 1970s, Yakult Honsha invested heavily in the recruitment of capable scientists and forming academic and corporate alliances in order to make its new venture in pharmaceuticals a success.[148] Researchers at the firm, alongside scientists at Showa University were able to synthesize an effective substance in 1983.[149] In 1984, Yakult formed an alliance with Daiichi Pharmaceuticals to develop the drug.[150]

Launched in 1994, Yakult's new anticancer drug, irinotecan, became a global blockbuster drug. It was the first drug that was found to be effective for colorectal cancer in 40 years. In the domestic market, irinotecan was launched as Campto by Yakult and Topotecin by Daiichi in April 1994.[151] Overseas, irinotecan was introduced in France as Campto by Rhône-Poulenc in 1995, and as Camptosar in the United States by Pharmacia & Upjohn in the following year. By March 2006, irinotecan was approved in 100 countries, and sold in 88. Until the introduction of its successor drug, oxaliplatin, irinotecan formed the backbone of Yakult's pharmaceutical operations; with annual sales over 15 billion yen, it comprised over

90 per cent of Yakult's pharmaceutical sales.[152] With 80 per cent of its sales from overseas markets, it was more of a global, rather than Japanese drug.[153] Yakult's success with irinotecan solidified the firm's position in the anticancer drug market, and helped the launch of a new anticancer drug.

This new drug, oxaliplatin, was an anticancer drug that was actually discovered in 1976 by a researcher at Nagoya City University.[154] But Japanese researchers had abandoned clinical testing in the 1970s. In 1989, however, Debiopharm, a Switzerland-based pharmaceutical firm, licensed-in oxaliplatin. Debiopharm specialized in ethical drug development and registration; the firm licensed-in potential compounds and licensed-out the developed drug. Debiopharm developed oxaliplatin into a drug, which was approved for colorectal cancer in France, the UK and the US in 1996, 1999 and 2004, respectively.[155] In Japan, however, Yakult did not gain approval for oxaliplatin/Elplat until 2005.[156] At a high launch price, oxaliplatin gained sales of 9 billion yen in 2005 in Japan, and surpassed irinotecan sales in Japan the following year.[157] The inability to develop such home-grown discoveries and launch them swiftly in the domestic market limited Japan's ability to become a global leader in pharmaceuticals.

Technology, patient empowerment and the modernization of medical practice

While Japanese physicians did not historically disclose to cancer patients their full and accurate diagnoses, Japan's medical culture began to change over the 1990s. The growth of Internet use, in particular, empowered patients who accumulated information on cancer and cancer therapies. This meant that physicians were more likely to prescribe drugs with the conspicuous side effects of cancer chemotherapy, and that there was more demand for such drugs. Japanese cancer patients began to help expand demand for innovative anticancer drugs and pressure authorities to accelerate drug approval.

The Internet not only empowered cancer patients with knowledge of their condition and possible therapies, but also fostered patient networks that campaigned for anticancer drugs that had yet to be approved in Japan. Patient groups such as Japan's Cancer Patients Support Organization (CANPS), for example, were instrumental in obtaining approval for oxaliplatin in Japan.[158] The national organization for cancer patients was only established in 2005, but quickly gained political influence through connections with government, firms and academia.[159] Patient groups concentrated primarily on the rapid approval of drugs for cancer or orphan diseases that were not available in Japan, but already approved in other countries.[160] For pharmaceutical firms, patient groups could also act as a vehicle to promote potential approvals. Much of the funding for CANPS campaigns, for example, came from pharmaceutical firms. Foreign pharmaceutical firms have been particularly keen in funding and disseminating information on their new drugs that had yet to be approved in Japan.[161] The absence of more empowered cancer patients had previously undermined the development of Japan's anticancer drug sector.

Barriers to entrepreneurship

The legal barriers to entrepreneurship faced by Japanese university academics until the late 1990s also hindered the translation of innovative research in anticancer drugs into commercial therapies. As mentioned in the overview chapter, until 1998, academics at national or public universities were prohibited from receiving income in private industry or establishing firms to commercialize their research.[162] In the meanwhile, American academic start-ups such as Genentech had played a key role in launching new anticancer drugs in the United States.[163]

The comparatively smaller size of Japanese firms appeared to disadvantage prospects for innovative discoveries due to the limited size of R&D that smaller firms could possibly afford. Dominant players in the Japanese anticancer drug market such as Taiho, Nippon Kayaku and Kyowa Hakko were not only much smaller than global leaders such as Novartis, Bristol–Myers Squibb or Aventis, but were also more diversified firms with considerable business outside of pharmaceuticals.[164] Yet it is unclear whether firm size impacted upon the ability to innovate. Smaller firms have the flexibility to concentrate on specialized research, while larger firms may achieve economies of scale in R&D. Also, from a historical perspective, drug discovery has not been as fruitful in recent years despite the growing size of leading firms, massive increases in R&D investment, advances in technology and greater knowledge of both drugs and disease.[165] Firm size was not a major reason why Japan did not become a leader in anticancer drugs.

Opening up

Japan's protectionist policies had created a distinctly domestic anticancer drug market. At the turn of the century, it remained the only market where domestic firms, rather than global multinationals dominated the market. Global leaders such as Bristol–Myers Squibb, Johnson & Johnson, AstraZeneca and Aventis had remarkably little presence in Japan.[166] Aside from Takeda, most of the leading firms such as Kyowa Hakko, Taiho and Nippon Kayaku were younger, mid-sized, less renowned firms. With differences in language and culture, an intricate distribution network and distinct domestic laws, most foreign firms found entry barriers still high enough to opt for licensing contracts rather than direct entry, despite substantial reforms since the 1990s.

But Japan's anticancer drug sector had begun to open up and modernize in the 1990s. R&D incentives to innovate improved significantly following the modernization of Japanese pharmaceutical regulations, the MOSS discussions of the 1980s, distribution reforms and the harmonization of regulation with the United States and Europe in the early 1990s.[167] Criteria for drug approval were more transparent, quality, safety and efficacy guidelines were modernized and innovative drugs were priced with a much higher premium compared to less innovative drugs. But while incentives had improved, conditions remained more favourable in other advanced nations. In the United States, for example, drug evaluation times were shorter, and while approval standards were more rigorous, approval decisions were based more on science than politics.[168] Moreover, compared to the medical practices in many Western countries, it was less common for Japanese physicians to provide cancer patients with complete and accurate disclosure of their illness.[169] In medical systems where the practice of informed consent was more common, patient demand was higher for potentially effective therapies, which tended to be highly invasive and toxic.

In a more global economy, where better incentives existed abroad, leading Japanese firms such as Takeda moved some of their core operations – such as R&D and marketing – overseas, hollowing out innovation in Japan. While these outward-oriented firms grew stronger, the more domestically oriented firms began to suffer in the face of foreign competition at home. Whether to strengthen their global reach or merely to survive, Japanese firms actively formed alliances with other firms during this period. Entrepreneurial initiatives taken by firms such as Takeda also reflected diverging fortunes among Japanese firms, whereby outward-looking firms prospered from expanding opportunities and inward-looking firms suffered from a shrinking home market.

Takeda

The best-selling anticancer drug in Japan today was launched by Takeda, one of the oldest of Japanese pharmaceutical firms. Founded in 1781 as wholesaler of Chinese medicines, Takeda had established its position as one of Japan's leading pharmaceutical firms by the Second World War – primarily through the import and distribution of Western medicines. In the post-war period, the firm grew primarily through its strengths in vitamins and antibiotics.[170]

Takeda's decision to invest in anticancer drugs was part of a company strategy to invest in R&D, rather than to develop anticancer drugs in particular. Over the decades, Takeda had cultivated its R&D capacity by forming ties with universities. In 1961, for example, Takeda launched an anticancer antibiotic, Toyomycin, with Morizō Ishidate at the University of Tokyo, who had developed nitromin in the early 1950s.[171]

The development of Takeda's anticancer drug, leuprorelin, emerged out of a company scheme to send its key scientists to learn from foreign research institutes. Like many large Japanese firms, Takeda had adopted the practice of sending its best scientists to study abroad to learn, adopt and build upon cutting edge technologies. In the mid 1960s, Takeda had sent Fujino Masahiko, later Takeda's chairman, to study at the Baylor College of Medicine in the United States where he studied two substances: TRH (thyrotropin releasing hormone) and LH-RH (luteinizing hormone releasing hormone).[172] Back in Japan, Fujino eventually found this substance to be effective towards prostate cancer.[173]

But facing a domestic market that appeared to offer few rewards for innovation, Takeda looked abroad to develop this drug. Leuprorelin marked one of the first of Japanese-origin drugs to be developed and launched abroad, as firms sought to capture the gains of greater market size, swift drug approval processes and the more favourable pricing regimes of countries such as the United States. In order to develop drugs in the United States, Takeda formed a joint venture with Abbott in 1977 – TAP Pharmaceutical Products Inc.[174] Taiho, too, established Taiho Pharma, its US subsidiary in 2002 to prioritize drug development in the United States.[175]

Leuprorelin was recognized for its effectiveness towards a wide range of cancers in international markets. Following FDA approval, leuprorelin was launched in the United States as Lupron Injection in May 1985 by TAP Pharmaceutical. By 1999, Leuprorelin had become the second best-selling drug in the world after Taxol/ paclitaxel (Bristol–Myers Squibb, 1991).[176] The drug was improved and approved for a wider range of indications in the following years, as Lupron Depot, Viadur and Eligard, in 1989, 2000 and 2002, respectively. However, Takeda's drug was only launched as Leuplin in Japan 9 years after the United States. Between 1988 and 1995, overseas sales soared from approximately 3.3 billion yen to 78.6 billion yen.[177] In 2007, Leuplin was still the top-selling anticancer drug in Japan.[178]

Japanese firms that developed drugs abroad also stood to benefit from superior pricing regimes. Poor economic conditions, downward price revisions and rising foreign competition in the home market, disincentivized firms such as Takeda from developing anticancer drugs in Japan. Instead, they increasingly sought opportunities abroad by investing heavily in R&D facilities abroad and strengthening overseas distribution networks.[179] The Japanese government had been loath to place high launch prices on drugs due to financial constraints of the Japanese health insurance system. But if a drug was already approved abroad, the government set prices to minimize the difference between domestic and overseas prices.[180] These policies further encouraged stronger firms such as Takeda to prioritize drug development outside of Japan. Without the profit potentials offered by larger cancer markets, and the absence of a generous pricing regime to reward innovation, the Japanese market could not support the development of a strong anticancer drug sector.

Summary of the period from 1990 to present

Over the 1990s, the Japanese cancer market had evolved markedly in both size and content. By 2001, the Japanese anticancer drug market stood at 14.4 per cent of the global market at $3.3 billion, compared to $10.9 billion in the United States and $1.6 billion in the United Kingdom.[181] The cancer market expanded amid an ageing population, wider options in pharmacological treatments and increased survival rates – as well as the comparatively high prices for new, innovative cancer therapies. By 2007, the Japanese anticancer drug market had expanded to 420.0 billion yen, led by Takeda's Leuplin, Taiho's UFT and AstraZeneca's Casodex, which recorded sales of 66 billion yen, 37 billion yen and 37 billion yen, respectively.[182] For firms, there were considerable pressures to invest in innovative therapies and survive intense competition – particularly as many leading drugs began to face patent expiry.

Case studies from the three firms that launched leading anticancer drugs during this period indicated that initial decisions to invest in anticancer drug research was often an ad-hoc product of corporate strategies to invest in R&D by individual firms who decided to invest in R&D – rather than a product of clearly defined research strategies by government or firms. Drug development, however, was very much influenced by government policy. Under a system that rewarded incremental innovations more than other Western countries, some firms, such as Taiho, developed a series of improved, domestic versions of anticancer drugs that were discovered abroad.

Other anticancer drug makers, such as Yakult and Takeda, began to circumvent inferior rewards to R&D in the Japanese market and sought opportunities overseas. These firms began to transfer their core R&D operations to countries where R&D was more rigorous and costly but where rewards to innovation were higher – and where their drugs could be translated more easily into multiple pharmaceutical markets. These firms were increasingly rootless: most of the managerial and sales operations were based in Japan, but the sources of innovation and potential for future growth were now based overseas.

While a handful of Japanese firms were able to launch innovative anticancer drugs, these were exceptions. There were several reasons for the relative weakness of Japan's anticancer drug sector. It was true that more drugs were approved on the basis of efficacy, even if they had significant side effects. The government did improve incentives to innovate by placing higher prices, for example, on innovative drugs – and many firms responded by investing more heavily in R&D. But innovation among many domestic firms suffered from lower prices than abroad, biannual price reductions, lack of venture capital, an undeveloped clinical testing environment and considerable delays in the drug approval process. Remnants of protectionist policies and the persistence of some non-tariff barriers, too, allowed comparatively weaker firms and drugs to survive in the domestic market. Finally, it was only after the millennium that the Japanese medical system was more equipped with the expertise and the facilities, or catered to patients empowered with knowledge over their condition, which created the final demand for innovative therapies.

Analysis of the anticancer drug sector

The Japanese anticancer drug sector was far less successful in drug discovery, development or sales – both in comparison with leading Western counterparts and the Japanese antibiotics sector. The experience of the anticancer drug sector sheds light upon the causes for the weakness in Japan's pharmaceutical industry. This section considers why Japan's anticancer sector remained underdeveloped.

Some scholars have suggested that the relative weakness of the Japanese anticancer drug sector stems from Japan's weak foundation in science compared to countries with stronger performance in this sector. Samuel Coleman and Steven Collins have argued that the Japan's weakness in pharmaceutical innovations stems from lack of investment in basic science and research at universities.[183] But Japanese universities engaged in rigorous cancer research in collaboration with government and industry since the early twentieth century.[184] In addition, most Japanese-origin anticancer drugs of global repute originated in academic laboratories. Japan's weakness in the anticancer drug sector cannot be explained by a weakness in basic science.

Another possible explanation for the weakness of the anticancer drug sector in Japan relates to industrial structure. The Japanese pharmaceutical industry was dominated by smaller firms for a longer period than in the leading pharmaceutical markets. Of the nearly 500 Japanese prescription drug makers in 2005, the leading firm, Takeda, was only a quarter of the size of the leading global firms, such as Pfizer or GlaxoSmithKline.[185] The difference between the market concentration of Japanese and other advanced Western markets, however, has not been significantly different.[186]

There is some value in explaining the weakness of Japan's anticancer drug sector in light of its industrial structure. Larger firms may have an advantage in developing anticancer drugs, which involve a much more costly and complex process compared to antibiotics. After all, producing cutting-edge anticancer drugs requires a much higher R&D investment than producing antibiotics.

Yet, it is unclear whether smaller firms are necessarily disadvantageous to the development of an anticancer drug sector. After all, smaller pharmaceutical ventures in the United States have also launched globally successful anticancer drugs and have contributed to the strength of the American industry. The considerable difference between the size of leading Japanese and global firms likely disadvantaged Japanese firms in achieving economies of scale in R&D, production and marketing. However, the optimal size of firm may not always be very large, especially given the limited market for a given anticancer drug. Industrial structure only provides a partial explanation for the weakness of Japan's anticancer drug sector.

A more convincing explanation for the weakness of Japan's anticancer drug sector lies in the research environment. For example, university professors faced considerable barriers in commercializing their research until 1998. The Law on National Public Employees, for example, effectively banned outside employment, while rigid labour markets and bankruptcy laws penalized failures in entrepreneurship.[187] The pre-1998 rules governing academics had a particularly acute impact on R&D intensive sectors such as anticancer drugs.

Because the development of antibiotics depended upon linear, incremental and evolutionary learning, restrictions to the transfer of academic know-how had a limited impact on the development of the antibiotics sector.[188] Antibiotic discovery had long been based on the random screening of a vast number of soil samples, and – while labour intensive – did not require the human capital and equipment needed to develop anticancer drugs. In contrast, anticancer drug development was much more sophisticated, and required more specialized expertise, equipment and more revolutionary knowledge spillovers from universities. Indeed, university affiliated start-ups such as Genentech played a large role in stimulating innovation and discoveries of anticancer drugs in the United States. While the pre-1998 rules hampered the development of the anticancer drug sector, it is not yet clear whether the change in the rules will result in a strong anticancer drug sector in Japan.

As in other Japanese industries, the locus of pharmaceutical R&D remained in the corporate laboratory. In the United States or Europe, university laboratories and biotechnology firms played a greater role in discovering new therapies. However, technology transfers between universities and industries in Japan was still difficult for the regulatory and cultural reasons mentioned earlier, and the country had few biotech companies.[189] The discovery and development of anticancer drugs not only required specialized expertise and high rewards for innovation, but also more revolutionary knowledge spillovers from universities. The centre of cancer research was located in universities, but academic scientists were less involved in pharmaceutical research.[190] Alliances between academia and industry existed more to exchange information and to act as channels for graduate employment rather than to exploit synergies for drug discovery and development. Moreover, Japanese industrial laboratories mostly employed researchers without doctoral degrees under a system of lifetime employment and seniority-based pay in hierarchical research units. The comparative lack of human capital and R&D incentives weakened Japan's ability to introduce new, original drugs.

One of the most powerful reasons for the relative weakness of Japan's anticancer drug sector was unhelpful government policy. More specifically, the weakness of Japan's anticancer drug sector stemmed largely from inferior R&D incentives, an undeveloped drug approval system and Japanese medical practice. It was true that other factors, such as industrial structure or legal barriers to entrepreneurship facing university professors, hindered the development of a strong, innovative industry. But these factors mattered less in explaining the causes for Japan's weakness in the anticancer drug sector.

To a certain extent, the ineffectiveness of government intervention in Japan's anticancer drug sector might be explained by the country's belated demand for drugs that treated diseases of affluence such as cancer compared to other advanced nations. On a practical level, it is also much more difficult for a government to intervene in the development of a complex product. Only a handful of firms equipped with high levels of human capital, capable and willing to undertake extraordinary risk and cost in the R&D process could acquire the capacity to discover and develop innovative anticancer drugs. Government policy is more effective and conducive in sectors such as antibiotics that can involve numerous firms in low-cost, labour-intensive and serendipitous methods of drug discovery for mass production.

The weakness of Japan's anticancer drug sector is most convincingly explained by its inferior R&D incentives. Japan's post-war pharmaceutical industry was shaped by the endurance of MHW's developmental health policies that prioritized improvements in public health over the development of industry. Public health objectives to deliver low-cost drugs to Japanese citizens under universal health insurance encouraged the government to set – effectively cap – prices and conduct periodic price reductions. While this helped contain healthcare costs for the government and facilitated public access to medicines, it also encouraged firms to long pursue incremental innovations rather than invest heavily in R&D. The introduction of product patents and capital liberalization should have incentivized firms to invest more heavily in R&D and develop more competitive drugs. But Japan's unique product standards, lower criteria for innovation and medical culture protected drugs of lesser quality from foreign competition. Japanese government policies that sustained less competitive drugs in the market help explain why Japan's anticancer drug sector remained weak.

At times, Japan's politicized, unscientific and non-transparent drug approval system also reduced R&D incentives and undermined the industry's prospects for growth. For firms, alliances with other firms and universities could substitute for or complement their lack of capacities in drug discovery, development or distribution, while affiliations with the government could facilitate drug approval. But in the 1970s and 1980s, firms unable to assess the government's approval criteria invested in developing political ties rather than R&D to facilitate drug approval. This helped prompt a massive expansion of the anticancer drug sector, which was supported by Japan's distinct product standards and medical system. If the safety and efficacy criteria for drug approval had been more transparent, more firms might have invested in R&D despite lower drug prices. At a time when many Western markets were launching new, innovative anticancer drugs, Japan's undeveloped drug approval system misdirected investments and undermined the industry's potential at a crucial time in its development.[191]

Just because a drug received approval in Japan did not mean it was recognized in other countries. A major factor limiting the ability of Japanese drug companies to export anticancer drugs was the fact that Western governments long viewed the Japanese regulatory system with scepticism. Until its pharmaceutical regulations were harmonized with the United States and Europe in the early 1990s, Japan's drug approval standards lacked the rigour and credibility of its Western counterparts. As a result, it was difficult for Japanese firms to use Japanese approval as a precedent to gain approval in other countries. Japan's drug approval process lacked credibility because of its non-transparent approval process and lack of clear, rigorous standards for laboratory or clinical trials.

Gaining recognition from regulatory authorities in advanced Western markets was particularly important in anticancer drugs. Cancer is a disease of affluence with most of its patients in the developed world. Japanese firms in the antibiotics sector could export their products to developing countries with less rigorous standards and higher demand for therapies to treat infectious diseases. But Japanese firms in the anticancer drug sector could not export their products to the developed world. Japanese antibiotics makers were therefore able to enjoy a degree of success in exports that their counterparts in the anticancer drug sector could not.

The weakness of the anticancer drug sector was also affected by Japan's medical system. Many physicians in Japan also dispensed drugs, and derived a portion of their income from dispensing drugs. Physicians were therefore incentivized to prescribe drugs that could be prescribed widely and had a greater difference between wholesale and retail prices. The cancer immunotherapy drugs of the 1970s and 1980s – unlike most anticancer drugs – had few side effects and were approved for various types of cancer. These drugs were popular because they could be prescribed to a large population of cancer patients who remained ignorant of their diagnosis, and could neither ascertain nor question the efficacy of drugs until long after they were taken. Cancer immunotherapy drugs were also popular because anticancer drugs were high-priced drugs that tended to have greater pharmaceutical price differentials. As a result, Japanese firms developed anticancer drugs of limited efficacy that could neither be approved in other advanced nations nor be delivered beyond the Japanese medical system.

The lack of oncologists and proper patient diagnoses not only undermined the capacity to conduct accurate clinical trials in Japan, but they also limited demand for innovative cancer therapies. As a complex, hospital-based therapy, the development of anticancer drugs was dependent on physicians and technicians with expertise in cancer and anticancer drugs to administer the drug – as well as hospitals equipped with the relevant equipment to deliver the drug. A strong anticancer drug sector also required a medical culture where physicians would provide patients with an accurate diagnosis to generate demand for an arduous treatment. The lack of such infrastructure for much of the post-war period also long hindered the development of Japan's anticancer drug sector.

Along with the pharmaceutical industry as a whole, Japan's anticancer drug sector increasingly resembled those of the advanced Western markets. The hollowing out of R&D in leading pharmaceutical firms, however, was particularly disappointing. More than the R&D capacity of Japanese firms, it had been the inadequacies of the R&D environment and the medical infrastructure that stifled the industry's development.

5 Conclusion

Reconsidering Japan's business in pharmaceuticals

This book has traced the history of the Japanese pharmaceutical industry since 1945. It explained how Japanese pharmaceutical firms recovered from the Second World War and then caught up with Western firms by importing technologies. The two case studies have also shown that Japanese pharmaceutical firms were able to develop a number of original, innovative therapies, some of which have proven successful in overseas markets.

The emphasis of this book, however, has not been on the achievements of the Japanese pharmaceutical industry, but rather on its relative weakness. Rather than invest heavily in R&D to pursue breakthrough discoveries, most Japanese firms opted to launch many new drugs with limited innovative value that could not be sold in other advanced markets. It was true that a handful of leading firms began to develop global blockbuster drugs and increase their overseas presence. But Japanese firms remained much smaller in terms of sales, workforce or R&D expenditures, and Japan remained a net importer of pharmaceuticals.

The aim of this book has been to explain why Japan's pharmaceutical industry did not become a global leader, and continues to lag behind the pharmaceutical industries of countries such as the United States, the United Kingdom and Switzerland. I used two classes of medicines, antibiotics and anticancer drugs, as case studies for exploring the overall history of the Japanese pharmaceutical industry. I showed that the experiences of these two sectors were very different, and that the antibiotics sector was the stronger of the two. Japanese pharmaceutical firms were able to develop many antibiotics that came to be produced under licence in other industrialized countries. Japan's anticancer drug sector was far less successful; it developed fewer globally competitive drugs and remained heavily reliant on imports.

There were several reasons why Japan's antibiotics sector became stronger than the anticancer drug sector. Both sectors were heavily shaped by government policy. The MHW's tendency to prioritize universal access to prescription drugs, however, had a disproportionate impact on the anticancer drug sector. The government's cost containment measures, to set drug prices and reduce them regularly, limited the profits that pharmaceutical firms in Japan could gain from launching new therapies. Japanese firms were reluctant to invest in anticancer drugs, which were much more expensive and difficult to develop compared to antibiotics.

As the previous chapters showed, the search for new antibiotics was a more low-cost, labour-intensive and serendipitous process compared to the search for new anticancer drugs. In addition, whereas a given antibiotic could treat many infectious ailments, a given anticancer drug could only treat a particular type and stage of cancer. Antibiotics were more suited to mass production and allowed R&D expenses to be recovered over a larger number of consumers.

Pharmaceutical firms in Japan had much less incentive to develop anticancer drugs compared to antibiotics. Moreover, the undeveloped medical infrastructure and opaque drug approval process increased the risk and cost of drug development. Moreover, well into the 1980s, there was little demand in Japan for efficacious anticancer drugs, as these tended to have strong side effects. There was also a cultural factor. Japanese physicians did not inform patients of their cancer diagnosis, and prescribed drugs with few side effects but of limited efficacy. Only in the 1990s did Japanese patients begin to make more informed decisions and generate final demand for more effective anticancer drugs. The antibiotics sector outperformed the anticancer drug sector in Japan because the returns to pharmaceutical R&D were limited; because antibiotics were easier to export compared to anticancer drugs; and because Japan's medical system did not generate demand for more effective anticancer drugs. The problems observed in the anticancer drug sector of the Japanese pharmaceutical industry illustrate some of the reasons why Japan did not become a leader in the global pharmaceutical industry.

Reasons for the unrealized potential of the Japanese pharmaceutical industry

This book showed that the major reasons for the weakness of the industry are: the weak incentives for pharmaceutical firms to invest in R&D; the government's protectionist policies; and Japanese medical culture. Other factors of secondary importance included: differences in therapeutic demand conditions between Japan and its potential export markets; different drug standards that acted as *de facto* trade barriers; the industrial structure of the Japanese pharmaceutical industry; the historical origins of Japanese pharmaceutical firms; barriers to entrepreneurship among university academics; and the lack of initiative taken by Japanese firms to expand into overseas markets.

The most important reason for the underperformance of Japan's pharmaceutical industry lay in weak R&D incentives. To a certain extent, the blame for this lay with government. The government did not offer strong incentives to invest in the discovery of innovative new drugs. The weakness of these R&D incentives stemmed from the fact that the industry was governed by the MHW, rather than the MITI. Whereas the MITI prioritized the growth of industry, the MHW prioritized improvements in public health. In order to increase access to drugs among Japanese citizens, the MHW set drug prices rather than allow pharmaceutical firms to determine prices in a free market. Under universal healthcare, the MHW continued to place downward pressures on drug prices. From the 1980s in particular, the government legislated regular reductions in drug prices so as to contain rising healthcare costs.

For many years, Japan's intellectual property regime also disincentivized Japanese firms from investing in the discovery of truly innovative therapies. Until 1975, Japan had a process patent regime. This was very different from the product patent regime that had already been adopted in Western countries such as the United States and the United Kingdom. Japan's patent regime encouraged firms to reverse engineer foreign-discovered drugs, because new patents could be filed for an alternative path to an existing product. While many Japanese firms began to invest in R&D to discover original therapies after product patents were introduced in 1976, most continued to pursue incremental improvements rather than breakthrough discoveries. The patent regime had a disproportionate impact on the development of new drugs in therapeutic sectors, such as anticancer drugs, that required greater, riskier investments in R&D. Japanese firms therefore developed drugs similar to drugs available abroad – and could not gain approval in these markets.

I showed that Japan's drug approval process was, at times, politicized and nontransparent. For pharmaceuticals firms, this reduced the incentive to invest in R&D because it was difficult to determine the risk involved in gaining drug approval. The development of anticancer drugs during the 1970s, in particular, revealed how firms that were unable to assess the government's drug approval criteria invested in forming political ties to facilitate drug approval. These misdirected investments undermined the industry's potential at a crucial time in its development. The very distinct features of the Japanese market also made firms reluctant to make the costly investments necessary to expand into overseas markets.

Had Japan's intellectual property regime introduced product patents earlier and penalized imitation, Japanese firms would likely have developed more original drugs that might have been recognized abroad. Had Japanese firms faced clearer standards and a more transparent and unbiased drug approval process, they might have invested in more pharmaceutical R&D to develop more original therapies. Had policies been different, firm responses and industrial performance would not have been the same. Institutions played a critical role in shaping Japan's post-war pharmaceutical industry.

The second major reason for the weakness of the Japanese pharmaceutical industry lay in the government's protectionist policies. Well into the 1970s, the government protected Japanese firms from foreign competition through a combination of capital controls, intellectual property laws and distinct product standards. Japanese firms could prosper without introducing original drugs. Had the government implemented less protectionist policies tailored to a more developed economy by the 1970s, Japanese firms might have pursued the discovery of highly innovative drugs that could have been marketed overseas. Had the government accounted for the idiosyncrasies of different therapeutic sectors to implement sector-specific policies, Japan might have developed stronger sectors in anticancer drugs and other therapies. Japan's pharmaceutical industry remained relatively weak, partly because the mix and degree of interventions by the state was less than optimal – for its level of development and for specific therapeutic sectors.

The third major cause of the weakness of Japan's pharmaceutical industry lay in firm size. Compared to countries such as the United States, the United Kingdom and Switzerland, the Japanese industry was dominated by numerous smaller firms. But in the pharmaceutical industry, larger firms have a crucial advantage in achieving economies of scale in R&D, production and marketing. As observed in the antibiotics and anticancer drug sectors, the size of pharmaceutical firms became increasingly important over the years. This was because R&D processes became more costly and complex, manufacturing processes incorporated rigorous quality controls and sophisticated marketing strategies came to play a crucial role in drug sales. It is true that the smaller specialized firms – ranging from biotechnology firms to contract research organizations – have played an important role in the discovery of innovative new drugs with the larger integrated pharmaceutical firms. It was the smaller size of Japan's integrated pharmaceutical firms that compromised their ability to compete with rivals in Western countries.

The fourth major cause for the weakness of Japan's pharmaceutical industry involves medical culture. The traditional practice among Japanese physicians to both prescribe and dispense pharmaceuticals created strong demand for newer drugs with higher prices, even if they had minimal innovative value. This was because Japanese physicians could profit from the difference between the wholesale and retail prices of drugs, and high-priced drugs tended to have greater price differentials. In addition, country-specific approaches to medical therapy, most notably in the area of cancer treatments, created demand for pharmaceuticals that were not recognized beyond Japan. The Japanese pharmaceutical industry remained a domestic rather than global industry because Japanese firms developed drugs that were not recognized by drug regulators abroad.

It is also important to remember that Japan's research environment discouraged the pursuit of breakthrough discoveries that might have led to more globally recognized drugs. For example, Japanese scientists who long emphasized applied research at the expense of basic research lacked the deep knowledge base to search for innovative new drugs. In terms of career prospects, scientists working in hierarchical research units under lifetime employment faced greater political gain by adhering to existing ways of research rather than proposing risky original projects that might fail and undermine the credibility of the group's senior researchers. These political incentives were made stronger because of the lack of external markets beyond a specific organization – in both industry and academia.

Several secondary factors also accounted for the weakness of Japan's pharmaceutical industry. The historical origins of Japanese pharmaceutical firms are part of the explanation. Many Japanese pharmaceutical firms began as import houses specializing in the distribution of German drugs. When these firms later began to produce these drugs for the Japanese market, many remained reliant on foreign technology and launched domestic versions of foreign-discovered drugs. A distinct feature of Japan's pharmaceutical industry was its development, not through the discoveries of original therapies, but through the borrowing of foreign technologies. The importation of technology allowed Japanese firms to leapfrog over earlier phases of pharmaceutical innovation. But Japanese pharmaceutical firms were path-dependent, and many firms continued to focus on acquiring or improving the capacity to produce rather than discover or develop leading drugs.

In addition, the incidence of diseases in Japan was different from other industrialized countries. Infectious diseases such as tuberculosis, for example, remained common causes of death in Japan for much longer than other developed countries. Even after diseases of affluence became the leading causes of death, patterns of disease in Japan were not identical to other markets. As a result, Japanese pharmaceutical firms launched therapies in response to domestic needs, which were not necessarily the same as those abroad.

As I have showed, drug standards in Japan were not harmonized with those of the United States and Europe until the 1990s. Before that time, drugs developed in Japan were not recognized as drugs that could be launched in these markets, and vice versa. The immense cost involved in re-developing drugs for overseas markets both deterred Japanese firms from expanding abroad, and protected Japanese firms from foreign competition.

I also showed that barriers to entrepreneurship imposed on university academics in Japan prevented the translation of academic research into commercial products. For several decades, academics could not work in private enterprise. In addition, the lack of infrastructure – the absence of qualified physicians, the low numbers of examiners and a less rigorous clinical trial system – undermined the ability of Japanese firms to develop highly innovative drugs.

Finally, the belated initiative taken by Japanese firms to seek opportunities abroad hindered the development of a more globally competitive pharmaceutical industry. Since 2000, Japanese firms such as Takeda and Astellas have transferred their core R&D operations to the United States to develop drugs for the American, European and Japanese markets.[1] Had these firms taken the initiative at an earlier stage to develop drugs that could have been marketed in multiple markets, Japan might have developed a pharmaceutical industry with a stronger international profile.

Policy lessons from the Japanese experience

The Japanese experience, then, offers several policy lessons for other countries in developing their pharmaceutical industries. First, governments must create strong incentives for firms to invest in R&D. For this, they might introduce product patents as domestic firms become able to reproduce existing drugs, establish clear standards and processes for drug approval, as well as reward innovative drugs with high prices. As a second, related point, governments should open the domestic market to foreign competition once domestic firms can reproduce foreign-discovered drugs. In so doing, domestic firms would be expected to launch drugs that can at least compete with drugs available overseas. Third, governments might identify therapeutic sectors that suit the comparative advantages of the domestic market, and target those specific sectors for development.

What's more, governments would also do well to create an environment that facilitates M&A, and enables firms to achieve economies of scale in R&D, manufacturing and distribution. They could do so by enhancing corporate disclosure practices, ensuring strong shareholder rights and by pursuing further deregulation. In terms of strategy, firms should also be encouraged to adopt a long-term perspective and develop their drugs for a larger, global market rather than a limited, domestic market.

Furthermore, the healthcare system must be continuously monitored and improved. A modern medical system is essential to the discovery, development and delivery of innovative new drugs. For this purpose, governments might ensure the adequate training of medical specialists and equip hospitals with leading medical technologies. Related to this, a clinical trial system equipped with adequate numbers of medical specialists, patient participants and well-trained examiners is crucial to retaining R&D in the country. Governments should also encourage physicians to prescribe the most effective drugs as well as penalize the prescription of less effective drugs. They might take steps to minimize pharmaceutical price differentials and allow pharmacists to have generic substitution rights.

While perhaps not fully articulated by the case studies alone, it should also be noted that the government might also introduce measures to strengthen links between academia and industry, both in terms of collaborative research projects as well as entrepreneurship among university academics. Offering funding for collaborative research projects in targeted areas and reducing barriers to entrepreneurship should further encourage the translation of academic discoveries into commercial products. Encouraging the adoption of more fluid organizational structures in Japan's research environment, by emphasizing merit over seniority and facilitating the movement of researchers across different organizations should encourage the cross-pollination of ideas and help strengthen Japan's R&D capacity to discover innovative products in pharmaceuticals – and beyond.

Contributions to existing scholarship

This book has contributed to five areas of scholarship. These areas are: the global histories on the pharmaceutical industry; works on Japanese industrial policy; the literature on late economic development; and existing works that highlight the relevance of New Institutional Economics in economic development. It also contributes to existing debates on Japanese capitalism and discussions on the role of cultural variables in shaping economic development.

My first contribution is to broaden our understanding of the global history of the pharmaceutical industry by expanding the geographic coverage beyond the North Atlantic region – particularly to demonstrate the role of culture in shaping the industry's development. The second contribution is to illustrate the role of government policy on the development of the pharmaceutical industry. This book demonstrates not only that industrial policy played a powerful role in shaping the industry, but also that unhelpful policies harmed its development. While the government's import substitution policy in the early post-war period was crucial to enabling Japanese firms to produce modern pharmaceuticals, its continued protection made firms content to profit from incrementally innovative drugs.

The third contribution of my book is to show the importance of strong, rigorous and credible institutions in developing a world-leading pharmaceutical industry. Japan's lack of transparent, credible institutions, for example, hindered the development of a world-leading industry, as Japanese firms invested in forming political ties that would facilitate drug approval, rather than invest in developing drugs that could be marketed abroad. The fourth contribution of this book is to show that the concept of late development advanced by Alexander Gerschenkron can be applied to the pharmaceutical sector.[2] Unlike Germany, Britain or the United States, the history of Japan's pharmaceutical industry was shaped by a developmental state, the borrowing of foreign technology and incremental innovations of production technology.

The fifth contribution of my book relates to debates on whether the distinct features of capitalism in Japan are suitable to economic development in a high technology age. Japanese capitalism has been most strongly characterized by the long-term relationships of firms with the government, other firms and their employees, such as through industrial policy, *keiretsu* structures and lifetime employment. The experience of the Japan's pharmaceutical industry suggests that these features weakened the capacity of Japanese firms to compete with foreign firms.

Future prospects of the Japanese pharmaceutical industry

Since the millennium, the Japanese government has issued two so-called vision statements on the pharmaceutical industry. These were attempts to reverse what the government saw as a 'crisis situation'.[3] In both the 2002 and 2007 statements, the government observed that Japan was producing fewer globally competitive drugs in an environment that was still inhospitable to pharmaceutical R&D and marketing. They pointed to Japan's persistent drug lag and the shrinking share of Japan origin drugs in the domestic market, and reiterated that reform was essential for the industry's survival.

As we have observed, Japan's pharmaceutical industry has certainly undergone significant changes since 1990. For example, Japanese firms have loosened their *keiretsu* ties and have dissolved their joint ventures with foreign firms to license in existing drugs and expand their product line-up. They have streamlined their business operations and have merged to invest in large-scale R&D projects to discover first generation drugs. Facing a saturated market, the leading Japanese firms have globalized and now prioritize overseas markets for drug development. Japan's leading pharmaceutical firms, at least, are converging with leading global pharmaceutical firms. After all, they are governed by the same laws to develop, manufacture and distribute drugs and compete in the same markets. Yet Japan also retains its tier of domestically oriented, small to medium sized firms that do not develop innovative drugs.

Perhaps reflective of this conflicting dichotomy within the domestic market, the future prospects of Japan's pharmaceutical industry remain mixed. Globally, there are great pressures to reform, particularly as the world pharmaceutical industry faces a host of patent expirations. Industry analysts estimate that about 15 per cent of revenue from patented drugs are expected to be lost in 2010, as firms such as Pfizer, Merck, Eisai and Astellas lose patent protection of their best-selling drugs.[4] Unable to fill the pipelines, firms that once shunned the generics market, for example, are reconsidering. Just in Japan, Daiichi Sankyo purchased the Indian generics maker Rambaxy in 2008, and Pfizer has announced plans to enter the Japanese generics market in 2011.[5] Other companies such as Merck and Takeda have been launching combination drugs to offset losses from generic entry.[6]

In some ways, this industry-wide restructuring actually offers an opportunity for Japanese firms to develop a more competitive edge in a new environment – particularly as patent expiry is not the only driver of change. The ageing population, for example, is changing disease patterns and intensifying cost pressures on the healthcare system, and is altering the type of and prices of drugs in demand. Advances in medical technology, ranging from genomic medicine, personalized medicine, to regenerative medicine are also reshaping the industry – by changing who develops what drugs in what way. New media, such as social networking sites, are also adding new dimensions to pharmaceutical marketing. For Japan, any potential leadership in the industry will depend on its ability to fully embrace and utilize these new technologies in this new environment.

This book has shown how Japan's pharmaceutical industry has been shaped by a complex interplay of factors. The industry would have evolved very differently had the government provided greater rewards for R&D, had Japanese firms been larger or had Japanese medical culture been more similar to those of the advanced Western markets. It is hoped that further studies on the history of the Japanese pharmaceutical industry will provide additional insights into Japanese industrial policy, late development and Japanese capitalism. To some extent, the history of Japan's pharmaceutical industry helps explain why Japan has struggled to maintain global leadership in a more knowledge-based economy. It reveals some of the complexities of an economy that remains caught between imitation and innovation, collectivism and individualism, tradition and modernity. It also shows the glimmer of hope that Japan's high technology industries – such as pharmaceuticals – might still become global leaders in the twenty-first century.

Appendices

Appendix 1: value of pharmaceutical production[1]

Table A1.1 Nominal value of pharmaceutical production for all categories of drugs (in millions of yen)

	All categories			
	All drugs		*Prescription drugs*	
	Total production	*Total production*	*Domestic production*	*Bulk imports*
1945	335			
1946	1,872			
1947	5,176			
1948	17,092			
1949	31,031			
1950	31,916			
1951	42,376			
1952	58,564			
1953	75,647			
1954	78,468			
1955	89,539			
1956	103,767			
1957	125,147			
1958	134,476			
1959	149,258			
1960	176,012			
1961	218,075			
1962	265,596			
1963	341,141			
1964	423,225			
1965	457,639			
1966	507,108			
1967	563,257			
1968	688,953	488,316	316,152	172,164
1969	842,514	615,800	398,789	217,012
1970	1,025,319	770,451	478,781	291,670
1971	1,060,424	826,173	506,850	319,323
1972	1,091,791	843,531	511,288	332,242
1973	1,367,138	1,081,285	656,800	424,486
1974	1,699,688	1,381,833	856,627	525,207

Table A1.1 Continued

	All categories			
	All drugs		Prescription drugs	
	Total production	Total production	Domestic production	Bulk imports
1975	1,792,406	1,464,030	905,892	558,139
1976	2,162,436	1,799,418	1,079,856	719,562
1977	2,458,294	2,056,991	1,280,655	776,326
1978	2,793,878	2,350,579	1,484,128	866,450
1979	3,042,302	2,562,029	1,665,834	896,194
1980	3,482,177	2,978,437	1,981,278	997,159
1981	3,679,139	3,135,703	2,161,243	974,460
1982	3,980,232	3,406,516	2,339,005	1,067,510
1983	4,032,057	3,438,567	2,382,616	1,055,950
1984	4,027,996	3,429,482	2,450,987	978,495
1985	4,001,807	3,383,710	2,386,022	997,688
1986	4,280,732	3,649,842	2,547,249	1,102,593
1987	4,825,398	4,141,820	2,897,396	1,244,424
1988	5,059,459	4,309,824	2,991,784	1,318,040
1989	5,502,271	4,676,456	3,230,933	1,445,523
1990	5,595,435	4,720,333	3,324,858	1,395,475
1991	5,697,244	4,812,216	3,357,206	1,455,010
1992	5,574,220	4,680,204	3,309,315	1,370,889
1993	5,695,068	4,819,341	3,457,673	1,361,668
1994	5,750,332	4,881,157	3,489,218	1,391,939
1995	6,168,062	5,243,575	3,747,649	1,495,927
1996	6,100,046	5,156,439	3,770,744	1,385,696
1997	6,147,833	5,187,140	3,766,935	1,420,206
1998	5,842,096	4,936,520	3,619,537	1,316,982
1999	6,290,023	5,438,173	4,012,085	1,426,088
2000	6,182,631	5,376,330	3,878,730	1,497,600
2001	6,504,318	5,728,874	4,062,517	1,666,358
2002	6,489,278	5,729,882	4,034,118	1,695,764
2003	6,533,108	5,813,704	4,120,441	1,693,263
2004	6,525,293	5,837,295	4,132,221	1,705,075
2005	6,390,722	5,741,280	4,247,218	1,494,062

Table A1.2 Nominal value of pharmaceutical production for antibiotics (in millions of yen)

| | Antibiotics | | | |
| | All drugs | Prescription drugs | | |
	Total production	Total production	Domestic production	Bulk imports
1950				
1951				
1952	9,288			
1953	12,750			
1954	12,331			
1955	12,511			
1956	12,193			
1957	16,950			
1958	18,399			
1959	14,180			
1960	17,224			
1961	22,010			
1962	28,224			
1963	36,018			
1964	52,247			
1965	58,554			
1966	64,506			
1967	72,992			
1968	95,432			
1969	114,447			
1970	157,020			
1971	176,647			
1972	174,196			
1973	238,916			
1974	331,380			
1975	363,392	363,308	153,062	210,246
1976	522,392	522,313	222,686	299,627
1977	583,908	583,906	275,360	308,546
1978	636,418	636,416	303,817	332,598
1979	658,009	658,008	328,546	329,462
1980	814,320	814,320	425,852	388,467
1981	780,136	780,136	422,796	357,340
1982	865,148	865,148	474,935	390,213
1983	735,888	735,888	417,591	318,296
1984	742,496	742,496	490,469	252,027
1985	690,505	690,505	446,162	244,343
1986	683,361	683,361	431,409	251,953
1987	733,974	733,974	444,721	289,253
1988	702,485	702,485	421,660	280,825
1989	724,523	724,523	438,035	286,488
1990	624,117	624,117	393,867	230,250
1991	589,014	589,244	370,236	219,009
1992	441,097	441,097	287,206	153,891
1993	444,048	444,048	298,683	145,365
1994	386,639	386,639	263,475	123,164
1995	451,477	451,477	314,763	136,714
1996	394,150	394,150	283,377	110,773
1997	433,475	433,475	321,076	112,399
1998	402,483	402,483	305,863	96,620
1999	437,812	437,812	345,470	92,343
2000	373,949	373,949	291,170	82,778
2001	410,413	410,413	304,430	105,983
2002	369,764	369,764	271,224	98,540
2003	386,923	386,923	293,816	93,107
2004	362,813	362,813	276,499	86,314
2005	346,951	346,097	255,367	90,730

Table A1.3 Nominal value of pharmaceutical production for anticancer drugs (in millions of yen)

	Anticancer drugs			
	All drugs	Prescription drugs		
	Total production	Total production	Domestic production	Bulk imports
1950				
1951				
1952				
1953				
1954				
1955	47			
1956	59			
1957	63			
1958	76			
1959	94			
1960	162			
1961	236			
1962	347			
1963	410			
1964	1,029			
1965	508			
1966	435			
1967	589			
1968	607			
1969	481			
1970	517			
1971	885			
1972	726			
1973	1,602			
1974	4,661			
1975	9,898	9,894	4,929	4,965
1976	32,376	32,376	16,753	15,623
1977	60,236	60,236	37,726	22,510
1978	84,474	84,474	57,325	27,149
1979	93,782	93,782	61,344	32,438
1980	107,351	107,351	72,662	34,689
1981	122,620	122,620	86,937	35,683
1982	124,511	124,511	91,242	33,270
1983	134,725	134,725	98,925	35,800
1984	143,627	143,618	121,344	22,275
1985	138,601	138,591	117,740	20,851
1986	160,822	160,799	137,751	23,047
1987	180,659	180,633	153,687	26,946
1988	193,045	193,031	164,273	28,759
1989	190,927	190,911	144,983	45,927
1990	164,151	164,134	116,044	48,090
1991	166,989	166,987	106,673	60,314
1992	166,810	166,810	98,702	68,108
1993	169,707	169,707	100,568	69,139
1994	169,476	169,476	98,267	71,209
1995	170,149	170,149	99,653	70,496

1996	156,920	156,920	97,364	59,555
1997	151,216	151,216	93,866	57,350
1998	135,378	135,378	83,881	51,497
1999	139,925	139,925	85,782	54,142
2000	146,995	146,995	88,041	58,954
2001	153,155	153,155	90,232	62,924
2002	167,748	167,748	88,581	79,166
2003	144,300	144,300	91,857	52,443
2004	147,811	147,811	101,282	46,528
2005	137,993	137,993	108,436	29,557

Appendix 2: pharmaceutical R&D[2]

Table A2.1 Nominal value of R&D expenditures (in millions of yen)

	R&D expenditures
1960	3,696
1961	6,794
1962	7,081
1963	9,983
1964	13,214
1965	14,602
1966	15,903
1967	18,068
1968	24,651
1969	20,656
1970	45,410
1971	55,740
1972	55,011
1973	64,406
1974	79,157
1975	95,191
1976	109,537
1977	120,537
1978	134,714
1979	176,905
1980	189,838
1981	218,435
1982	239,817
1983	289,896
1984	295,284
1985	341,880
1986	341,978
1987	380,701
1988	416,220
1989	455,950
1990	516,062
1991	590,105
1992	643,415
1993	629,179
1994	632,802
1995	642,190

Table A2.1 Continued

	R&D expenditures
1996	667,145
1997	643,291
1998	681,118
1999	689,449
2000	746,214
2001	839,400
2002	965,723
2003	883,653
2004	906,749
2005	1,047,747

Table A2.2 R&D expenditures as a percentage of sales

	R&D expenditures/sales
1960	2.2
1961	2.0
1962	2.5
1963	2.3
1964	2.9
1965	3.0
1966	3.1
1967	2.8
1968	3.0
1969	3.3
1970	3.4
1971	3.9
1972	4.3
1973	4.1
1974	4.4
1975	4.9
1976	5.1
1977	4.8
1978	5.0
1979	5.5
1980	5.5
1981	5.9
1982	5.6
1983	6.6
1984	6.5
1985	7.0
1986	6.9
1987	7.0
1988	6.9
1989	7.5
1990	8.0
1991	8.7
1992	8.7
1993	8.2
1994	7.8

1995	8.0
1996	8.1
1997	8.1
1998	8.1
1999	8.1
2000	8.6
2001	8.5
2002	8.9
2003	8.4
2004	8.6
2005	10.0

Appendix 3: value of pharmaceutical trade[3]

Table A3.1 Nominal value of pharmaceutical trade for all categories of drugs (in millions of yen)

	Imports	*Exports*
1947	521	7
1948	698	45
1949	934	146
1950	598	514
1951	2,141	1,082
1952	3,352	1,605
1953	4,145	2,165
1954	3,600	3,267
1955	3,522	3,001
1956	3,376	3,882
1957	4,001	5,258
1958	4,026	4,947
1959	5,131	5,539
1960	6,265	6,457
1961	9,690	7,388
1962	9,728	8,996
1963	13,945	9,125
1964	19,425	9,821
1965	21,517	11,911
1966	28,434	12,057
1967	35,292	13,411
1968	45,997	14,440
1969	56,822	18,229
1970	77,873	23,743
1971	81,337	29,989
1972	79,096	25,590
1973	97,938	27,185
1974	133,160	40,122
1975	130,688	36,806
1976	163,200	43,100
1977	164,422	48,401
1978	172,736	47,012
1979	202,471	57,902
1980	243,568	66,826
1981	253,619	72,736

Table A3.1 Continued

	Imports	Exports
1982	311,107	75,856
1983	288,447	82,709
1984	298,917	84,433
1985	308,166	93,281
1986	290,591	86,500
1987	305,188	85,152
1988	340,586	91,889
1989	366,659	98,923
1990	395,452	111,133
1991	419,134	146,763
1992	464,942	172,941
1993	436,288	163,993
1994	430,939	158,081
1995	461,687	173,359
1996	489,522	205,494
1997	512,668	235,849
1998	490,215	250,585
1999	524,149	274,683
2000	513,377	294,529
2001	611,895	331,628
2002	677,236	351,825
2003	716,502	368,708
2004	769,196	383,028
2005	905,966	367,664

Table A3.2 Nominal value of pharmaceutical trade for antibiotics (in millions of yen)

	Imports	Exports
1950		3
1951	1,558	280
1952	2,064	321
1953	2,266	499
1954	1,540	741
1955	840	303
1956	572	511
1957	638	908
1958	580	853
1959	648	1,040
1960	1,009	1,027
1961	632	320
1962	1,034	688
1963	1,911	688
1964	2,409	742
1965	2,922	845
1966	4,148	937
1967	5,230	981
1968	7,666	1,170
1969	9,107	1,511
1970	15,319	1,511

1971	17,538	2,437
1972	15,147	2,720
1973	19,813	3,579
1974	35,189	5,044
1975	44,595	5,891
1976	62,937	7,174
1977	54,671	8,680
1978	53,991	8,880
1979	57,725	12,007
1980	69,467	14,530
1981	69,145	15,941
1982	85,916	18,839
1983	71,661	22,153
1984	76,665	25,741
1985	69,889	29,400
1986	62,984	27,273
1987	65,264	29,249
1988	68,435	33,926
1989	73,674	36,523
1990	75,792	46,566
1991	70,826	57,850
1992	67,940	67,218
1993	57,254	58,947
1994	52,202	54,639
1995	63,458	56,255
1996	67,217	63,744
1997	66,874	62,418
1998	64,317	68,464
1999	70,355	60,089
2000	59,887	58,960
2001	62,249	57,704
2002	65,010	68,988
2003	66,592	55,472
2004	59,900	55,472
2005	66,247	59,971

Notes

1 Introduction: Why didn't Japan become a leader in pharmaceuticals?

1 This article refers to the pharmaceutical industry in terms of the prescription drugs industry. Prescription drugs refer to medication that can be purchased with a physician's prescription.

2 IMS Health, IMS Health Midas, December 2009.

3 Takeda Pharmaceutical, Co. *Annual Report 2009* (Osaka: Takeda Pharmaceutical, Co., 2009), 2; Astellas Pharma, Inc., *Annual Report 2009* (Tokyo: Astellas Pharma, Inc., 2009), 4; Daiichi Sankyo, Co. *Annual Report 2009* (Tokyo: Daiichi Sankyo Co., 2009), 4; Eisai, Co., *Annual Report 2009* (Tokyo: Eisai, Co., 2009), 11; Otsuka Pharmaceutical Co., *Kessan Jōhō* [Financial Information] http://www.otsuka.co.jp/company/profile/finance/ (accessed 10 May 2009).

4 P.E. Barral, *20 Years of Pharmaceutical Research Results Throughout the World* (Antony: Rohne-Poulenc Rorer Foundation, 1996), 24. An international drug is defined as a drug that has been launched in at least four of the G7 countries.

5 Organisation for Economic Co-operation and Development, *Health at a Glance 2009: OECD Indicators* (Paris: Organisation for Economic Co-operation and Development, 2009), 167. Japanese figures are for 2006. OECD figures for pharmaceuticals include both prescription and OTC drugs.

6 The automobiles market refers to the new car market. Datamonitor, 'Pharmaceuticals in the United States', *Industry Profile* (London: Datamonitor, 2009); Datamonitor, 'New Cars in the United States', *Industry Profile* (London: Datamonitor, 2009).

7 Past scholarship on the Japanese pharmaceutical industry revolved around the topical issues of the time. These have evolved from writings on capital liberalization and product patents to R&D, deregulation and industry reorganization. Recent works include, for example, Shinichi Ishii, 'Kigyō no Gaiburenkei ni taisuru Ninshiki to Gaiburenkei no Jisshi: Sangakurenkei to Iyakuhin Kigyō o Chūshin to Shita Hikakubunseki [The Perception and Reality of External Collaborations: A Comparative Analysis of University–Industry Collaborations in the Pharmaceutical Industry]', *Keiei Kenkyū* 53, no. 3 (2002): 205–217; Takuji Hara, *Innovation in the Pharmaceutical Industry: The Process of Drug Discovery and Development* (Cheltenham: Edward Elgar, 2003); Ryūhei Wakasugi and Harue Wakasugi, 'Iyakuhin no Kenkyū Kaihatsu to Hōseido [Pharmaceutical R&D and the Legal System]', *Mitagakkai Zasshi* 99, no. 1 (April 2006): 57–74.

8 Hiroyuki Odagiri, 'Iyakuhin Sangyō ni okeru Araiansu [Alliances in the Pharmaceutical Industry]', *Iryō to* Shakai 17, no. 1 (2008): 3–18; Kazuyuki Motohashi, 'Baiobenchā no Katsudō ni Kansuru Nichibei Hikakubunseki [A Comparison of Bioventures in Japan and the United States]', *Iryō to Shakai* 17, no. 1 (2008): 55–70; Tsurihiko Nanbu, ed. *Iyakuhin Sangyō Soshikiron* [Studies on the Organization of the Pharmaceutical Industry] (Tokyo: University of Tokyo Press, 2002); Ichirō Kataoka,

Mitsuaki Shimaguchi and Mimura Yumiko, eds, *Iyakuhin Ryūtsūron* [Studies on Distribution in the Pharmaceutical Industry] (Tokyo: University of Tokyo Press, 2003).

9 Takeda Pharmaceutical Co., *Takeda 200-nen* [200 Years of Takeda] (Osaka: Takeda Pharmaceutical Co., 1984); Daiichi Pharmaceutical Co., *Daiichi Seiyaku 90-nenshi* [Daiichi Pharmaceutical, a 90-year History] (Tokyo: Daiichi Pharmaceutical Co., 2007); Sankyo Co., *Sankyō 100-nenshi* [Sankyo, a 100-year History] (Tokyo: Sankyo Co., 1999); Fujisawa Pharmaceutical Co., *Fujisawa Yakuhin 100-nenshi* [Fujisawa Pharmaceutical, a 100-year History] (Osaka: Fujisawa Pharmaceutical Co., 1995); Yamanouchi Pharmaceutical Co., *Yamanouchi Seiyaku 50-nenshi* [Yamanouchi Pharmaceutical, a 100-year History] (Tokyo: Yamanouchi Pharmaceutical Co., 1975). Daiichi Sankyo and Astellas were both formed in 2005 as the result of mergers between Daiichi and Sankyo, and Fujisawa and Yamanouchi, respectively.

10 Nihon Yakushi Gakkai, *Nihon Iyakuhin Sangyōshi* [The History of the Japanese Pharmaceutical Industry] (Tokyo: Yakuji Nippōsha, 1995).

11 Takashi Nishikawa, *Kusuri Kara Mita Nihon; Shōwa 20-nendai no Genfūkei to Konnichi* [Looking at Japan from 'Medicine': Scenes from the 1940s to the Present] (Tokyo: Yakuji Nippōsha, 2004).

12 Julia Yongue, 'Origins of Innovation in the Japanese Pharmaceutical Industry: The Case of Yamanouchi Pharmaceutical Company (1923–1976)', *Japanese Research in Business History* 22 (2005): 109–136; Julia Yongue, 'Research Culture in the Pharmaceutical Industry', *Kenkyū Gijutsu, Keikaku* 8, no. 3 (1993): 239–248.

13 Alfred D. Chandler, *Shaping the Industrial Century: The Remarkable Story of the Modern Chemical and Pharmaceutical Industries* (Cambridge, MA: Harvard University Press, 2005), 3–6.

14 Ibid., 5.

15 Marvin B. Lieberman and David B. Montgomery, 'First-mover Advantages', *Strategic Management Journal* 9, no. 1 (1988): 41–58; Marvin B. Lieberman and David B. Montgomery, 'First-mover (Dis)advantages: Retrospective and Resource-based View', *Strategic Management Journal* 19, no. 12 (1998): 1111–1125.

16 Lacy Glenn Thomas, *The Japanese Pharmaceutical Industry: The New Drug Lag and the Failure of Industrial Policy* (Northampton: Edward Elgar, 2001).

17 Jeremy Howells and Ian Neary, *Intervention and Technological Innovation: Government and the Pharmaceutical Industry in the UK and Japan* (Basingstoke: Macmillan, 1995).

18 Steven W. Collins, *The Race to Commercialize Biotechnology: Molecules, Markets, and the State in the United States and Japan* (London: RoutledgeCurzon, 2004).

19 Chalmers Johnson and Daniel Okamoto explored the impact of selective industrial targeting policy on Japanese development in Chalmers A. Johnson, *MITI and the Japanese Miracle: The Growth of Industrial Policy, 1925–1975* (Stanford, CA: Stanford University Press, 1982); Daniel I. Okimoto, *Between MITI and the Market: Japanese Industrial Policy for High Technology* (Stanford, CA: Stanford University Press, 1989). Government support for the electronics industry, for example, was examined Dimitris Kazis, *Post-war Industrial Policy and the Electronics Industry in Japan* (Athens: Centre of Planning and Economic Research, 1988), 111–118.

20 Michael Reich, 'Why the Japanese Don't Export More Pharmaceuticals: Health Policy as Industrial Policy', *California Management Review* 32, no. 2 (1990): 124–150; Tomofumi Anegawa, 'Nihon no Iyakuhin Sangyō: Sono Seikō to Shippai [The Japanese Pharmaceutical Industry: Its Success and Failure]', *Iryō to Shakai* 12, no. 2 (2002): 49–78.

21 Morris Low, Shigeru Nakayama and Hitoshi Yoshioka, eds, *Science, Technology and Society in Contemporary Japan* (Cambridge: Cambridge University Press, 1999).

22 Chie Nakane, *Japanese Society* (Tokyo: Charles E. Tuttle, 1984); Robert Kneller, 'Autarkic Drug Discovery in Japanese Pharmaceutical Companies: Insights into National Differences in Industrial Innovation', *Research Policy* 32 (2003): 1805–1827.

23 Shigeru Nakayama and Morris Low, 'The Research Function of Universities in Japan', *Higher Education* 34 (1997): 245–258.
24 Ministry of Education, *Kyōiku Shihyō no Kokusai Hikaku* [International Comparison of Education Benchmarks] (Tokyo: Office of the Prime Minister, 1985–2005).
25 Steven Collins and Hikoji Wakoh, 'Universities and Technology Transfer in Japan: Recent Reforms in Historical Perspective', *The Journal of Technology Transfer* 25 (June 2000): 213–222.
26 Kenneth Lipartito, 'Culture and the Practice of Business History', *Business and Economic History* 24, no. 2 (1995): 1–42.
27 Steven Kent Vogel, *Japan Remodeled: How Government and Industry are Reforming Japanese Capitalism* (Ithaca, NY: Cornell University Press, 2006).
28 Marie Anchordoguy, *Reprogramming Japan: The High Tech Crisis Under Communitarian Capitalism* (Ithaca, NY: Cornell University Press, 2005).
29 For example, market dynamics differ markedly among chronic vs. acute ailments.
30 Ministry of Health, Labour and Welfare, 'Deaths by Leading Cause of Death, Population and Households', http://www.stat.go.jp/english/data/chouki/02.htm (accessed 1 December 2007).
31 Datamonitor, 'Japan – Antibacterial Drugs', *Industry Profile* (London: Datamonitor, 2002); Datamonitor, 'Japan – Cancer Drugs', *Industry Profile* (London: Datamonitor, 2002).
32 In value. See Ministry of Health and Welfare, *Yakuji Kōgyō Seisan Dōtai Chōsa Tōkei* [Annual Survey on Production in the Pharmaceutical Industry] (Tokyo: Yakugyō Keizai Kenkyūjo, 1953–1967); Ministry of Health and Welfare, *Yakuji Kōgyō Seisan Dōtai Chōsa Tōkei* [Annual Survey on Production in the Pharmaceutical Industry] (Tokyo: Yakugyō Keizai Kenkyūjo, 1968–2000); Ministry of Health, Labour and Welfare, *Yakuji Kōgyō Seisan Dōtai Chōsa Tōkei* [Annual Survey on Production in the Pharmaceutical Industry] (Tokyo: Jihō, 2001–2006).
33 US Department of Labor, Bureau of Labor Statistics, 'Consumer Price Index History Table', US Department of Labor, http://www.bls.gov/cpi/home.htm (accessed 1 July 2008).
34 Statistical Survey Department, Statistics Bureau, Ministry of Internal Affairs and Communications, 'General Index Excluding Imputed Rent for Japan', Ministry of Internal Affairs and Communications, http://www.e-stat.go.jp/SG1/estat/List.do?bid =000000730006&cycode=0 (accessed 1 July 2008).

2   A historical overview of Japan's pharmaceutical industry

1 The Ministry of Health and Welfare, established in 1938, became the Ministry of Health, Labour and Welfare in 2001. The Ministry of International Trade and Industry, established in 1949, became the Ministry of Economy, Trade and Industry in 2001.
2 Developments on Japan's post-war pharmaceutical industry are well documented in the white papers released annually by the Ministry of Health. See, Ministry of Health and Welfare, *Kōsei Hakusho* [White Paper on Health and Welfare] (Tokyo: Ōkurashō Insatsukyoku, 1955–2000); and Ministry of Health, Labour and Welfare, *Kōsei Rōdō Hakusho* [White Paper on Health, Labour and Welfare] (Tokyo: Ōkurashō Insatsukyoku, 2001–2007).
3 Japan learned of Western medicine by hiring foreign teachers, sending students overseas and establishing numerous schools of pharmacy.
4 This included the Rules to Control Pharmaceutical Sales [*Baiyaku Torishimari Kisoku*] in 1870, Rules for Pharmaceutical Sales [*Baiyaku Kisoku*] in 1877 and the Regulations on Pharmaceutical Operations and Products in 1889 [*Yakuhin Eigyo Narabi ni Yakuhin Torishimari Kisoku*] in 1889. The Japanese Pharmacopoeia was also introduced in 1886. See, Ministry of Health and Welfare, *Chikuji Kaisetsu Yakujihō* [Explanatory

Notes on the Pharmaceutical Affairs Law] (Tokyo: Gyōsei, 1973), 1–13. See also, Nihon Kōgakukai [Japan Federation of Engineering Societies], *Meiji Kōgyōshi* [History of Industry in the Meiji Period] (Tokyo: Nihon Kōgakukai, 1925), 992–1015; Hajime Sōda, '*Ishinki no Seiyaku* [Manufacturing Pharmacy during the Times of the Meiji Restoration]', *Iyaku Jānaru* (August 1972): 38–42. Also Hajime Sōda, '*Ishinki no Seiyaku* [Manufacturing Pharmacy during the Times of the Meiji Restoration]', *Iyaku Jānaru* (September 1972): 57–60.

5 Jonathan Liebenau, 'Industrial R&D in Pharmaceutical Firms in the Early Twentieth Century', *Business History* 26 (November 1984): 329–346.

6 For developments in Japan's pharmaceutical industry from the First World War up to the Second World War, see Yakugyō Keizai Kenkyūjo, *Yakuji Nenkan* [Pharmaceutical Affairs Annual] (Osaka: Nihon Yakugyō Shimbunsha, 1951), 241–246. See Keizai Shunjūsha, ed. '*Meiji Hyakunen Kigyō no Rekishi* [Company Histories 100 Years after Meiji] (Tokyo: Keizai Shunjūsha, 1968), 239–240. In addition to publicizing data on research conducted at the government's research laboratories (*Naimushō Eisei Kenkyūjo*) on specific production methods, the government provided subsidies to industry via the Law to Promote Chemical and Pharmaceutical Production (*Senryō Iyakuhin Seizō Shōrei hō*). This prompted production at a range of firms, including Tanabe, Dainihon, Shionogi, Sankyo and Takeda. The Wartime Act on Intellectual Property Rights (*Kōgyō Shoyūken Senjihō*) also voided the patent rights of enemy countries, legally enabling the production of patented pharmaceuticals for profit.

7 Anthelmentics refer to medicines that rid the body of worms. Sulfa drugs were discovered by Gerhard Dogmak in the early 1930s as one of the first chemotherapeutic substances that could cure bacterial infections.

8 In 1938, the military began to control imports of medicine and the allocation of raw materials for drug production, which were soon followed by controls over the production and prices of drugs. As rations were introduced in 1941, the government procured and distributed drugs to rationing posts. Developments during the Second World War are often documented in company histories. See, for example, Takeda Pharmaceutical Co., *Takeda 200-nen* [200 Years of Takeda], 79–81.

9 Yakugyō Keizai Kenkyūjo, *Yakuji Nenkan* [Pharmaceutical Affairs Annual] (Osaka: Nihon Yakugyō Shimbunsha, 1957), 289. As consumer price indices are not available for dates prior to 1947, these values were converted using the domestic corporate goods index produced by the Bank of Japan. This data is reprinted in Ministry of Internal Affairs and Communication, *Historical Statistics of Japan*, vol. 4 (Tokyo: Japan Statistical Association, 2006), 492–495.

10 Yakugyō Keizai Kenkyūjo, *Yakuji Nenkan* [Pharmaceutical Affairs Annual] (1957), 289.

11 Ibid.

12 Ibid.

13 'Trade and Industry: Pharmaceuticals', *Oriental Economist* 22 February 1947, 140. This is also documented in numerous company histories and corporate security filings of the 1940s. See also, Katsuhiro Matsumura, 'Seiyaku Kigyō no Saihen Seibi to Gōrika Katei, Shōwa 20-nen kara 25-nen zenhan made [The Reorganization and Rationalization of the Pharmaceutical Industry, from 1945 to early 1950]' *Iyaku Jānaru* 12 (March 1973): 42–48.

14 This is documented in the security filings of various firms in the late 1940s.

15 A steady supply of penicillin was particularly important because many American soldiers in Japan had acquired the venereal disease, syphilis, which could be cured with this drug.

16 General Headquarters, Supreme Commander for the Allied Powers, Public Health and Welfare Section, *Public Health and Welfare in Japan. Annual Summary: 1949* (Tokyo: Supreme Commander for the Allied Powers. Public Health and Welfare Section,

1949), 121. See also, Takashi Nishikawa, *Kusuri Kara Mita Nihon: Shōwa 20-nendai no Genfūkei to Konnichi* [Looking at Japan from 'Medicine': Scenes from the 1940s to the Present]. A brief overview of developments in the Occupation period has been written by Tōru Yamazaki, 'Sengo Yakugyōshi [A Postwar History of the Pharmaceutical Industry] (1)', *Yakkyoku* 16, no. 8 (August 1965): 3–8; Kinoichi Tsunematsu, 'Senryōka ni Okeru Yakuji Eisei Taisaku [Public Health and Welfare Policy under the Occupation]', *Iyaku Jānaru* 9 (July 1970): 56–58.

17 Yakugyō Keizai Kenkyūjo, *Yakuji Nenkan* [Pharmaceutical Affairs Annual] (1957), 227.

18 See for example, *Yakuji hō*, 29 July 1948, Law no. 197; General Headquarters, Supreme Commander for the Allied Powers, Public Health and Welfare Section, J.M. Bransky Narcotic Investigator, Memorandum for Record, 'Conference Relative to Raising Standards of Pharmaceutical Education', 11 June 1946. Declassified EO 12065 Section 3-402/NNDG no. 775024 (NDL); General Headquarters Supreme Commander for the Allied Powers, Public Health and Welfare Section, B.N. Riordan Chief, Supply Division, Memorandum for Record, 'Meeting of Pharmaceutical Education Council', 19 July 1946, 17 January, 14 March 1947, 12 January, 6 July 1951. Declassified EO 12065 Section 3-402/NNDG no. 775024 (NDL); General Headquarters Supreme Commander for the Allied Powers. Charles Band Chief, Supply Division. Public Health and Welfare Section, Memorandum for Record, 'Reorganization of the Pharmaceutical and Supply Bureau: Ministry of Welfare', 26 March, 29 March, 1 October 1949. Declassified EO 12065 Section 3-402/NNDG no. 775024 (NDL); Ministry of Health and Welfare, *Yakkyokuhō, Dairokuji Kaisei* [Japanese Pharmacopoeia, 6th revision] (Tokyo: Ministry of Health and Welfare, 1951).

19 The American efforts at improving public health conditions in Japan is well documented in an interview with Crawford Sams, who was the head of the GHQ's Public Health and Welfare Section. See Crawford F. Sams, interview by Darryl Podoll, 3 May 1979, interview OH037, transcript, Washington University School of Medicine Oral History Project, Bernard Becker Medical Library, St Louis, Missouri, http://beckerexhibits.wustl.edu/oral/interviews/sams.html (accessed 8 November 2010).

20 For an overview of the history of foreign direct investment in Japan, see Ralph Paprzycki and Kyoji Fukao, 'The Extent and History of Foreign Direct Investment in Japan', in *Foreign Direct Investment in Japan* (Cambridge: Cambridge University Press, 2008), 17–55; Mark Mason, 'The Screen Door. 1950–1870' in *American Multinationals in Japan: The Political Economy of Japanese Capital Controls* (Cambridge, MA: Harvard University Press, 1992), 150–198.

21 Even before the yen could freely be exchanged with foreign currencies in 1963, a few foreign firms such as Roche, Schering and Pfizer had established manufacturing operations in Japan. Between 1957 and 1963, foreign firms were allowed to invest over 50 per cent in yen-based firms. But after FDIs became subject to government approval in 1963, new pharmaceutical ventures were virtually excluded from the market.

22 See Katsuhiro Matsumura, 'Seiyaku Kigyō no Keiei Kiban Kyōka Katei, Shōwa 25-nen Zenhan kara 30-nen Goro made [Pharmaceutical Firms Strengthen the Foundations of their Business, from the Early 1950s to around 1955]', *Iyaku Jānaru* 12 (May 1973): 46–52. Many corporate histories also document this. See, for example, Sankyo Co., *Sankyō 100-nenshi* [Sankyo, a 100-year History], 107; Daiichi Pharmaceutical Co., *Daiichi Seiyaku 80-nenshi* [Daiichi Pharmaceutical, an 80-year History] (Tokyo: Daiichi Pharmaceutical Co., 1996), 99–100.

23 Tōru Yamazaki, 'Sengo Yakugyōshi [A Postwar History of the Pharmaceutical Industry] (2)', *Yakkyoku* 16, no. 9 (September 1965): 7–12.

24 Unless otherwise, all figures are in real terms in order to illustrate change over time. In nominal terms, technology imports increased from $1.6 million to $2.8 million. Yakugyō Keizai Kenkyūjo, *Yakuji Nenkan* [Pharmaceutical Affairs Annual] (Osaka: Nihon Yakugyō Shimbunsha, 1961), 123.

25 Ibid., 120–124.
26 In nominal terms, production levels grew from 58.6 million yen to 420.2 billion yen. Yakugyō Keizai Kenkyūjo, *Yakuji Nenkan* [Pharmaceutical Affairs Annual] (1961), 1; Ministry of Health and Welfare, *Yakuji Kōgyō Seisan Dōtai Chōsa Tōkei* [Annual Survey on Production in the Pharmaceutical Industry] (Tokyo: Yakugyō Keizai Kenkyūjo, 1953–1967); Angus Maddison and Organisation for Economic Co-operation and Development Centre, *The World Economy*, Vol. 2. (Paris: Organisation for Economic Co-operation and Development, 2006), 552.
27 See Yakugyō Keizai Kenkyūjo, *Yakuji Nenkan* [Pharmaceutical Affairs Annual] (1957), 230–231; Tōru Yamazaki, 'Sengo Yakugyōshi [A Postwar History of the Pharmaceutical Industry] (2)'.
28 Examples included Eisai's *Chokora-kai*, Sankyo's *Sankyo-kai* and Takeda's *Uroko-kai.*
29 Kunihiko Futaba, 'Sengo no Iyakuhin Ryūtsūshi: Dōran ni Yoru Kakkyō to Ranbai Mondai no Hassei [The History of Distribution in the Pharmaceutical Industry: The Korean War Boom and Emerging Problems with Dumping]', *Iyaku Jānaru* 11 (June 1972): 40–54. See also, Kunihiko Futaba, 'Sengo no Iyakuhin Ryūtsūshi: Kajō Seisan ni Taisuru Shijō no Kakudai to Tōsei no Hōsaku [The History of Distribution in the Pharmaceutical Industry: Strategies for Controlling a Market Expanding with Overproduction]' *Iyaku Jānaru* 11 (July 1972): 58–70. See also, Yakugyō Keizai Kenkyūjo, *Yakuji Nenkan* [Pharmaceutical Affairs Annual] (1961), 49.
30 Kunihiko Futaba, 'Sengo no Iyakuhin Ryūtsūshi: Dōran ni Yoru Kakkyō to Ranbai Mondai no Hassei [The History of Distribution in the Pharmaceutical Industry: The Korean War Boom and Emerging Problems with Dumping]'; Kunihiko Futaba, 'Sengo no Iyakuhin Ryūtsūshi: Kajō Seisan ni Taisuru Shijō no Kakudai to Tōsei no Hōsaku [The History of Distribution in the Pharmaceutical Industry: Strategies for Controlling a Market Expanding with Overproduction]'; Yakugyō Keizai Kenkyūjo, *Yakuji Nenkan* [Pharmaceutical Affairs Annual] (1961), 49.
31 Organisation for Economic Co-operation and Development, *Pharmaceuticals: Gaps in Technology* (Paris: Organisation for Economic Cooperation and Development, 1969), 48.
32 Lacy Glenn Thomas, III, 'Implicit Industrial Policy: The Triumph of Britain and the Failure of France in Global Pharmaceuticals', *Industrial and Corporate Change* 3 (1994): 451–489.
33 Stefan Timmermans and Valerie Leiter, 'The Redemption of Thalidomide: Standardizing the Risk of Birth Defects', *Social Studies of Science* 30, no. 1 (2000): 41–71; for an overview of the thalidomide disaster, see *Sunday Times* Insight Team, *Suffer the Children: The Story of Thalidomide* (London: Andre Deutsch, 1979); Harvey Teff, *Thalidomide: The Legal Aftermath* (Farnborough: Saxon House, 1976).
34 The American response to the Thalidomide tragedy has been documented in many articles and books. See, for example, Philip Hilts, 'Thalidomide', in *The FDA, Business, and One Hundred Years of Regulation* (New York: Knopf, 2003), 144–165.
35 'Drug Is Defended by Germany Maker: Thalidomide's Link to Baby Deformities Held Lacking', *New York Times*, 4 August 1962, 20.
36 Hideo Fujiki and Mitsuhiro Kida, eds, *Yakuhin Kōgai to Saiban: Saridomaido Jiken no Kiroku kara* [Drug Accidents and Trials: From the Records of the Thalidomide Disaster] (Tokyo: University of Tokyo Press, 1974). Mitsushiro Kida, *Thalidomide Embryopathy in Japan* (Tokyo: Kodansha, 1987).
37 See Shūzō Nishimura, 'Iryō Sangyō [The Health Care Industry]', in *Sengo Nihon Sangyōshi* [A History of Japanese Industries in the Post-war Period], edited by Sangyō Gakkai [The Society for Industrial Studies] (Tokyo: Tōyō Keizai Shinpōsha, 1995), 769–786.
38 See, 'Yakka Saeki Nen ni 1-chō 3-zen-oku en: Kusuridai Sōgaku no 4-bun no 1

[Pharmaceutical Price Differentials amount to 1.3 Trillion Yen a Year, or a Quarter of Drug Prices]', *Asahi Shimbun* 9 November 1989.

39 Eric Feldman, 'Medical Ethics the Japanese Way', *The Hastings Center Report* 15, no. 5 (1985): 21–24; William E. Steslicke, 'Doctors, Patients, and Government in Modern Japan', *Asian Survey* 12, no. 11 (1972): 913–931.

40 In terms of production. As historical sales values are not available, production values have used as proxy to estimate the size of the pharmaceutical market. Organisation for Economic Co-operation and Development, *Pharmaceuticals: Gaps in Technology*, 32.

41 Ibid., 47, 59.

42 GCP refers to quality standards for pharmaceutical R&D in the laboratory. GPMSP refers to quality standards to monitor drugs in a clinical setting after marketing.

43 This is evident in drug development records. See Yakuji Nippōsha, *Saikin no Shinyaku* [New Drugs in Japan] (Tokyo: Yakuji Nippōsha, 1950–2006).

44 MITI refers to the Ministry of International Trade and Industry.

45 In nominal terms, R&D expenditures between 1960 and 1975 increased from 3.7 billion yen to 95.2 billion yen. Office of the Prime Minister, *Kagaku Gijutsu Kenkyū Chōsa Hōkoku* [Report on the Survey of Research and Development] (Tokyo: Office of the Prime Minister, 1961–1984); National Science Foundation, *Survey of Industrial Research and Development Historical Database 1953–1998*, http://www.nsf.gov/statistics/iris (accessed 13 November 2009).

46 Ibid.; Pharmaceutical Research and Manufacturers of America (PhRMA), *Pharmaceutical Industry Profile 2008* (Washington DC: PhRMA, March 2008), 53; Great Britain, Business Statistics Office, *Industrial Research and Development Expenditure and Employment: 1975* (London: HMSO, 1979), 27.

47 Pharmaceutical trade refers to the sum of imports and exports in pharmaceuticals. In nominal terms, Japanese trade in pharmaceuticals increased from 12.7 billion yen in 1961 to 167.5 billion yen in 1975. See Ministry of International Trade and Industry, *Tsūshō Hakusho* [White Paper on Trade] (Tokyo: Ōkurashō Insatsukyoku, 1958–1973).

48 Mostly Asia. See Yakugyō Keizai Kenkyūjo, *Yakugyō Keizai Nenkan* [Pharmaceutical Economics Annual] (Tokyo: Yakuji Nippōsha, 1967), 132–137.

49 See Organisation for Economic Co-operation and Development, *Pharmaceuticals: Gaps in Technology*, 127.

50 Yakugyō Keizai Kenkyūjo, *Yakugyō Keizai Nenkan* [Pharmaceutical Economics Annual] (1967), 77, 322; Ibid., (1979), 178, 179, 254.

51 Yakugyō Keizai Kenkyūjo, *Yakugyō Keizai Nenkan* [Pharmaceutical Economics Annual] (1967), 236–244.

52 Yakugyō Jihōsha, *Nihon no Iyakuhin Sangyō* [The Japanese Pharmaceutical Industry] (Tokyo: Yakugyō Jihōsha, 1973), 160–161; Kōseishō 50-nenshi Henshū Iinkai [Editorial Committee for the 50-year History of the Ministry of Health and Welfare], 'Jiyūka to Kokusaika no Shinten [Progress in Capital Liberalisation and Internationalisation]', in *Kōseishō 50-nenshi* [A 50-year History of the Ministry of Health and Welfare] (Tokyo: Kōsei Mondai Kenkyūkai, 1988), 1624–1626.

53 Organisation for Economic Co-operation and Development, *Pharmaceuticals: Gaps in Technology*. However, the profitability among firms was heavily bolstered by the healthcare system and is not an accurate indicator of the ability of Japanese firms to compete against foreign counterparts.

54 Administrative guidance refers to informal legislation in the form of official or unofficial announcements from the government. The Japanese government used administrative guidance as an instrument of industrial policy to provide guidelines for business. See Kaoru Tabuchi, 'GMP no Ayumi to sono Tenbō [History and Prospects of GMP]', *Gekkan Yakuji* 21 (November 1979): 243–247; Shinji Nitta, 'Iyakuhin no Shinsa Gyōsei [Governing the Examination of Pharmaceuticals]', *Gekkan Yakuji* 21 (November 1979): 53–65.

55 This legislation created the distinction between prescription and OTC drugs by establishing criteria for drug approval in Japan. The 1967 guidelines, for example, specified the necessary documentation required to pursue a new drug application. Among other criteria, the guidelines also asked producers of prescription medicines to disclose adverse effects and provide a stable supply of medicines.

56 Ministry of Health and Welfare, *Yakuji Kōgyō Seisan Dōtai Chōsa Tōkei* [Annual Survey on Production in the Pharmaceutical Industry] (1953–1967); Ministry of Health and Welfare, *Yakuji Kōgyō Seisan Dōtai Chōsa Tōkei* [Annual Survey on Production in the Pharmaceutical Industry] (Tokyo: Yakugyō Keizai Kenkyujo, 1968–2000).

57 An NCE is a chemical compound that has not been previously approved for use in humans.

58 Robert Neimeth, 'Japan's Pharmaceutical Industry Postwar Evolution', in *The Changing Economics of Medical Technology*, edited by Annetine Gelijns and Ethan Halm, Committee on Technological Innovation in Medicine, Institute of Medicine (Washington DC: National Academy Press, 1991), 158–159.

59 Mitsibishi Bank, Ltd, 'Nihon Shijō ni Chūryoku suru Iyakuhin Gaishi [Foreign Pharmaceutical Firms Eye the Japanese Market', *Mitsubishi Bank Research Report* 369 (January 1986): 32.

60 Yakugyō Jihōsha, *Yakuji Handobukku* [Pharmaceutical Affairs Handbook] (1968–2000).

61 Ministry of Health and Welfare, *Kōsei Hakusho*, [White Paper on Health and Welfare] (1974).

62 In nominal terms, production levels rose from 218.1 million yen to 1.8 trillion yen. Ministry of Health and Welfare, *Yakuji Kōgyō Seisan Dōtai Chōsa Tōkei* [Annual Survey on Production in the Pharmaceutical Industry] (1953–1967); Ministry of Health and Welfare, *Yakuji Kōgyō Seisan Dōtai Chōsa Tōkei* [Annual Survey on Production in the Pharmaceutical Industry] (1968–2000).

63 Yano Keizai Kenkyūjo, 'Tasangyō kara no Kigyō Shinshutsu [New Entrants from Other Sectors]', *Iyaku Sangyō Nenkan* (Tokyo: Yano Keizai Kenkyūjo, 1975), 78. Between 1970 and 1980, the number of facilities related to pharmaceutical manufacture increased from 20,993 to 22,497. See Ministry of Health and Welfare, 'Pharmaceutical Business Facilities (C.Y. 1944–1996, F.Y. 1997–2004)', http://www.stat.go.jp/data/chouki/24.htm (accessed 27 July 2008).

64 Ministry of Health and Welfare, *Iyakuhin Sangyō Jittai Chōsa Hōkoku* [Report on the Status of the Pharmaceutical Industry] (Tokyo: Ministry of Health and Welfare, 1988–2000). Reprinted in Japan Pharmaceutical Manufacturers Association, *Data Book* (Tokyo: Japan Pharmaceutical Manufacturers Association, 2007), 2.

65 Tokai Bank, Ltd, 'Hanbai-mō no Kyōka o Isogu Iyakuhinkai [The Pharmaceutical Industry Rushes to Strengthen its Distribution Network]', *Tokai Ginkō Chōsa Geppō* 222 (January 1966): 17–26. See also, Kunihiko Futaba, 'Sengo no Iyakuhin Ryūtsushi: Iyakuhin Kōgyō no Kiki to Dakai e no Mosaku [The History of Distribution in the Pharmaceutical Industry: Seeking Solutions to the Challenges of the Pharmaceutical Industry]', *Iyaku Jānaru* 11 (September 1972): 44–53.

66 P.E. Barral, *20 Years of Pharmaceutical Research Results Throughout the World* 24. See also, Elma S. Hawkins and Michael R. Reich, 'Japanese-originated Pharmaceutical Products in the United States from 1960 to 1989: An Assessment of Innovation', *Clinical Pharmacology and Therapeutics* 51 (January 1992): 1–11. A global drug has been defined as a drug that has been launched in at least four of the G7 countries.

67 Ministry of Health and Welfare, 'Iyakuhin Sangyō nado no Genjō to Shomondai [Current Status and Problems in the Pharmaceutical Industry]' in *Kōsei Hakusho* [White Paper on Health] (1977).

68 Japan Pharmaceutical Manufacturers Association, *Seiyakukyō 20-nen no Ayumi* [A 20-year History of the Japan Pharmaceutical Manufacturers Association] (Tokyo: Japan Pharmaceutical Manufacturers Association, 1988), 57–58, 63–64.

69 Ministry of International Affairs and Communications, 'Nenrei Kakusai Danjobetsu Jinkō [Population by Single Years of Age and Sex] (1884–2000)', http://www.stat. go.jp/data/chouki/02.htm (accessed 20 March 2007).

70 Ministry of Health and Welfare, 'Densenbyō oyobi Shokuchūdoku no Kanjasū to Shibōshasū [Patients and Deaths of Infectious Diseases and Food Poisoning] (1876 1999)', http://www.stat.go.jp/data/chouki/02.htm (accessed 20 March 2007).

71 Jihō, *Iryō Iyakuhin Gyōkai no Ippan Chishiki* [General Information on the Healthcare and Pharmaceutical Industries] (Tokyo: Jihō, 2005), 60.

72 In nominal terms, production values fell from 3.40 trillion yen in 1982 to 3.38 trillion yen in 1985. Ministry of Health and Welfare, *Yakuji Kōgyō Seisan Dōtai Chōsa Tōkei* [Annual Survey on Production in the Pharmaceutical Industry] (1968–2000).

73 Jihō, *Iryō Iyakuhin Gyōkai no Ippan Chishiki* [General Information on the Health Care and Pharmaceutical Industries], 60.

74 Mitsubishi Bank, Ltd, 'Nihon Shijō ni Chūryoku suru Iyakuhin Gaishi [Foreign Pharmaceutical Firms Eye the Japanese Market', 22–32.

75 Yano Keizai Kenkyūjo, *Iyaku Sangyō Nenkan* (Tokyo: Yano Keizai Kenkyūjo, 1980), 12–15; Kinoichi Tsunematsu, 'Saihen Katei no Iyakuhin Sangyō [The Pharmaceutical Industry under Reorganisation]', *Iyaku Jānaru* 9 (September 1970): 20–23.

76 US Department of Commerce, International Trade Administration, Market Access and Compliance, 'MOSS Agreement on Medical Equipment and Pharmaceuticals', US Department of Commerce, http://www.mac.doc.gov/japan/source/menu/medpharm/ta860109.html (accessed 15 May 2007).

77 'Yūsei na Kaihatsuryoku de Kyūseicho o Tsuzukeru Zainichi Gaishi [With Stronger Development Capacities, Foreign Firms in Japan Continue to Grow Rapidly]', *Detailman* (May 1992): 28–35.

78 GLP, GCP and GMP are quality standards for the laboratory, for clinical trials and for manufacturing, respectively. Yakugyō Jihōsha, *Yakuji Handobukku*, [Pharmaceutical Affairs Handbook] (Tokyo: Yakugyō Jihōsha, 1968–1999).

79 The partial revision to the patent law, Law no. 27 in 1987, became effective in 1988. See Ministry of Health and Welfare, 'Iyakuhin no Kenkyū Kaihatsu no Shien: Gutaiteki na Shiensaku [Supporting R&D in Pharmaceuticals: Specific Support Policies]', in *Kōsei Hakusho* (1988), http://wwwhakusyo.mhlw.go.jp/wpdocs/hpaz198701/b0053.html (accessed 15 November 2010); Kazuyuki Motohashi, 'Japan's Patent System and Business Innovation: Reassessing Pro-patent Policies', RIETI Discussion Paper Series 03-E-020, http://www.rieti.go.jp/en/publications/act_dp2003.html (accessed 15 May 2008). The actual term of a Japanese patent was 15 years from the date of examined publication, but not more than 20 years from the filing date before 1 July 1995. Since 1 July 1995, the term of a patent has simply been 20 years from the filing date.

80 In nominal terms, R&D expenditures between 1975 and 1990 rose from 95.2 billion yen to 516.1 billion yen. See Ministry of Health and Welfare, 'Iyakuhin no Kenkyū Kaihatsu no Shien: Gutaiteki na Shiensaku [Supporting R&D in Pharmaceuticals: Specific Support Policies]', in *Kōsei Hakusho* (1988), http://wwwhakusyo.mhlw.go.jp/wpdocs/hpaz198701/b0053.html (accessed 15 November 2010).

81 This figure does need to be treated with caution, as the criteria for new drug approval was lower in Japan for other countries. However, the figure is used to illustrate the point that there were advances in drug discovery during this period. See European Federation of Pharmaceutical Industries and Associations (EFPIA), *The Pharmaceutical Industry in Figures* (Brussels: EFPIA, 1997): 12, and EFPIA, *The Pharmaceutical Industry in Figures* (Brussels: EFPIA, 2005), 20.

82 In nominal terms, Japanese exports increased from 36.8 billion yen to 111.1 billion yen. Ministry of International Trade and Industry, *Tsūshō Hakusho* [White Paper on Trade] (1958–1973); Ministry of International Trade and Industry, *Tsūshō Hakusho* [White Paper on Trade] (Tokyo: Gyōsei, 1974–2000).

83 Ministry of Health and Welfare, *Yakuji Kōgyō Seisan Dōtai Chōsa Tōkei* [Annual Survey on Production in the Pharmaceutical Industry] (1968–2000).

84 Ministry of Health, Labour and Welfare, *Iyakuhin Sangyō Jittai Chōsa Hōkokusho* [Report on the Pharmaceutical Industry] (2001); Yano Keizai Kenkyūjo *Iyaku Sangyō Nenkan* (Tokyo: Yano Keizai Kenkyūjo), reprinted in Japan Pharmaceutical Manufacturers Association, *Data Book* (2007), 21.

85 In 1990, Takeda, Japan's leading pharmaceutical firm, was still the only Japanese company that ranked within the top 25 global pharmaceutical companies (in sales). See PJB Publications, *Scrip: Pharmaceutical Company League Tables 1991* (Richmond: PJB Publications, 1991), 2.

86 Yakugyō Jihōsha, *Yakuji Handobukku* [Pharmaceutical Affairs Handbook]; Yakuji Nippōsha *The Japanese Pharmaceutical Industry in the New Millennium* (Tokyo: Yakuji Nippōsha, 2001).

87 See for example, Bank of Tokyo-Mitsubishi, Ltd, 'Honkakuteki na Kyōsō Jidai o Mukaeru Iyakuhin Gyōkai [The Pharmaceutical Industry to Face an Era of Real Competition]', *Chōsa Geppō* [Monthly Research Report] 107 (February 2005): 1–9.

88 Ministry of Health, Labour and Welfare, *Iyakuhin Sangyō Jittai Chōsa Hōkokusho* [Report on the Pharmaceutical Industry] (Tokyo: Ministry of Health, Labour and Welfare, 2001); Yano Keizai Kenkyūjo *Iyaku Sangyō Nenkan* (Tokyo: Yano Keizai Kenkyūjo), reprinted in Japan Pharmaceutical Manufacturers Association, *Data Book* (2007), 21.

89 See Yakugai Konzetsu Fōramu, *Yakugai Eizu wa Naze Okitaka* [Why the HIV Drug Tragedy Occurred]', (Tokyo: Kirishobō, 1996); Eric A. Feldman, 'HIV and Blood in Japan, Transforming Private Conflict in Public Scandal', in *Blood Feuds: Aids, Blood and the Politics of Medical* Disaster (Oxford: Oxford University Press, 1999), 59–94; Takao Takahashi, 'Medical Business Ethics: The HIV-tainted Blood Affair in Japan', in *Taking Life and Death Seriously: Bioethics from Japan*, edited by Takao Takahashi (Amsterdam: Elsevier, 2005), 253–273.

90 Kuniaki Yasuda, 'Nihon ni Okeru Shiniyakuin no Shōnin Shinsa Kikan [Approval Times for New Drugs in Japan]', *Research Paper Series, Office of Pharmaceutical Industry Research, Japan Pharmaceutical Manufacturers Association* 35 (December 2006); US Food and Drug Administration, CDER Drug and Biological Approval Reports, http://www.fda.gov/cder/rdmt/default.htm (accessed 4 May 2008).

91 Office of Pharmaceutical Industry Research, 'Seiyaku Sangyō no Shōraizō [The Future Image of the Pharmaceutical Industry]' *Office of Pharmaceutical Industry Research, Japan Pharmaceutical Manufacturers Association* (May 2007), 124.

92 Problems with this system have been widely discussed. See for example, Shūmei Tanaka, 'Iyakuhin no Ryūtsu o Meguru Mondaiten [Problems in Pharmaceutical Distribution]', in *Shakai Yakugaku Nyūmon* (Tokyo: Nankōdō, 1987), 156–168.

93 US Department of Commerce, International Trade Administration, Office of Japan Market Access and Compliance, 'U.S.–Japan Structural Impediments Initiative (SII)', US Department of Commerce, http://www.mac.doc.gov/japan/market-opening/market-opening.htm (accessed 2 May 2008).

94 The new price settlement system was called 'Shin-shikirika-sei'. See Ministry of Health and Welfare, 'Iyakuhin, Iryōryōgu no Ryūtsu Kindaika [Modernisation of Distribution in Pharmaceuticals and Medical Equipment]', in *Kōsei Hakusho* [White Paper on Health and Welfare] (1974); Japan, House of Representatives, Health and Welfare Committee, *Official Report of Debates*, 126th Diet, 6th Session, 2 April 1993; Japan, House of Councillors, Health and Welfare Committee, *Official Report of Debates*, 126th Diet, 7th Session, 20 April 1993; Japan, House of Councillors, Health and Welfare Committee, *Official Report of Debates*, 126th Diet, 11th Session, 30 June 1993.

95 See Tadashi Inoue, 'Iryōyō Iyakuhin Shijō no Tokushusei to Ryūtsū Kaikaku [Special Features of the Prescription Pharmaceutical Market and Distribution Reform]'.

Waseda Shakaigaku Kenkyū 49 (October 1994): 55–65. See also Japan Business History Association, *Banyū Seiyaku 85-nenshi* [Banyu Pharmaceutical: an 85-year History] (Tokyo: Banyu Pharmaceutical, 2002), 304–308. Banyu Pharmaceutical's then president Kenjirō Nagasaka spearheaded the industry's distribution reforms.

96 P. Reed Maurer, 'Why Japanese Pharmaceutical Wholesalers Merge'. *Pharma Marketletter*, 4 June 1999; Ministry of Health and Welfare, *Iyakuhin Sangyō Jittai Chōsa Hōkoku* [Report on the Status of the Pharmaceutical Industry].

97 These figures are in terms of the number of companies who were members of the Federation of Japan Pharmaceutical Wholesalers Association. Actual figures are expected to be higher, and the fall in the number of wholesalers much more dramatic. Federation of Japan Pharmaceutical Wholesalers Association, 'Nihon Iyakuhin Oroshigyō Rengōkai Kaiin Kōseiinsū/Honshasū Suii [Changes in the Number of Member Firms/ Headquarters of the Federation of Japan Pharmaceutical Wholesalers Association]', http://www.jpwa.or.jp/jpwa/index.html (accessed 4 May 2007). Jihō, *Yakuji Handobukku* [Pharmaceutical Affairs Handbook] (2002), 215.

98 This was called the bulk-line method. Most drugs had been revised at the 90th percentile point. From 1982, drugs with significant differences in wholesale and retail prices were revised at the 81st percentile point.

99 Japan Pharmaceutical Association, 'Iyakuhin Bungyō Shinchoku Jōkyō [Progress on the Separation on the Prescribing and Dispensing of Medicines]'.

100 The International Conference on Harmonisation of Technical Requirements for Registration of Pharmaceuticals for Human Use (ICH), http://www.ich.org (accessed 15 May 2007).

101 Established in 1990, the ICH is a project that aims to harmonize the pharmaceutical regulations of Europe, Japan and the United States.

102 Yano Keizai Kenkyūjo, *Iyaku Sangyō Nenkan* (Tokyo: Yano Keizai Kenkyūjo), reprinted in Japan Pharmaceutical Manufacturers Association, *Data Book* (2007), 21. In 1990, for example, there were 37 manufacturing facilities and 44 sales offices abroad. In 2005, there were 102 manufacturing facilities and 206 sales offices abroad.

103 The impact of foreign firms on the Japanese pharmaceutical industry has been reported in Mizuho Corporate Bank, Ltd, 'Ōbei Seiyaku Kigyō no Saihen Dōkō to Wagakuni Seiyakugyōkai e no Inpurikēshon', *Mizuho Sangyō Chōsa* 17 (March 2005): 1–42.

104 In sales. PJB Publications, *Scrip: Pharmaceutical Company League Tables 1991*, 42.

105 Jihō, *Yakuji Handobukku* [Pharmaceutical Affairs Handbook] (2007), 473. This excludes firms solely dedicated to the bulk production of drugs.

106 Yakugyō Jihōsha, *Yakuji Handobukku* [Pharmaceutical Affairs Handbook] (1968– 1999); Jihō, *Yakuji Handobukku* [Pharmaceutical Affairs Handbook] (2000–2007).

107 Ministry of Health and Welfare, 'Standards for the Implementation of Clinical Trials on Pharmaceutical Products', MHW Ordinance no. 28, 27 March 1997; and Ministry of Health and Welfare, 'Application of Standards for the Implementation of Clinical Trials on Pharmaceutical Products', Notification no. 445 of Pharmaceuticals and Cosmetics Division/Notification no. 68 of the Safety Division, Pharmaceutical Affairs Bureau, 29 May 1997. Information on contract research organizations in Japan may be found at Japan CRO Association, http://www.jcroa.gr.jp/ (accessed 4 May 2008).

108 This status changed with the incorporation of national universities in Japan in April 2004. See Ministry of Education, Culture, Sports, Science and Technology, 'Incorporation of National Universities', in *FY2003 White Paper on Education, Culture, Sports, Science and Technology* (Tokyo: Ministry of Education, Culture, Sports, Science and Technology, 2004).

109 See Steven Collins and Hikoji Wakoh, 'Universities and Technology Transfer in Japan: Recent Reforms in Historical Perspective', 213–222; Kenji Kushida, 'Japanese Entrepreneurship: Changing Incentives in the Context of Developing a New Economic Model', *Stanford Journal of East Asian Affairs* 1 (Spring 2001): 86–95.

110 Barriers to entrepreneurship has been discussed in Yoshiaki Nakamura and Hiroy-uki Odagiri, 'Nihon no Biobenchā Kigyō: Sono Igi to Jittai [Japanese Bioventures: Meaning and Current Status]', *REITI Discussion Paper Series* 02-J-007 (June 2002). An assessment of recent changes in legislation has been written by Michael Lynskey 'The Commercialisation of Biotechnology in Japan: Bioventures as a Mechanism of Knowledge Transfer from Universities', *International Journal of Biotechnology* 6 (2004): 155–185. The limitations on relying predominantly on in-house R&D have also been discussed in Robert Kneller, 'Autarkic Drug Discovery in Japanese Pharma-ceutical Companies: Insights into National Differences in Industrial Innovation'.

111 Steven W. Collins, *The Race to Commercialize Biotechnology: Molecules, Markets, and the State in the United States and Japan*, 151.

112 Hiroyuki Fukuhara, 'Iyakuhin no Sekai Hatsu Jōshi kara Kakkokuni okeru Jōshi made no Kikan [Time Differences between Initial Global Launches and Domestic Launches of Drugs across Different Countries]', *Research Paper Series, Office of Pharmaceuti-cal Industry Research, Japan Pharmaceutical Manufacturers Association* 31 (May 2006).

113 P. Reed Maurer, interview by author, Tokyo, Japan, 11 July 2007.

114 Takao Saruta, 'Chiken no Shitsuteki Reberuappu no tame no Teian: Tantōi no Tachiba kara [Suggestions to Improve the Quality of Clinical Trials: From a Physician's Stand-point]', *Yakuri to Chiryō* 23, no. 3 (1995): 561–564; Mitsuyoshi Nakajima, 'Chiken no Shitsuteki Reberuappu no tame no Teian: Kontorōrā no Tachiba kara [Suggestions to Improve the Quality of Clinical Trials: From a Controller's Standpoint]', *Yakuri to Chiryō* 23, no. 4 (1995): 777–783; Shigeyuki Nakano, 'Chiken ni Sanka Suru Hiken-sha no Meritto [Patient Benefits to Participating in Clinical Trials]', *Yakuri to Chiryō* 23, no. 5 (1995): 1085–1093.

115 Kōji Todaka, '"GRP"; Nihon ni okeru Yakuzai Kaihatsu no Infura to shite no Ishi no Yakuwari ["GRP"; The Role of Physicians in Helping to Develop Drugs in Japan]', *Rinshō Hyōka* 31, no. 3 (2004): 567.

116 Ministry of International Affairs and Communications', Nenrei Kakusai Danjobetsu Jinkō [Population by Single Years of Age and Sex] (1884–2000)'.

117 The impact of the regular price reductions has been widely discussed. See for exam-ple, Tsuruhiko Nanbu, 'Iyakuhin no Sangyō Soshiki: Yakka Kisei no Keizaiteki Kōka [Industrial Organisation in Pharmaceuticals: The Consequences of Price Regulation in Japan]', *Iryō to Shakai* 7 (January 1997): 1–15.

118 US Department of Commerce, *Pharmaceutical Price Controls in OECD Countries: Implications for US Consumers, Pricing, Research and Development, and Innovation* (Washington DC: US Department of Commerce, 2004), 15.

119 Government funds for pharmaceutical R&D are provided to universities. Firms are indirectly subsidised through joint projects conducted with universities.

120 Developments in drug discovery technologies has been written by Leland J. Gershell and Joshua H. Atkins, 'A Brief History of Novel Drug Discovery Technologies', *Nature Reviews Drug Discovery* 2 (April 2003): 321–327. See also, James R. Broach and Jeremy Thorner, 'High-throughput Screening for Drug Discovery', *Nature* 384 (November 1996): 14–16.

121 Thomson Reuters, *The Japanese Generic Drug Market: Opportunities and Strategies for Success* (London: Thomson Reuters, 2009).

122 Fuji Keizai, 'Jenerikku Iyakuhin Kokunai Shijō no Shuyō 24 Yakkō Ryōiki o Chōsa [Investigating 24 Therapeutic Sectors in the Domestic Generic Medicines Market]', https://www.fuji-keizai.co.jp/market/08096.html (accessed 7 May 2010).

123 Development Bank of Japan, 'Iyakuhin Gyōkai no Genjō to Jenerikku Iyakuhin Shijō [The Current Status of the Pharmaceutical Industry and the Generics Market]', *Kon-getsu no Topikkusu* [Topic of the Month] report no. 145–2 (24 March 2010); Sumi-tomo Trust & Banking Co., Kakudai suru Jenerikku Iyakuhin Gyōkai no Yukue [The Future of the Expending Generics Market]', *Chōsa Geppō* (January 2006).

124 'M&A Continues in Pharma/Biotech, but are Mega Acquisitions a Thing of the Past?' *Pharma Marketletter*, 5 January 2009; 'Teva in Generics JV with Japan's Kowa', *Pharma Marketletter*, 26 September 2008.

125 Management and Coordination Agency, Statistics Bureau & Statistics Centre, *Kagaku Gijutsu Kenkyū Chōsa Hōkoku* [Report on the Survey of Research and Development] (Tokyo: Management and Coordination Agency, 1985–2000); Ministry of Internal Affairs and Communications, Statistics Bureau, *Kagaku Gijutsu Kenkyū Chōsa Hōkoku* [Report on the Survey of Research and Development] (Tokyo: Ministry of Internal Affairs and Communications, 2001–2006). It is recognized that these figures do not accurately represent the strength of Japanese firms. The figures, for example, obscure the number of foreign pharmaceutical firms that, rather than licensing out to Japanese firms, marketed their drugs through their own distribution networks in Japan.

126 Jihō, *Yakuji Handobukku* [Pharmaceutical Affairs Handbook] (2002), 159.

127 Organisation for Economic Co-operation and Development, *International Trade, by Commodities Statistics Database*, http://www.sourceoecd.org (accessed 20 May 2010). Note that OECD figures include both medical and pharmaceutical products.

128 Centre for Medicines Research International, 'Japan in Focus: Strategies for Innovation and Global Drug Development, What Differentiates Japanese Pharma Companies from their Western Counterparts', *R&D Briefing* 28 (1999): 4.

129 Japan Pharmaceutical Manufacturers Association, *JPMA Databook* (Tokyo: JPMA, 2009), 15, 69; It is also important to note that the number of Japanese firms that derive a substantial portion of sales from abroad is still very limited.

130 See Yakugyō Jihōsha, *Yakuji Handobukku* [Pharmaceutical Affairs Handbook] (1968–1999); Jihō, *Yakuji Handobukku*, [Pharmaceutical Affairs Handbook] (2000–2007). The experience of globally successful Japanese firms are documented in 'Kokusaiteki Hitto Shōhin no Jōken [The Criteria for an Internationally Successful Drug]', *Detailman* (September 1991): 29–45; and 'Kaigai de Katsuyaku suru Kokusan Shinyaku no Genjō [The Current Status of Japanese-origin Drugs Abroad]', *Gekkan Mix* (June 1996): 44–62.

131 Eiji Ueda, 'Wagakuni no Chiken no Genjō to Mondaiten [The Current Environment and Issues around Clinical Trials in Japan', *Modan Media* 50, no. 2 (2004): 12.

132 Office of Pharmaceutical Industry Research, 'Sōyaku no Ba to shite no Kyōsōryoku Kyōka ni Mukete [Creating a Stronger, More Competitive Environment for Drug Discovery]', *Office of Pharmaceutical Industry Research, Japan Pharmaceutical Manufacturers Association* (November 2005), 75–78.

133 Even in 2006, Japan had 197 personnel to evaluate drug approvals, compared to 2,200 in the United States (FDA), 693 in the United Kingdom (MHRA), and 1,100 in Germany. Ibid., 113–114. See also, Robert Kneller, 'University–Industry Collaboration in Biomedical Research in Japan and the United States: Implications for Biomedical Industries', in *Industrializing Knowledge: University–Industry Linkages in Japan and the United States*, edited by Lewis M. Branscomb, Fumio Kodama and Richard L. Florida (Cambridge, MA: MIT Press, 1999), 410–438.

134 Mitsubishi Pharma Corp., *Yūka Shōken Hōkokusho* (Tokyo: Ōkurashō Insatsukyoku, 2006), 4.

135 Astellas Pharma Inc., *Yūka Shōken Hōkokusho* (Tokyo: Ōkurashō Insatsukyoku, 2006), 4; Dainippon Sumitomo Pharma Co., 'Kaisha Enkaku [Company History]', http://www.ds-pharma.co.jp/profile/history.html (accessed 28 July 2008); Daiichi Sankyo Co., *Yūka Shōken Hōkokusho* (Tokyo: Ōkurashō Insatsukyoku, 2006): 3.

136 Jiho, *Yakuji Handobukku* (2009), 481.

137 'Drugs Mergers; Everybody Get Together', *The Economist* 8 April 1989, 78; 'Drug Company Mergers; Love Potion No. 9', *The Economist* 5 August 1989, 58.

138 Office of Pharmaceutical Industry Research, 'Seiyaku Sangyō no Shōraizō [The Future Image of the Pharmaceutical Industry]', 52. See also, Michiyo Nakamoto and David

Pilling, 'Drugs Market Set for Change: Japan's Pharma Industry is Slowly Opening Up', *Financial Times* 3 April 2002.

139 Chugai Pharmaceutical Co., 'History', http://www.chugai-pharm.co.jp/profile/about/history.html (accessed 4 May 2008).

140 Centre for Medicines Research International, 'Japan in Focus: Strategies for Innovation and Global Drug Development. What Differentiates Japanese Pharma Companies from their Western Counterparts', 2.

141 American Chamber of Commerce in Japan FDI Task Force, 'Pharmaceuticals', *Specific Policy Recommendation* 3, February 2004, 3.

3 Developing a modern industry: The antibiotics sector

1 *Yakuji Kōgyō Seisan Dōtai Chōsa Tōkei* [Annual Survey on Production in the Pharmaceutical Industry] (1968–2000); Ministry of Health, Labour and Welfare, *Yakuji Kōgyō Seisan Dōtai Chōsa Tōkei* [Annual Survey on Production in the Pharmaceutical Industry] (Tokyo: Jihō, 2001–2006). Japan recorded a trade surplus in antibiotics in 1993, 1994 and 1998. Ministry of International Trade and Industry, *Tsūshō Hakusho* [White Paper on Trade] (Tokyo: Yakugyō Keizai Kenkyūjo, 1974–2000).

2 N.R. Kleinfeld, 'Intense Battle for Antibiotics', *The New York Times* 13 June 1983.

3 Eric Schmitt, 'What's Hot in Imported Products; Antibiotics Made Jointly', *The New York Times* 30 November 1986.

4 Jenny Wilson, *Antibacterial Products and Markets*, Scrip Reports (Richmond: PJB Publications, 1997), 137.

5 Datamonitor, 'Japan – Antibacterial Drugs', *Industry Profile* (London: Datamonitor, 2002), 9.

6 ICH refers to the International Conference on Harmonisation of Technical Requirements for Registration of Pharmaceuticals for Human Use. See also Chapter 2.

7 See 'Gyōkai Tenbō: Seiyaku Kōgyōkai [Industry Prospects: The Pharmaceutical Industry]', *Kigyō Chōsa* 63 (September 1948): 3.

8 Alexander Fleming, 'On the Antibacterial Action of Cultures of a Penicillium, with Special Reference to Their Use in the Isolation of H. Influenzae', *British Journal of Experimental Pathology* 10 (June 1929): 226–236.

9 For a general history on the development of penicillin, see, for example, Gladys L. Hobby and Milton Wainwright, *Penicillin: Meeting the Challenge* (New Haven: Yale University Press, 1985); John Parascandola, ed., *History of Antibiotics* (Madison: American Institute of the History of Pharmacy, 1980). Textbooks generally define antibacterials as synthetic chemicals more toxic to bacteria than to mammals while antibiotics are defined as substances produced by microorganisms that are toxic to bacteria. The distinctions between these two categories have, however, blurred over the years as scientists developed synthetic means to produce antibiotics.

10 W.H. Helfand, H.B. Woodruff, K.M.H. Coleman and D.L. Owen, 'Wartime Industrial Development of Penicillin in the United States, in *The History of Antibiotics: A Symposium*, edited by John Parascandola (Madison: American Institute of the History of Pharmacy, 1980): 31–55.

11 Gwyn Macfarlane, *Alexander Fleming: The Man and the Myth* (Oxford: Oxford University Press, 1984), 139.

12 See for example, Jonathan Liebenau, 'The British Success with Penicillin', *Social Studies of Science* 17, no. 1 (1987): 69–86; M. Lawrence Podolsky and Daniel E. Koshland, 'The Oxford Incidents', in *Cures out of Chaos: How Unexpected Discoveries Led to Breakthroughs in Medicine and Health* (Amsterdam: Harwood, 1997), 177–224.

13 Details of this discovery have been written in Fusako Tsunoda, *Hekiso: Nihon Penishirin Monogatari* [Hekiso: The Story of Penicillin in Japan] (Tokyo: Shinchōsha,

1978): 3–22. A brief overview of Japan's wartime penicillin project was also written by a scientist involved in the project: Hamao Umezawa, 'Kōsei Busshitsu no Kenkyūshi (1) [A History of Research in Antibiotics (1)]', *Shizen* 17, no. 2 (1962): 83–89.

14 Manfred Kiese, 'Chemotherapie mit Antibakteriellen Stoffen aus Niederen Pilzen und Bakterien', *Journal of Molecular Medicine* 22 (1943): 505–511.

15 Katsuhiko Inagaki, interview by Nihon Penishirin Kyōkai, 'Penishirin no Nihon Inyū [The Transfer of Penicillin into Japan], in Nihon Penishirin Kyōkai [Japan Penicillin Association]', *Penishirin no Ayumi: 1946–1961* [The History of Penicillin: 1946–1961] (Tokyo: Nihon Penishirin Kyōkai, 1961); Katsuhiko Inagaki, interview by Kihachirō Shimizu, 'Nihon ni Okeru Penishirin Kaihatsu no Keii [The Development of Penicillin in Japan]', *Today's Therapy* 19, no. 2 (1995): 26–34. Inagaki's involvement in the development of penicillin in Japan was later published by Haruhiko Inagaki, *Hekiso: Kokusan Penishirin Kaihatsu no Hatafuri, Inagaki Gun'i Shosa to Ichikōsei Gakuto Dōin* [Hekiso: Pioneering the Development of Penicillin in Japan, Lieutenant Medic Inagaki and the Mobilized Students of the Imperial University] (Tokyo: Nikkei Jigyō Shuppan Sentā, 2005).

16 Chāchiru Inochi Biroi, Zuruhon zai o Oginau Penishirin [Churchill's Life Is Saved: Penicillin, Instead of Sulfa Drugs, Is the Drug of Choice]', *Asahi Shimbun* 27 January 1944.

17 Yukimasa Yagisawa, 'Early History of Antibiotics in Japan', in *The History of Antibiotics: A Symposium*, edited by John Parascandola (Madison: American Institute of the History of Pharmacy, 1980), 69–90.

18 Katsuhiko Inagaki, Penishirin Iinkai no Kotodomo [Notes on the Penicillin Committee], 16 November 1944, Naito Museum of Pharmaceutical Science and Industry, Kagamihara, Japan. See also, Penishirin Iinkai, Penishirin Iinkai Gijiroku [Minutes of the Penicillin Committee], February to December 1944, Naito Museum of Pharmaceutical Science and Industry, Kagamihara, Japan.

19 Ibid.

20 See, Hamao Umezawa, 'Kōsei Busshitsu o Motomete (1) [Searching for Antibiotics (1)]' *Shokun* 1, no. 1 (1980): 294. Umezawa estimated that the development of penicillin in the 1940s cost the Japanese 1.5 billion yen while it cost the United States 50 billion yen in 1980 values. This article discusses the development of penicillin in Japan during the Second World War.

21 Katsuhiko Inagaki, Penishirin Iinkai no Kotodomo [Notes on the Penicillin Committee], 11.

22 Katsuhiko Inagaki, Penishirin Iinkai no Kotodomo [Notes on the Penicillin Committee] and Penishirin Iinkai, Penishirin Iinkai Gijiroku [Minutes of the Penicillin Committee].

23 Ibid. Both firms had been linked to key members of the Penicillin Committee. President Hanzaburo Matsuzaki of Morinaga and Katsuhiko Inagaki were fellow alumni of the University of Tokyo. President Koichi Iwadare of Banyu and Hamao Umezawa's (one of the lead scientists of the project) were also alumni of the University of Tokyo.

24 'Trade and Industry: Penicillin', *The Oriental Economist* 13 September 1947, 749. See also Katsuhiko Inagaki, interview by Nihon Penishirin Kyōkai, 'Penishirin no Nihon Inyū [The Transfer of Penicillin into Japan], in Nihon Penishirin Kyōkai [Japan Penicillin Association]', *Penishirin no Ayumi: 1946–1961* [The History of Penicillin: 1946–1961].

25 This is well documented in the company security filings in the late 1940s. See also, Chōbei Takeda, 'Wakakuni no Iyakuhin Kōgyō to Bōeki [Pharamceutical Industry and Trade in Our Country]', *Kankeiren* 16 (January 1949): 19–21.

26 Ministry of Health and Welfare, 'Densenbyō Oyobi Shokuchūdoku no Kanjasū to Shibōshasū' [Patients and Deaths of Infectious Diseases and Food Poisoning]

(1876–1999)', Statistics Bureau, Ministry of International Affairs and Communications, http://www.stat.go.jp/data/chouki/24.htm (accessed 20 March 2007).

27 Eiji Takemae, *Inside GHQ: The Allied Occupation of Japan and its Legacy* (London: Continuum, 2002), 409. See also Crawford F. Sams and Zabelle Zakarian, *'Medic': The Mission of an American Military Doctor in Occupied Japan and Wartorn Korea* (London: M.E. Sharpe, 1998), 81.

28 'Furyō Iyakuhin Torishimari Kyoka: Yamitorihiki wa Genbatsu [Strengthening Regulations over Unauthentic Medicines: Strict Penalties for Black Market Transactions]', *Iji Tsūshin* 1 (November 1946): 3; 'Yami no Penishirin wa Inchiki [Black Market Penicillin is Fraudulent]', *Directives and Important Releases of G.H.Q.* 26 (December 1946): 10.

29 'Penishirin Saihanbai Kyoka [Penicillin Resale Approval]', *Nihon Iji Shinpō* 10 (May 1946): 11.

30 General Headquarters, Supreme Commander for the Allied Powers, Public Health and Welfare Section, *Public Health and Welfare in Japan* (Tokyo: General Headquarters, Supreme Commander for the Allied Powers, Public Health and Welfare Section, 1949), 190. See also General Headquarters, Supreme Commander for the Allied Powers, Public Health and Welfare Section, *Mission and Accomplishments of the Occupation in the Public Health and Welfare Fields* (Tokyo: Supreme Commander for the Allied Powers, Public Health and Welfare Section, 1949), 32.

31 'Penishirin no Daiikkai Haikyū [The First Ration of Penicillin]', *Iyaku Tsūshin* 1 (July 1946): 3. The Recreation and Amusement Association was an organization established by the Japanese government to form brothels and provide prostitution services to the Occupation forces. Yoshiwara was a red-light district in Tokyo.

32 General Headquarters, Supreme Commander for the Allied Powers, Public Health and Welfare Section, *Public Health and Welfare in Japan* (1949), 121. Licensed Agencies for Relief in Asia (LARA) was an American volunteer organization established in April 1946 under the American Council of Voluntary Agencies for Foreign Service to provide aid to the impoverished regions of Asia (particularly Japan, Korea and Okinawa) after the Second World War. Cooperative for American Remittances to Europe (CARE) was also an American humanitarian aid organization founded in 1945 to provide relief to survivors of the Second World War.

33 Sey Nishimura, 'Censorship of Medical Journals in Occupied Japan', *Journal of the American Medical Association* 274 (August 1995): 456. See also Chapter 2.

34 Japan Business History Association, ed., *Banyū Seiyaku 85-nenshi* [Banyu Pharmaceutical: an 85-year History], 95–96.

35 See, for example, 'Penishirin no Seisankeikaku [Production Plan for Penicillin]', *Akarui Bōeki* 2, no. 2 (1947): 11. Penicillin, along with other medicines – such as antibiotics and vaccines – were mostly rationed via 'purchasing passbooks' to dealers authorized by the prefectural government, such as clinics, veterinary hospitals, pharmacies and other retailers.

36 Yakugyō Keizai Kenkyūjo, *Yakuji Nenkan* [Pharmaceutical Affairs Annual] (Osaka: Nihon Yakugyō Shimbunsha, 1951), 247.

37 Nihon Penishirin Kyōkai [Japan Penicillin Association], *Penishirin no Ayumi: 1946–1961* [The History of Penicillin: 1946–1961], 58–67.

38 Ibid., 68–69. See also, Japan Antibiotics Research Association, 'Honkai no Gaiyō [About Us]', http://www.antibiotics.or.jp/jara/news/jara.htm (accessed 28 April 2008). The Japan Penicillin Research Association was renamed as the Japan Antibiotics Research Association (JARA) in 1951. JARA currently operates under the Ministry of Health, Labour and Welfare, Pharmaceutical and Food Safety Bureau, Evaluation and Licensing Division.

39 Crawford F. Sams, 'Address to Tokyo Pharmacists', 7 March 1946. Declassified EO 12065 Section 3-402/NNDG no. 775024, 3 (NDL).

40 Eiji Takemae, *Inside GHQ: The Allied Occupation of Japan and its Legacy*, 49. See

also, Crawford F. Sams, interview by Darryl Podoll, 3 May 1979, interview OH037, transcript, Washington University School of Medicine Oral History Project, Bernard Becker Medical Library, St Louis, Missouri, http://beckerexhibits.wustl.edu/oral/interviews/sams.html (accessed 8 November 2010).

41 Yukimasa Yagisawa, 'Early History of Antibiotics in Japan', 79–80.

42 Barry Woodruff, 'A Soil Microbiologist's Odyssey', *Annual Review of Microbiology* 35 (1981): 8.

43 Jackson W. Foster, 'Three Days' Symposium on Penicillin Production, Held at Welfare Ministry, Tokyo, Japan, November 13–15, 1946', *Journal of Antibiotics* 1 (March 1947): 1–28.

44 Yukimasa Yagisawa, 'Early History of Antibiotics in Japan', 79.

45 Ibid., 80.

46 Nihon Yakushi Gakkai, *Nihon Iyakuhin Sangyōshi* [A History of the Japanese Pharmaceutical Industry] (Tokyo: Nihon Yakushi Gakkai, 1995), 113.

47 Nippon Kayaku Co., *Nihon Kayaku no Ayumi: Kono 10-nen o Chūshin to shite* [The History of Nippon Kayaku: With Special Attention to the Past 10 Years] (Tokyo: Nippon Kayaku Co., 1976), 186; Junichi Aoyagi, *Inochi o Kangaete 85-nen: Banyu Seiyaku no Ayumi* [85 Years for Life: The History of Banyu] (Tokyo: Banyu Pharmaceutical, Co., 2000), 153.

48 General Headquarters, Supreme Commander for the Allied Powers, Public Health and Welfare Section, *Public Health and Welfare in Japan* (Tokyo: Supreme Commander for the Allied Powers, Public Health and Welfare Section, 1950), 83.

49 Joichi Kumazawa and Morimasa Yagisawa, 'The History of Antibiotics: The Japanese Story', *Journal of Infection and* Chemotherapy 8, no. 2 (2002): 125. See also, General Headquarters, Supreme Commander for the Allied Powers, Public Health and Welfare Section, *Public Health and Welfare in Japan* (Tokyo: Supreme Commander for the Allied Powers, Public Health and Welfare Section, 1952), 123; and Crawford F. Sams and Zabelle Zakarian, *'Medic': The Mission of an American Military Doctor in Occupied Japan and Wartorn Korea*, 136.

50 'Trade and Industry: Penicillin', *The Oriental Economist* 1 May 1948, 352–353.

51 Kuniaki Tatsuta and Morimasa Yagisawa, *Kōseibusshitsu: Seisan no Kagaku* [Antibiotics: The Science of Production] (Tokyo, Nihon Kagakukai [The Chemical Society of Japan], 1994). 9.

52 'Trade and Industry: Penicillin', *The Oriental Economist* 13 September 1947, 749; 'Trade and Industry: Penicillin', *The Oriental Economist* 1 May 1948, 352–353.

53 'Trade and Industry: Penicillin', *The Oriental Economist* 3 September 1949, 863; Hamao Umezawa, 'Kōsei Busshitsu no Kenkyūshi (2) [A History of Research in Antibiotics (2)]' *Shizen* 17, no. 3 (1962): 86, 87.

54 Penicillin was out of reach of ordinary citizens in the early post-war period. In 1946, for example, the smallest dose of 10,000 unit penicillin was priced at 450 yen at a time when ordinary citizens could only withdraw 500 yen for living expenses from blocked deposits. See Yukimasa Yagisawa, 'Early History of Antibiotics in Japan', 77.

55 General Headquarters, Supreme Commander for the Allied Powers, Public Health and Welfare Section, *Public Health and Welfare in Japan* (1949), 123.

56 This rule refers to the Shitei Seisan Shizai Wariate Kisoku. See Takeda Pharmaceutical Co., *Takeda 200-nen* [200 Years of Takeda] (Osaka: Takeda Pharmaceutical Co., 1984), 128–129.

57 Ibid.

58 Nihon Penishirin Kyōkai [Japan Penicillin Association], *Penishirin no Ayumi: 1946–1961* [The History of Penicillin: 1946–1961], 166.

59 Ibid., 170.

60 Federal Trade Commission, United States, *Economic Report on Antibiotics Manufacture* (Washington: Government Printing Office, 1958), 82.

61 General Headquarters, Supreme Commander for the Allied Powers, Public Health and Welfare Section, *Public Health and Welfare in Japan* (1950), 89.

62 Mark Mason, *American Multinationals in Japan: The Political Economy of Japanese Capital Controls* (Cambridge, MA: Harvard University Press, 1992), 105–109.

63 'Drug Production Begun: Two Plants Now Devoted to Making of Streptomycin', *The New York Times* 21 August 1946; Albert Schatz, Elizabeth Bugie and Selman Waksman, 'Streptomycin, A Substance Exhibiting Antibiotic Activity against Gram-positive and Gram-negative Bacteria', *Proceedings of the Society for Experimental Biology and Medicine* 55 (1944): 66–69.

64 GARIOA was a US government aid programme for American occupied territories after the Second World War. US government aid through this programme provided mainly foodstuffs, fertilizers and pharmaceuticals to Japan between 1947 and 1951.

65 General Headquarters, Supreme Commander for the Allied Powers, Public Health and Welfare Section, *Public Health and Welfare in Japan* (1949), 128–129.

66 Stuart G. Smith to Selman A. Waksman, 19 July 1948, personal correspondence; Selman A. Waksman to W. Fujita, 15 March 1949, personal correspondence, Selman A. Waksman Papers, Box 20, Folder 1, Rutgers University.

67 General Headquarters, Supreme Commander for the Allied Powers, Public Health and Welfare Section, *Public Health and Welfare in Japan* (1949), 122–123.

68 Ibid., 122. This council was comprised of officials from the GHQ's Public Health and Welfare Section, Japan's Ministry of Health, university professors and hospital directors.

69 General Headquarters, Supreme Commander for the Allied Powers, Public Health and Welfare Section, *Public Health and Welfare in Japan* (1950), 81; Ibid. (1952), 123–124.

70 Yukimasa Yagisawa, 'Early History of Antibiotics in Japan', 82.

71 Selman A. Waksman to Russel E. Watson, 12 October 1951, personal correspondence, Selman A. Waksman Papers, Box 20, Folder 1, Rutgers University.

72 Yukimasa Yagisawa, 'Early History of Antibiotics in Japan', 82.

73 Russell E. Watson to Selman A. Waksman, 18 October 1951, personal correspondence, Selman A. Waksman Papers, Box 20, Folder 1, Rutgers University.

74 General Headquarters, Supreme Commander for the Allied Powers, Public Health and Welfare Section, *Public Health and Welfare in Japan* (1952), 124.

75 Yakugyō Keizai Kenkyūjo, *Yakuji Nenkan* [Pharmaceutical Affairs Annual] (Osaka: Nihon Yakugyō Shimbunsha, 1957), 59–60.

76 See for example, Yusuke Sumiki to Selman A. Waksman, 28 November 1950 and 14 February 1950, personal correspondence, Selman A. Waksman Papers, Box 20, Folder 1, Rutgers University; Selman A. Waksman to Yusuke Sumiki, 4 December 1950, 6 February 1951 and 18 June 1951, personal correspondence, Selman A. Waksman Papers, Box 20, Folder 1, Rutgers University.

77 Japan's older, more traditional firms such as Takeda, Daiichi and Sankyo often produced drugs such as hexyresourcinol, DDT and sulfa drugs.

78 Katsuichi Matsuo, 'Korisuchin oyobi Korisuchin Metan Suruhonsan Natoriumu no Kaihatsu [The Development of Colistin and Colistin Methanesulfonate]', in *Sangyō Gijutsu no Rekishi no Shūtaisei-Taikeika o Okonaukoto ni Yoru Inobēshon Sōshutsu no Kankyō Seibi ni Kansuru Chōsa Kenkyu Hōkokusho* [Investigation and Research Report on the Compilation and Organization on the History of Industrial Technology to Develop an Environment more Suitable for Innovation], edited by Japan Machinery Federation (Tokyo: Japan Machinery Federation, 2006), 74–80, 242–275.

79 Yasuo Koyama, Akio Kurosasa, Atsushi Tsuchiya and Kinsuke Takakuta, 'A New Antibiotic "Colistin" Produced by Spore-forming Soil Bacteria', *The Journal of Antibiotics* 3, no. 7 (1950): 457–459.

80 Ibid.

81 Yakuji Nippōsha, 'Colistin', in *Saikin no Shinyaku* [New Drugs in Japan] (Tokyo, Yakuji Nippōsha, 1952), 21–23.

82 FDA/Center for Drug Evaluation and Research, 'Label and Approval History', Drugs@ FDA, FDA Approved Drug Products, http://www.accessdata.fda.gov/scripts/cder/ drugsatfda/index.cfm?fuseaction=Search.Label_ApprovalHistory#apphist (accessed 8 May 2008); Seiyaku Kigyō Kondankai [Council of Pharmaceutical Firms], *Seiyaku Kigyō no Genjō to Kōsatsu* [An Evaluation of the Current Status of Pharmaceutical Firms] (Tokyo: Seiyaku Kigyō Kondankai, 1965).

83 In 1969, the firm was recognized by the MITI for its contribution towards Japanese exports. Katsuichi Matsuo, 'Korisuchin oyobi Korisuchin Metan Suruhon san Natoriumu no Kaihatsu [The Development of Colistin and Colistin Methanesulfonate]', 74.

84 Minoru Aizawa and United Nations Industrial Development Organization, *Review of the Development of Antibiotic Industry in Selected Countries: Technical Report: Antibiotic Industry in Japan, History and Development* (Vienna: United Nations Industrial Development Organization, 1985), 74.

85 Converted into 2005 yen. Sankyo Co., *Yūka Shōken Hōkokusho* [Annual Securities Report] (Tokyo: Ōkurashō Insatsukyoku, 1960).

86 Shionogi & Co., *Yūka Shōken Hōkokusho* [Annual Securities Report] (Tokyo: Ōkurashō Insatsukyoku, 1960).

87 Takeda Pharmaceutical Co., *Yūka Shōken Hōkokusho* [Annual Securities Report] (Tokyo: Ōkurashō Insatsukyoku, 1960).

88 Yakugyō Keizai Kenkyūjo, *Yakuji Nenkan* [Pharmaceutical Affairs Annual] (Osaka: Nihon Yakugyō Shimbunsha, 1961), 123.

89 Ibid., 124–145.

90 Ibid.

91 Trade in this context refers to the sum of imports and exports.

92 Yakugyō Keizai Kenkyūjo, *Yakuji Nenkan* [Pharmaceutical Affairs Annual] (1957), 292–293, 300–301.

93 Yakugyō Keizai Kenkyūjo, *Yakuji Nenkan* [Pharmaceutical Affairs Annual] (1961), 37–38.

94 Ibid., 44–45.

95 Ibid., 42.

96 Yakugyō Keizai Kenkyūjo, *Yakuji Nenkan* [Pharmaceutical Affairs Annual] (1961), 37–38.

97 Ibid., 44–45.

98 Minoru Aizawa and United Nations Industrial Development Organization, *Review of the Development of Antibiotic Industry in Selected Countries: Technical Report: Antibiotic Industry in Japan, History and Development*, 74.

99 See Japan Antibiotics Research Association, 'Honkai no Gaiyō [About Us]'; Yukimasa Yagisawa, 'Early History of Antibiotics in Japan', 88.

100 This is documented in various company histories. See, for example, Takeda. Pharmaceutical Co., *Takeda 200-nen* [200 Years of Takeda]; Fujisawa Pharmaceutical Co., *Fujisawa 100-nenshi* [Fujisawa Pharmaceutical, a 100-year History] (Osaka: Fujisawa Pharmaceutical Co., 1995); and Daiichi Pharmaceutical Co., *Daiichi Seiyaku 80-nenshi* [Daiichi Pharmaceutical, an 80-year History] (Tokyo: Daiichi Pharmaceutical Co., 1998).

101 Hamao Umezawa was one of the central scientific researchers in Japan's wartime penicillin project. See, for example, Katsuhiko Inagaki, Penishirin Iinkai no Kotodomo [Notes on the Penicillin Committee], 16 November 1944, Naito Museum of Pharmaceutical Science and Industry, Kagamihara, Japan.

102 Hamao Umezawa, 'Kōseibusshitsu o Motomete (2): Kanamaishin no Hakken [Searching for Antibiotics (2): The Discovery of Kanamycin]', *Shokun* 12, no. 2 (1980): 294–305.

103 Hamao Umezawa, Masahiro Ueda, Kenji Maeda, Koki Yagishita, Shinichi Kondo, Yoshiro Okami, Ryozo Itahara, Yasuke Osato, Kazuo Nitta and Tomio Takeuchi, 'Production and Isolation of a New Antibiotic, Kanamycin', *The Journal of Antibiotics Series A* 10 (September 1957): 181–188.

104 Takeshi Nakagawa, interview by Shōzō Tsunabuchi in 'Meiji Seika: Ishokudōgen Baio o Mezasu [Meiji Seika Aims to Develop Biotechnology Businesss]', *Will* (December 1982): 48–51.

105 Nihon Penishirin Kyōkai [Japan Penicillin Association], *Penishirin no Ayumi: 1946–1961* [The History of Penicillin: 1946–1961], 170.

106 For a history of Meiji Seika, see Meiji Seika Kaisha, Ltd, *Meiji Seika no Ayumi: Kaukide Tsukutte 60-nen* [A History of Meiji Seika: Selling What We Want to Buy for 60 Years] (Tokyo: Meiji Seika Kaisha, Ltd, 1977); Meiji Seika Kaisha, Ltd, *Meiji Seika no Ayumi: Sōgyō kara 70-nen* [A History of Meiji Seika: 70 Years since Establishment] (Tokyo: Meiji Seika Kaisha, Ltd, 1987).

107 Hamao Umezawa, 'Kanamycin', in *Saikin no Shinyaku* [New Drugs in Japan], edited by Yakuji Nippōsha (Tokyo: Yakuji Nippōsha, 1959), 13–17.

108 Yakuji Nippōsha, *Saikin no Shinyaku* [New Drugs in Japan] (Tokyo: Yakuji Nippōsha, 1959), 22.

109 Hamao Umezawa, 'Kōsei Busshitsu o Motomete (2) [Searching for Antibiotics (2)]', 301.

110 Ibid.; Hamao Umezawa, 'Kanamycin'; Hamao Umezawa, 'Kanamycin: Its Discovery', *Annals of the New York Academy of Sciences* 76, no. 2 (1958): 20–26.

111 Meiji Seika Kaisha, Ltd, *Meiji Seika no Ayumi: Sōgyō kara 80-nen* [The History of Meiji Seika: 80 Years from Establishment] (Tokyo: Meiji Seika Kaisha, Ltd, 1997), 20. See for example, Meiji Seika Kaisha, Ltd, *Yūka Shōken Hōkokusho* [Annual Securities Report] (Tokyo: Ōkurashō Insatsukyoku, 1960). By fiscal year 1960, Meiji Seika derived 20 per cent of sales, or 16.2 yen (in 2005 yen) from pharmaceuticals, with most of its sales from penicillin, streptomycin and kanamycin.

112 Takeshi Nakagawa, interview by Shōzō Tsunabuchi in 'Meiji Seika: Ishokudōgen Baio o Mezasu [Meiji Seika Aims to Develop Biotechnology Businesss]', 48. These are nominal values. In 2005 values, Meiji Seika had risked 1.09 billion yen to pursue R&D of kanamycin at a time when the firm had a capital of 4.57 billion yen.

113 Yakuji Nippōsha, *Saikin no Shinyaku* [New Drugs in Japan] (Tokyo, Yakuji Nippōsha, 1959), 22.

114 Nihon Yakushi Gakkai, *Nihon Iyakuhin Sangyōshi* [The History of the Japanese Pharmaceutical Industry], 110.

115 Hamao Umezawa, 'Kōsei Busshitsu o Motomete (2) [Searching for Antibiotics (2)]', 297.

116 This is evident in the various drug development processes. See Yakuji Nippōsha, *Saikin no Shinyaku* [New Drugs in Japan] (Tokyo: Yakuji Nippōsha, 1950–2006).

117 Ministry of Health and Welfare, *Yakuji Kōgyō Seisan Dōtai Chōsa Tōkei* [Annual Survey on Production in the Pharmaceutical Industry] (Tokyo: Yakugyo Keizai Kenkyujo, 1953–1967); Ministry of Health and Welfare, *Yakuji Kōgyō Seisan Dōtai Chōsa Tōkei* [Annual Survey on Production in the Pharmaceutical Industry] (1968–2000).

118 Ministry of Health and Welfare, *Yakuji Kōgyō Seisan Dōtai Chōsa Tōkei* [Annual Survey on Production in the Pharmaceutical Industry] (1968–2000).

119 See Organisation for Economic Co-operation and Development, *Pharmaceuticals: Gaps in Technology* (Paris: Organisation for Economic Cooperation and Development, 1969), 32, 69; and Yakugyō Keizai Kenkyūjo, *Yakugyō Keizai Nenkan* [Pharmaceutical Economics Annual] (Tokyo: Yakuji Nippōsha, 1967), 132–299.

120 Minoru Aizawa and United Nations Industrial Development Organization, *Review of the Development of Antibiotic Industry in Selected Countries: Technical Report: Antibiotic Industry in Japan, History and Development*, 74–75.

121 Yakugyō Keizai Kenkyūjo, *Yakugyō Keizai Nenkan* [Pharmaceutical Economics Annual] (1967), 50, 51, 70, 71.
122 Michael Reich, 'Why the Japanese Don't Export More Pharmaceuticals: Health Policy as Industrial Policy', *California Management Review* 32, no. 2 (1990): 135.
123 See, for example, Yukimasa Yagisawa, 'Shinbunya o Kirihiraita Kōseibusshitsu [A New Field Created by Antibiotics]', *Iyaku Jānaru* 9 (February 1970): 20–23.
124 GCP refers to quality standards for pharmaceutical R&D in the laboratory. GPMSP refers to quality standards to monitor drugs in a clinical setting after marketing.
125 Joichi Kumazawa and Morimasa Yagisawa, 'The History of Antibiotics: The Japanese Story', 125–133; Morimasa Yagisawa, 'Antibiotics, Chemotherapeutics and Other Microbial Products Originated from Japan', unpublished document sent to author.
126 Yamanouchi Pharmaceutical Co., Ltd, *Yūka Shōken Hōkokusho* [Annual Securities Report] (Tokyo: Ōkurashō Insatsukyoku, 1950), 8.
127 Yamanouchi Pharmaceutical Co., Ltd, *Yūka Shōken Hōkokusho* [Annual Securities Report] (Tokyo: Ōkurashō Insatsukyoku, 1961), 7.
128 Antibiotic sales grew from 3.8 billion yen in 1960 to 15.2 billion yen in 1970. In nominal terms, Yamanouchi's antibiotic sales grew from 722 million yen to 5.1 billion yen between 1960 and 1970. Ibid., 17. Yamanouchi Pharmaceutical Co., Ltd, *Yūka Shōken Hōkokusho* [Annual Securities Report] (Tokyo: Ōkurashō Insatsukyoku, 1971), 18. The firm's history has been documented in Yamanouchi Pharmaceutical Co., *Yamanouchi Seiyaku 50-nenshi* [A 50-year History of Yamanouchi Pharmaceutical Co.] (Tokyo: Yamanouchi Pharmaceutical Co., 1975).
129 Yamanouchi Pharmaceutical Co., *Yamanouchi Seiyaku 50-nenshi* [A 50-year History of Yamanouchi Pharmaceutical Co.] (1975), 221.
130 Yakuji Nippōsha, 'Josamycin', in *Saikin no Shinyaku* [New Drugs in Japan] (Tokyo: Yakuji Nippōsha, 1970), 86–87.
131 Takashi Osono, Yoshihiko Oka, Shunichi Watanabe, Yōzō Numazaki, Kiruko Moriyama, Hitoshi Ishida, Kiyoshi Suzaki, Yoshirō Okami and Hamao Umezawa, 'A New Antibiotic Josamycin I: Isolation and Physicochemical Characteristics', *The Journal of Antibiotics Series A* 20, no. 3 (1967): 174–180; and Kazuo Nitta, Kuniichiro Yano, Fumio Miyamoto, Yoshiharu Hasegawa, Toshihisa Sato, Noriko Kamoto and Shintaro Matsumoto, 'A New Antibiotic, Josamycin. II: Biological Studies', *The Journal of Antibiotics Series A* 20 no. 3 (1967): 181–187.
132 Yakuji Nippōsha, 'Josamycin', in *Saikin no Shinyaku* [New Drugs in Japan] (Tokyo: Yakuji Nippōsha, 1970), 86–87.
133 Yamanouchi Pharmaceutical Co., *Yamanouchi Seiyaku 50-nenshi* [A 50-year History of Yamanouchi Pharmaceutical Co.] (1975), 311–312.
134 Yamanouchi Pharmaceutical Co., *Yūka Shōken Hōkokusho* [Annual Securities Report] (Tokyo: Ōkurashō Insatsukyoku, 1976), 7.
135 In nominal terms, Yamanouchi's antibiotic sales grew from 5.1 billion yen to 15.9 billion yen between 1970 and 1980. Yamanouchi Pharmaceutical Co., *Yūka Shōken Hōkokusho* [Annual Securities Report] (Tokyo: Ōkurashō Insatsukyoku, 1971), 18; Yamanouchi Pharmaceutical Co., *Yūka Shōken Hōkokusho* [Annual Securities Report] (Tokyo: Ōkurashō Insatsukyoku, 1981), 12.
136 Fujisawa Pharmaceutical Co., *Yūka Shōken Hōkokusho* [Annual Securities Report] (Tokyo: Ōkurashō Insatsukyoku, 1963), 7.
137 Fujisawa Pharmaceutical Co., *Yūka Shōken Hōkokusho* [Annual Securities Report] (Tokyo: Ōkurashō Insatsukyoku, 1960–1965). For a history of Fujisawa, see Fujisawa Pharmaceutical Co., *Fujisawa Yakuhin 80-nenshi* [Fujisawa Pharmaceutical, an 80-year History] (Osaka: Fujisawa Pharmaceutical Co., 1976); Fujisawa Pharmaceutical Co., *Fujisawa Yakuhin 100-nenshi* [Fujisawa Pharmaceutical, a 100-year History] (Osaka: Fujisawa Pharmaceutical Co., 1995).
138 Yakugyō Keizai Kenkyūjo, *Yakuji Nenkan* [Pharmaceutical Affairs Annual] (Osaka: Nihon Yakugyō Shimbunsha, 1961), 187.

139 Minoru Nishida, Tadao Matsubara, Takeo Murakawa, Yasuhiro Mine, Yoshiko Yokota, Sachiko Goto and Shogo Kuwahara, 'Cefazolin, a New Semisynthetic Cephalopsorin Antibiotic II. In vitro and In vivo Antimicrobial Activity', *The Journal of Antibiotics* 23, no. 3 (1970): 137–148. See also Fujisawa Pharmaceutical Co., *Fujisawa Yakuhin 80-nenshi* [Fujisawa Pharmaceutical, an 80-year History], 342.

140 Fujisawa Pharmaceutical Co., *Fujisawa Yakuhin 100-nenshi*, 165.

141 Fujisawa Pharmaceutical Co., *Fujisawa Yakuhin 80-nenshi* [Fujisawa Pharmaceutical, an 80-year History], 342. Cefazolin was valued for its wide bacterial spectrum towards gram positive and negative bacteria. It was also stable and well absorbed in the body, without causing bodily dysfunction or allergic reactions. It was also found to be effective to various bacterial strains that had become resistant to penicillin. See Minoru Nishida, Tadao Matsubara, Takeo Murakawa, Yasuhiro Mine, Yoshiko Yokota, Sachiko Goto and Shogo Kuwahara, 'Cefazolin, a New Semisynthetic Cephalopsorin Antibiotic II. In vitro and In vivo Antimicrobial Activity'.

142 In nominal terms, Fujisawa's antibiotic sales grew from 11.6 billion yen to 41.4 billion yen between 1960 and 1970. Fujisawa Pharmaceutical Co., *Yūka Shōken Hōkokusho* [Annual Securities Report] (Tokyo: Ōkurashō Insatsukyoku, 1972), 10; Fujisawa Pharmaceutical Co., *Yūka Shōken Hōkokusho* [Annual Securities Report] (Tokyo: Ōkurashō Insatsukyoku, 1977), 9.

143 Yakuji Nippōsha, 'Cefamedine', in *Saikin no Shinyaku* [New Drugs in Japan] (Tokyo: Yakuji Nippōsha, 1971), 66; Yakuji Nippōsha, 'Cefaloridin', in *Saikin no Shinyaku* [New Drugs in Japan] (Tokyo: Yakuji Nippōsha, 1966), 51–53; and Yakuji Nippōsha, 'Cefalotin', in *Saikin no Shinyaku* [New Drugs in Japan] (Tokyo: Yakuji Nippōsha, 1967), 45–46.

144 Minoru Aizawa and United Nations Industrial Development Organization, *Review of the Development of Antibiotic Industry in Selected Countries: Technical Report: Antibiotic Industry in Japan, History and Development*, 74.

145 Robert Neimeth, 'Japan's Pharmaceutical Industry Postwar Evolution', in *The Changing Economics of Medical Technology*, edited by Annetine Gelijns and Ethan Aalm, Committee on Technological Innovation in Medicine, Institute of Medicine (Washington DC: National Academy Press, 1991), 160.

146 Ibid. As historical data for sales are not available, production values have been used as a measure of market size.

147 In nominal terms, production levels rose from 22.0 billion yen to 363.4 billion yen. Ibid.

148 Ministry of Health and Welfare, *Kōsei Hakusho* [White Paper on Health and Welfare] (Tokyo, Ōkurashō Insatsukyoku, Ministry of Finance, 1974).

149 Ibid.

150 In nominal terms, trade values increased from 2.0 billion yen in 1960 to 50.5 billion yen in 1975. Ministry of International Trade and Industry, *Tsūshō Hakusho* [White Paper on Trade] (Tokyo: Ōkurashō Insatsukyoku, 1958–1973); Ministry of International Trade and Industry, *Tsūshō Hakusho* [White Paper on Trade] (1974–2000).

151 In nominal terms, antibiotic imports grew from 1.0 billion yen to 44.6 billion yen while antibiotic exports grew from 1.0 billion yen to 5.9 billion yen. Ibid.

152 In nominal terms, antibiotic imports in 1975 from the United States, Singapore and the United Kingdom were 26.6 billion yen, 9.5 billion yen and 6.2 billion yen, respectively. Yakugyō Keizai Kenkyūjo, *Yakugyō Keizai Nenkan* [Pharmaceutical Economics Annual] (Tokyo: Yakuji Nippōsha, 1979), 167.

153 Between 1945 and 1972, Okinawa was ruled by the United States.

154 Yakugyō Keizai Kenkyūjo, *Yakugyō Keizai Nenkan* [Pharmaceutical Economics Annual] (1979), 168.

155 Michael Reich, 'Why the Japanese Don't Export More Pharmaceuticals: Health Policy as Industrial Policy', 135.

156 Eric Feldman, 'Medical Ethics the Japanese Way', *The Hastings Center Report* 15, no. 5 (1985): 21–24; William E. Steslicke, 'Doctors, Patients, and Government in Modern Japan', *Asian Survey* 12, no. 11 (1972): 913–931.

157 P. Reed Maurer, interview by author, Tokyo, Japan, 11 July 2007.

158 In nominal terms, the production level of antibiotics increased from 363.4 billion to 814.3 billion yen. Ibid.

159 Yakugyō Jihōsha, *Yakuji Handobukku* [Pharmaceutical Affairs Handbook] (Tokyo: Yakugyō Jihōsha, 1968–1999).

160 In nominal terms, antibiotic production stood at 624.1 billion yen in 1990. Ministry of Health and Welfare, *Yakuji Kōgyō Seisan Dōtai Chōsa Tōkei* [Annual Survey on Production in the Pharmaceutical Industry] (1968–2000).

161 Ibid.

162 M. Itō, 'Nichi-bei-ō ni okeru Kōkinyaku no Rinshōhyōkahō [A Clinical Evaluation of Antibacterial Agents in the United States, Europe and Japan]', *Saishin Igaku* 44, no. 12 (1989): 2461. Per capita consumption calculated based on demographic data available at Organisation for Economic Co-operation and Development, *OECD Health Data 2008: Statistics and Indicators for 30 Countries* (Paris: Organisation for Economic Co-operation and Development, 2008) in SourceOECD, http:www.sourceoecd.org.

163 In nominal terms, antibiotic production from bulk imports changed from 210.2 billion yen to 230.2 billion yen. Ministry of Health and Welfare, *Yakuji Kōgyō Seisan Dōtai Chōsa Tōkei* [Annual Survey on Production in the Pharmaceutical Industry] (1968–2000).

164 For general information on quinolone drugs, see Peter Ball, 'The Quinolones: History and Overview', in *The Quinolones*, edited by Vincent T. Andriole (San Diego: Academic Press, Inc., 1988), 1–33; David C. Hooper and Ethan Rubinstein, 'Introduction', in *Quinolone Antimicrobial Agents* (Washington DC: American Society for Microbiology Press, 2003), viii–ix.

165 Hisashi Takahashi, Isao Hayakawa and Takeshi Akimoto, 'The History of the Development and Changes of Quinolone Antibacterial Agents', *Yakushigaku Zasshi* 38, no. 2 (2003): 161–179.

166 Walter Sneader, *Drug Discovery: A History* (Chichester: John Wiley & Sons, 2005), 395.

167 Kyorin Pharmaceutical Co., *Yūka Shōken Hōkokusho* [Annual Securities Report] (Tokyo: Ōkurashō Insatsukyoku, 1995), 3.

168 This is documented in the scholarly articles published.

169 Akira Ito, Keiji Hirai, Matsuhisa Inoue, Hiroshi Koga, Seigo Suzue, Tsutomu Irikura and Susumu Mitsuhashi, 'In Vitro Antibacterial Activity of AM-715, a New Nalidixic Acid Analog', *Antimicrobial Agents and Chemotherapy* 17, no. 2 (1980): 103–108. Earlier quinolones were largely ineffective towards gram-negative bacteria. Keiji Hirai, Akira Ito, Yasuo Abe, Seigo Shizue, Tsutomu Irikura, Matsuhisa Inoue and Susumu Mitsuhashi, 'Comparative Activities of AM-715 and Pipemedic and Nalidixic Acids Against Experimentally Induced Systemic and Urinary Tract Infections', *Antimicrobial Agents and Chemotherapy* 19, no. 1 (1981): 188–189.

170 Yakuji Nippōsha, 'Norfloxacin', in *Saikin no Shinyaku* [New Drugs in Japan] (Tokyo: Yakuji Nippōsha, 1985), 128–129.

171 PJB Publications, *Scrip's Antibacterial Report* (London: PJB Publications, 1990), 26. See also, 'Merck Introduces Two Drugs in the U.S.', *Chemical Week* 26 November 1986, 16.

172 Martha Glaser, 'Market-share Battle Marks Cardiovasculars, Antiarthritics; 48th Annual Prescription Review', *Drug Topics* 131 (March 1987): 43; Martha Glaser, 'Quinolones, Antidepressants Gained in 1988: PDS; Pharmaceutical Data Services', *Drug Topics* 133 (April 1989): 73.

173 K. Sato, Y. Matsuura, M. Inoue, T. Une, Y. Osada, H. Ogawa and S. Mitsuhashi, 'In

Vitro and In Vivo Activity of DL-8280, a New Oxazine Derivative', *Antimicrobial Agents and Chemotherapy* 22, no. 4 (1982): 548–553.

174 For Daiichi's history, see Daiichi Pharmaceutical Co., *Daiichi Seiyaku 70-nen no Ayumi* [Daiichi Pharmaceutical, a 70-year History] (Tokyo: Daiichi Pharmaceuticals Co., 1986); Daiichi Pharmaceutical Co., *Daiichi Seiyaku 80-nenshi* [Daiichi Pharmaceutical, an 80-year History]; or Daiichi Pharmaceutical Co., *Daiichi Seiyaku 90-nenshi* [Daiichi Pharmaceutical, a 90-year History] (Tokyo: Daiichi Pharmaceutical Co., 2007).

175 Daiichi Pharmaceutical Co., *Daiichi Seiyaku 70-nen no Ayumi* [Daiichi Pharmaceutical, a 70-year History] (1986), 35, 77; Daiichi Pharmaceutical Co., *Daiichi Seiyaku 80-nenshi* [Daiichi Pharmaceutical, an 80-year History] (1998), 242.

176 Yakuji Nippōsha, 'Ofloxacin', in *Saikin no Shinyaku* [New Drugs in Japan] (Tokyo: Yakuji Nippōsha, 1986), 125–126.

177 In nominal terms, Daiichi's antibiotic sales grew from 21.1 billion yen to 70.4 billion yen. Exports grew from 7.3 billion yen to 11.2 billion yen. Daiichi Pharmaceutical Co., *Daiichi Seiyaku 80-nenshi* [Daiichi Pharmaceutical, an 80-year History], 399; Daiichi Pharmaceutical Co., *Yūka Shōken Hōkokusho* [Annual Securities Report] (Tokyo: Ōkurashō Insatsukyoku, 1986), 10, 13; Daiichi Pharmaceutical Co., *Yūka Shōken Hōkokusho* [Annual Securities Report] (Tokyo: Ōkurashō Insatsukyoku, 1991), 19; Daiichi Pharmaceutical Co., *Yūka Shōken Hōkokusho* [Annual Securities Report] (Tokyo: Ōkurashō Insatsukyoku, 1996), 24.

178 'Ofloxacin/Levofloxacin', *Gekkan Mix* [Monthly Medical Information Express] (December 1996): 55–56.

179 Daiichi Pharmaceutical Co., *Daiichi Seiyaku 70-nen no Ayumi* [Daiichi Pharmaceutical, a 70-year History], 277; John Elmsey, 'Flourine Helps the Medicine Go Down' *The Independent* 18 March 1991, 17.

180 PJB Publications, *Scrip's Antibacterial Report*, 136.

181 See, Matthew Lynn, *The Billion-dollar Battle: Merck v Glaxo* (London: Mandarin, 1992).

182 Yakuji Nippōsha, 'Meropenem', in *Saikin no Shinyaku* [New Drugs in Japan] (Tokyo: Yakuji Nippōsha, 1996), 103–109.

183 Saburō Fukai, ed., *Konnichi no Shinyaku: Kindai Iyakuhin no Hensen* [New Drugs Today: Changes in Modern Pharmaceutials] (Tokyo: Yakuji Jihōsha, 1995), 878. See also, Yutaka Takeuchi, Yoshiaki Takebayashi, Makoto Sunagawa, Yutaka Isobe, Yukari Hamazume, Akura Uemura and Tetsuo Noguchi, 'The Stability of a Novel Carbapenem Antibiotic, Meropenem (SM-7338), in a Solid State Formulation for Injection', *Chemical & Pharmaceutical Bulletin* 41, no. 11 (1993): 1998–2002.

184 FDA/Center for Drug Evaluation and Research, 'Label and Approval History'.

185 In nominal terms, meropenem reached 13.6 billion yen in sales. PJB Publications, *Scrip's Antibacterial Report*, 46; Jenny Wilson, *Antibacterial Products and Markets*, *Scrip Reports*, 78.

186 The degree of international competitiveness (according to rates of overseas licensing) has varied according to types of antibiotics. The number of Japanese-origin antibiotics, for example, has been highest in b-lactam antibiotics at 39 substances, or 39 per cent of all discoveries.

187 Joichi Kumazawa and Morimasa Yagisawa, 'The History of Antibiotics: The Japanese Story', 127; Morimasa Yagisawa, 'Antibiotics, Chemotherapeutics and Other Microbial Products Originated from Japan'.

188 Morimasa Yagisawa, 'Antibiotics, Chemotherapeutics and Other Microbial Products Originated from Japan'.

189 In nominal terms, antibiotic trade grew from 50.5 billion yen in 1975 to 122.4 billion yen in 1990. Ministry of International Trade and Industry, *Tsūshō Hakusho* [White Paper on Trade] (1974–2000).

190 In nominal terms, between 1975 and 1990, antibiotic imports increased from 44.6

billion yen to 75.8 billion yen while antibiotic exports increased from 5.9 billion yen to 46.5 billion yen. Ibid.

191 Most of these were semisynthetic b-lactam, aminoglycoside and macrolide antibiotics or synthetic quinolone antibiotics.

192 Specific patient populations refer to patient groups whose response to a given drug may differ from an average healthy adult. Such groups include children, pregnant women, the elderly and patients undergoing other types of treatment.

193 See, for example, Harold C. Neu, 'The Crisis in Antibiotic Resistance', *Science* 257, no. 5073 (1992): 1064–1073; and John Travis, 'Reviving the Antibiotic Miracle?', *Science* 264, no. 5157 (1994): 360–362.

194 See, for example, Yano Keizai Kenkyūjo, *Iyaku Sangyō Nenkan* [Pharmaceutical Industry Annual], (Tokyo: Yano Keizai Kenkyūjo, 1985), 2–12.

195 The US antibiotics market at the time would have been approximately $9 billion in 2005 values. Eric Schmitt, 'What's Hot in Imported Products; Antibiotics Made Jointly'.

196 Ministry of Health and Welfare, *Yakuji Kōgyō Seisan Dōtai Chōsa Tōkei* [Annual Survey on Production in the Pharmaceutical Industry] (1968–2000). See Naoki Ikegami and John Creighton Campbell, 'Health Care Reform in Japan: The Virtues of Muddling Through', *Health Affairs* 18 (May/June 1999): 56–75.

197 G. Philip White, *Antibiotics: Market Review and Development Trends* (London: FT Healthcare, 1999), 27.

198 Japan Pharmaceutical Association, *Iyakuhin Bungyō Shinchoku Jōkyō* [Progress on the Separation on the Prescribing and Dispensing of Medicines], Japan Pharmaceutical Association, http://www.nichiyaku.or.jp/contents/bungyo/default.html (accessed 20 April 2008).

199 The impact of biennial price reductions on reducing demand has been widely discussed. See for example, Hidenao Takahashi, 'Iyakuhin no Juyō no Kakaku Danryokusei no Suikei [The Price Elasticity of Demand in Pharmaceuticals: An Examination of the Biennial Price Reductions]', *Hitotsubashi University COE Working Paper* 12 (August 2005): 16.

200 Yakugyō Jihōsha, *Yakuji Handobukku* [Pharmaceutical Affairs Handbook] (Tokyo: Yakugyō Jihōsha, 1968–1999); Jihō, *Yakuji Handobukku* [Pharmaceutical Affairs Handbook] (Tokyo: Jihō, 2000–2007).

201 Ibid.

202 J.R. Broach and J. Thorner, 'High-throughput Screening for Drug Discovery', 14–16; Jürgen Drews, 'Drug Discovery: A Historical Perspective', *Science* 287, no. 5460 (17 March 2000): 1962.

203 Pharmacopoeia Drug Discovery, Inc., *Annual Report 2006* (Cranbury, NJ: Pharmacopoeia Drug Discovery, Inc., 2007), 2.

204 Joichi Kumazawa and Morimasa Yagisawa, 'The History of Antibiotics: The Japanese Story', 126; Morimasa Yagisawa 'Biseibutsu Taisha Sanbutsu Tansaku Kenkyū no Dōkō [Trends in Exploratory Research of Microbial Metabolite Part 2; 20 Years after Antibiotics]', *Baiosaiensu to Indasutorī* 58, no. 2 (2000): 92. The difficulty of drug discovery despite advances in phenomenal advances in drug discovery technologies has been widely discussed. See, for example, Gerry Higgs, 'Molecular Genetics: the Emperor's Clothes of Drug Discovery?', *Drug Discovery Today* 9 (September 2004): 727–729.

205 In 1999, tuberculosis still affected 438,000 and killed 3,000 in Japan, but these figures were about 10 per cent and 2 percent of 1945 figures, respectively. Ministry of Health and Welfare, 'Densenbyō oyobi Shokuchūdoku no Kanjasū to Shibōshasū [Patients and Deaths of Infectious Diseases and Food Poisoning] (1876–1999)', Statistics Bureau, Ministry of International Affairs and Communications, http://www.stat.go.jp/data/chouki/24.htm (accessed 20 March 2007); and World Health Organization, Global TB database, http://www.who.int/tb/country/global_tb_database/en/index.html (accessed 1 November 2007).

206 *Yakuji Kōgyō Seisan Dōtai Chōsa Tōkei* [Annual Survey on Production in the Pharmaceutical Industry] (1968–2000); Ministry of Health, Labour and Welfare, *Yakuji Kōgyō Seisan Dōtai Chōsa Tōkei* [Annual Survey on Production in the Pharmaceutical Industry] (2001–2006); Yakuji Jihōsha, *Yakuji Handobukku* [Pharmaceutical Affairs Handbook] (1968–1999).

207 'Japan's Medicine Men Take Aim', *The Economist* 2 March 1991, 69.

208 Saburō Fukai, ed., *Konnichi no Shinyaku: Kindai Iyakuhin no Hensen* [New Drugs Today: Changes in Modern Pharmaceuticals], 928–941, 854–894.

209 Ministry of Health and Welfare, *Yakuji Kōgyō Seisan Dōtai Chōsa Tōkei* [Annual Survey on Production in the Pharmaceutical Industry] (1968–2000).

210 Ibid.

211 Nigel Thompson, *International Price Comparison: Japan* (Tokyo: Japan Pharmaceutical Manufacturers Association Long Term Vision Research Council, 1999).

212 See, for example, 'Global Drug Market: 30 Years of Growth', *Pharma Marketletter*, 4 January 1993; Peter Martin, 'Weak Link in the Chain: Distribution Difficulties Have Meant that Japan's Successes in the West's Car and Consumer Electronics Markets Have Not Been Equalled in Other Industries', *Financial Times* 6 March 1997.

213 For trade statistics, see Ministry of International Trade and Industry, *Tsūshō Hakusho* [White Paper on Trade] (1974–2000) and Ministry of Health and Welfare, *Yakuji Kōgyō Seisan Dōtai Chōsa Tōkei* [Annual Survey on Production in the Pharmaceutical Industry] (1968–2000); Management and Coordination Agency, Statistics Bureau & Statistics Centre, *Kagaku Gijutsu Kenkyū Chōsa Hōkoku* [Report on the Survey of Research and Development] (Tokyo: Management and Coordination Agency, 1985–2000). Various academic and popular articles have also documented Japan's strong performance in antibiotics. See, for example, Michael Reich, 'Why the Japanese Don't Export More Pharmaceuticals: Health Policy as Industrial Policy'; Eric Schmitt, 'What's Hot in Imported Products; Antibiotics Made Jointly'.

214 Datamonitor, 'Global – Antibacterial Drugs', *Industry Profile* (London: Datamonitor, 2002), 8.

215 Datamonitor, 'Japan – Antibacterial Drugs', *Industry Profile* (London: Datamonitor, 2002), 9. Most Japanese firms relied upon domestic sales for a significant portion of total revenue.

216 G. Philip White, *Antibiotics: Market Review and Development Trends*, 28.

217 Jenny Wilson, *Antibacterial Products and Markets*, *Scrip Reports*, 137.

218 James R. Bartholomew, *The Formation of Science in Japan* (New Haven: Yale University Press, 1989).

219 Eleanor Westney, 'Country Patterns in R&D Organization: The United States and Japan', in *Country Competitiveness: Technology and the Organizing of Work*, edited by Bruce Kogut (Oxford: Oxford University Press, 1993), 36–53; David T. Methé and Joan D. Pinner-Hahn, 'Globalization of Pharmaceutical Research and Development in Japanese Companies: Organizational Learning and the Parent-Subsidiary Relationship', in *Japanese Multinationals Abroad: Individual and Organizational Learning*, edited by Schon Beechler and Allan Bird (New York: Oxford University Press, 1999), 191–210.

220 See, for example, Christian Oberlaender, 'The Rise of Western "Scientific Medicine" in Japan: Bacteriology and Beriberi', in *Building a Modern Japan: Science, Technology and Medicine in the Meiji Era and Beyond*, edited by Morris Low (New York: Palgrave Macmillan, 2005), 11–36.

221 See Takehiko Hashimoto, 'The Hesitant Relationship Reconsidered: University–Industry Cooperation in Post-war Japan', in *Industrializing Knowledge: University–Industry Linkages in Japan and the United States*, edited by Lewis M. Branscomb, Fumio Kodama and Richard L. Florida (Cambridge, MA: MIT Press, 1999), 234–251; and Robert Kneller, 'The Beginning of University Entrepreneurship in Japan: TLOs and Bioventures Lead the Way', *Journal of Technology Transfer* 32 (2007): 435–456.

222   Louis Galambos and Jane Eliot Sewell, *Networks of Innovation: Vaccine Development at Merck, Sharp & Dohme, and Mulford, 1895–1995* (Cambridge: Cambridge University Press, 1996).

4 What went wrong? The anticancer drug sector

1   'Japanese Drug Companies Pull Ahead in the Race to Innovate', *The Economist* 24 September 1983, 93.
2   US Congress, Office of Technology Assessment, *Commercial Biotechnology: An International Assessment* (Washington DC: US Government Printing Office, 1984); Geoffrey M. Holdridge, ed., 'JTEC/WTEC Annual Report and Program Summary, 1993/1994' (Baltimore: Japan Technology Evaluation Center, 1994).
3   Yakugyō Jihōsha, *Yakuji Handobukku* [Pharmaceutical Affairs Handbook] (Tokyo: Yakugyō Jihōsha, 1968–1999); Jihō, *Yakuji Handobukku* [Pharmaceutical Affairs Handbook] (Tokyo: Jihō, 2000–2007).
4   National Cancer Institute, 'Dictionary of Cancer Terms', http://www.cancer.gov/dictionary/ (accessed 20 March 2007).
5   Jacqueline L. Longe and Deirdre S. Blanchfield, eds, *Gale Encyclopedia of Medicine* (Farmington Hills, MI: Gale Group, 2001), 635–636.
6   This is because most anticancer drugs available today cannot distinguish between benign and malign cells.
7   The government sets prescription drug prices in Japan. It reviews and reduces prices every two years, both to contain healthcare costs and to correct the difference between wholesale and retail prices (the price at which firms supply pharmacies and the government-set price paid by patients).
8   Hisao Endō, Matsurō Oka, Masaki Ozawa, Yoshiaki Kamoya and Nobuo Tanaka, 'Iryōyō Iyakuhin Shijō ni Okeru Kyōsō Keitai [Forms of Competition in the Ethical Pharmaceutical Market]', in *Iyakuhin Sangyō Soshikiron* [On the Organisation of the Pharmaceutical Industry], edited by Tsurihiko Nanbu (Tokyo: University of Tokyo Press, 2002), 49–74.
9   Japan Cancer Association, 'Gangakkai no Rekishi [The History of the Japan Cancer Association]', Japan Cancer Association, http://www.jca.gr.jp/b01.html (accessed 1 December 2007).
10 National Cancer Institute, 'The National Cancer Institute Act, 1937–2007: Celebrating 70 Years of Excellence in Cancer Research', The National Cancer Institute Act, http://www.cancer.gov/aboutnci/ncia (accessed 1 December 2007); Cancer Research UK, 'Our History', http://info.cancerresearchuk.org/cancerandresearch/historyandachievements/ourhistory/ (accessed 1 December 2007); German Cancer Research Center, 'History', http://www.dkfz.de/en/dkfz/geschichte.html (accessed 1 December 2007).
11 Robert F. Bud, 'Strategy in American Cancer Research After World War II: A Case Study', *Social Studies of Science* 8 (November 1978): 425–459.
12 Jonathan Liebenau, 'Industrial R&D in Pharmaceutical Firms in the Early Twentieth Century', *Business History* 26, no. 3 (1984): 229–346.
13 See, for example, Bowen C. Dees, 'Japanese Science and Technology Before 1945', in *The Allied Occupation and Japan's Economic Miracle: Building the Foundations of Japanese Science and Technology, 1945–52* (Richmond: Japan Library, 1997), 1–11.
14 L.S. Goodman, M.M. Wintrobe, W. Dameshek, M.J. Goodman, A. Gilman and M.T. McLennan, 'Nitrogen Mustard Therapy. Use of Methyl-bis(beta-chloroethyl)amine hydrochloride and Tris(beta-chloroethyl)amine Hydrochloride for Hodgkin's Disease, Lymphosarcoma, Leukemia, and Certain Allied and Miscellaneous Disorders', *Journal of the American Medical Association* 105 (1946): 475–476; C.P. Rhoads, 'Nitrogen Mustards in the Treatment of Neoplastic Disease: Official Statement', *Journal of the American Medical Association* 131 (1946): 656–658.

15 T. Yoshida, H. Sato and M. Ishidate, 'Yoshida Nikushu ni yoru Akusei Shuyō Kagakuryōhō no Jikkenteki Kenkyū 1 [Experimental Studies on Chemotherapy of Malignant Growth Employing Yoshida Sarcoma 1', *Gann* 41 (1950): 93–96; M. Ishidate, K. Kobayashi, Y. Sakurai, H. Sato and T. Yoshida, 'Experimental Studies on Chemotherapy of Malignant Growth Employing Yoshida Sarcoma Animals (II). The Effect of N-oxide Derivatives of Nitrogen Mustard', *Proceedings of the Japan Academy* 27 (1951): 493–498.

16 Yoshitomi Pharmaceutical Co., *Yoshitomi Seiyaku 50-nen no Ayumi* [A 50-year History of Yoshitomi Pharmaceutical Co.] (Tokyo: Yoshitomi Pharmaceutical Co., 1990), 55–57; Shinpei Miyata, 'Tomizo Yoshida: Yoshida Carcinoma and the Beginning of a New Era (Yoshida Tomizō: Shinjidai o Hiraita Yoshida Nikushu)', *Gekkan Gan* 33 (September 2002): 42–45.

17 In 1949, for example, sales to Takeda comprised 76 per cent of the firm's total sales, followed by the Ministry of Health and public hospitals, at 13 per cent and 4 per cent, respectively. Yoshitomi Pharmaceutical Industries, Ltd, *Yūka Shōken Hōkokusho* [Annual Securities Report] (Tokyo: Ōkurashō Insatsukyoku, 1949).

18 Yakuji Nippōsha, 'Nitromin', in *Saikin no Shinyaku* [New Drugs in Japan] (Tokyo: Yakuji Nippōsha, 1952), 118. Approved at 1,000 yen per five ampoules, nitromin was manufactured by Yoshitomi and distributed through Takeda.

19 Yoshitomi Pharmaceutical Industries, Ltd, *Yūka Shōken Hōkokusho* [Annual Securities Report] (Tokyo: Ōkurashō Insatsukyoku, 1961).

20 Methanol is an alcohol used as a raw material in many industrial and chemical processes. Acetone is a widely used solvent.

21 In 2005 values, this would be approximately 66.8 billion yen. Kyowa Hakko Kyogyo Co., *Yūka Shōken Hōkokusho* [Annual Securities Report] (Tokyo: Ōkurashō Insatsukyoku, 1960).

22 Yakuji Nippōsha, 'Mitomycin', in *Saikin no Shinyaku* [New Drugs in Japan] (Tokyo: Yakuji Nippōsha, 1960), 15–18; Shigetoshi Wakaki, 'Tōsha ni okeru Seiganzai no Kenkyū to Kaihatsu no Genjō [The Status of Anticancer Drug R&D at Our Company]', *Kagakukōgyō* (April 1976): 96–98.

23 Anticancer antibiotics are, like antibiotics, a substance produced by bacteria that is used to treat cancer. See, for example, National Cancer Institute, 'Dictionary of Cancer Terms: Antitumor Antibiotic', National Cancer Institute, http://www.cancer.gov/templates/db_alpha.aspx?CdrID=44488 (accessed 26 May 2008).

24 Kyowa Hakko Kyogyo Co., *Bara wa Bara: Kyōwa Hakkō 35-nenshi* [A Rose is a Rose: A 35-year History of Kyowa Hakko] (Tokyo: Kyowa Hakko Kyogyo Co., 1984), 70.

25 Toju Hata, Fumiwaka Koga, Yoshitomo Sano, Kokichi Kanamori, Akihiro Matsumae, Ryozo Sugawara, Tadashi Hoshi, Tatsuo Shima, Shinya Ito and Setsuo Tomizawa, 'Carzinophilin, New Tumor Inhibitory Substance Produced by Streptomyces', *Journal of Antibiotics* 7 (August 1954): 107–112.

26 Toju Hata, Yoshimoto Sano, Ryozo Sugawara, Akihiro Matsumae, Kokichi Kanamori, Tatsuo Shima and Tadashi Hoshi, 'Mitomycin, a New Antibiotic from Streptomyces I', *Journal of Antibiotics, Series A* 9 (July 1956): 141–146; Ryozo Sugawara and Toju Hata, 'Mitomycin C, a New Antibiotic from Streptomyces II', *Journal of Antibiotics, Series A* 9 (July 1956): 147.

27 S. Wakaki, H. Marumo and K. Tomioka, 'Isolation of New Fractions of Antitumour Mitomicins', *Antibiotics and Chemotherapy* 8, no. 8 (1958): 228–240.

28 As mentioned in the previous chapter, the government had supported academic research in antibiotics from the late 1940s. This funding was useful in the search for other therapeutic uses of substances produced by bacteria, including the treatment of cancer.

29 Thomas W. Ennis, 'Dr. Kanematsu Sugiura, 89, Dies; A Pioneer in Cancer Chemotherapy; Research Dates to 1912', *The New York Times* 23 October 1979. Since the

end of the Second World War, the Japanese American scientist Kanematsu Sugiura had liaised with Japanese scientists for collaborations in cancer research. See
also, John Hillaby, 'Cancer Increase is not Clear-cut; World Congress in London
Attributes Some of it to Regular Check-ups', *The New York Times* 9 July 1958; William L. Laurence, 'Science in Review: Reports of Progress in Fight on Cancer Hold
Out Hope of Cutting Death Toll', *The New York Times* 13 July 1958.

30 'Cancer Drug Rejected; U.S. Says Japanese Antibiotic has Significant Side-effects',
The New York Times 22 January 1959.

31 US Food and Drug Administration, Center for Drug Evaluation and Research, 'FDA
Oncology Tools Approval Summary for Mitomycin C', US Food and Drug Administration, http://www.accessdata.fda.gov/scripts/cder/onctools/summary.cfm?ID=273
(accessed 10 November 2007).

32 Kyowa Hakko Kyogyo Co., *Bara wa Bara: Kyowa Hakko 35-nenshi* [A Rose is a
Rose: A 35-year History of Kyowa Hakko], 70.

33 In nominal terms, Kyowa Hakko's yearly production level in 1965 was approximately
214,000 yen, 839,000 yen in terms of 2005 yen. Kyowa Hakko Kogyo Co., *Yūka
Shōken Hōkokusho* [Annual Securities Report] (Tokyo: Ōkurashō Insatsukyoku,
1965), 8, 16; Kyowa Hakko Kogyo Co., *Yūka Shōken Hōkokusho* [Annual Securities
Report] (Tokyo: Ōkurashō Insatsukyoku, 1966), 20.

34 Benzaburō Katō, 'Innen no Dōri ni Rikkyaku Shita Jigyō Keiei [Business Management Based on the Philosophy of Fate]', in *Gendai Toppu Keiei no Jigyō Tetsugaku*
[Business Philosophies among Today's Leading Managers], edited by Nihon Jitsugyō
Shuppansha (Tokyo: Nihon Jitsugyō Shuppansha, 1969). Benzaburō Katō became the
president of Kyowa Hakko in 1949 and its chairman in 1969.

35 Ibid.

36 Shigetoshi Wakaki, 'Tōsha ni Okeru Seiganzai no Kenkyū to Kaihatsu no Genjō [The
Status of Anticancer Drug R&D at Our Company]', 96–98.

37 In terms of production, Nippon Kayaku had particular strengths in aspirin and penicillin. Nippon Kayaku Co., *Yūka Shōken Hōkokusho* [Annual Securities Report] (Tokyo:
Ōkurashō Insatsukyoku, 1950), 1; Nippon Kayaku Co., *Yūka Shōken Hōkokusho* [Annual
Securities Report] (Tokyo: Ōkurashō Insatsukyoku, 1951), 19. The market positions
of Japanese firms are based on production, as sales values are not readily available.

38 Nippon Kayaku's pharmaceutical sales stood at 19.4 billion yen, or 19.5 per cent of
the firm's total sales five years after bleomycin's launch. In nominal terms, Nippon
Kayaku's pharmaceutical sales five years after launch stood at 9.3 billion yen. Nippon
Kayaku Co., *Yūka Shōken Hōkokusho* [Annual Securities Report] (Tokyo: Ōkurashō
Insatsukyoku, 1974), 20. A decade later, the firm's pharmaceuticals sales reached 24.0
billion yen, or 22.3 per cent of total sales. In nominal terms, Nippon Kayaku's pharmaceutical sales a decade after launch reached 17.8 billion yen. Nippon Kayaku Co.,
Yūka Shōken Hōkokusho [Annual Securities Report] (Tokyo: Ōkurashō Insatsukyoku,
1979), 22.

39 Nippon Kayaku Co., *Nippon Kayaku no Ayumi: Kono 10-nen o Chūshin ni Shite*
[The History of Nihon Kayaku: With Special Attention to the Past 10 Years] (Tokyo:
Nippon Kayaku Co., 1976), 93; Tokuji Ichikawa, 'Bureomaishin no Shōkai [An Intro-
duction to Bleomycin]', *Gan no Rinshō* 14 (1967): 149.

40 Hamao Umezawa, Kenji Maeda, Tomio Takeuchi and Yoshiro Okami, 'New Antibiotics, Bleomycin A and B', *Journal of Antibiotics, Series A* 19 (September 1966):
200–209; Hamao Umezawa, 'Kōseibusshitsu o Motomete (3): Michi no Ryōiki Gan
e no Chōsen [Searching for Antibiotics (3): Challenging Cancer]', *Shokun* 12, no. 3
(1980): 230–244.

41 Yakuji Nippōsha, 'Bleomycin', in *Saikin no Shinyaku* [New Drugs in Japan] (Tokyo:
Yakuji Nippōsha, 1969), 51–55. See also, Institute of Microbial Chemistry, *Institute of
Microbial Chemistry: 1962–1977* (Tokyo: Center for Academic Publications, 1977),
18–21.

42 Nippon Kayaku Co., *Nippon Kayaku no Ayumi: Kono 10-nen o Chūshin ni Shite* [The History of Nihon Kayaku: With Special Attention to the Past 10 Years], 94; US Food and Drug Administration, Center for Drug Evaluation and Research, 'FDA Oncology Tools Approval Summary for Bleomycin', US Food and Drug Administration, http://www.accessdata.fda.gov/scripts/cder/onctools/summary.cfm?ID=208 nnk (accessed 10 November 2007).

43 Tomizō Yoshida, 'Cancer Research in Japan', *Cancer Research* 16, no. 11 (1956): 1008.

44 See, for example, Susan B. Carter, Scott Sigmund Gartner, Michael R. Haines, Alan L. Olmstead, Richard Sutch and Gavin Wright, eds, 'Death rate, by cause: 1900–1998', Table Ab929-951 in *Historical Statistics of the United States, Earliest Times to the Present: Millennial Edition* (New York: Cambridge University Press, 2006), http://hsus.cambridge.org/HSUSWeb/index.do; John Charlton and Mike Murphy, eds, 'Trends in Causes of Mortality: 1841–1994 – An Overview', in *The Health of Adult Britain* (London: Stationery Office, 1997), 30–57.

45 Ministry of Health and Welfare, *Kanja Chōsa* [Patient Survey] (Tokyo: Ministry of Health and Welfare, 1953–1985).

46 To a certain extent, the government's funding for antibiotic research indirectly supported the development of anticancer antibiotics.

47 National Cancer Center, 'Cancer Statistics in Japan, 2007', http://ganjoho.ncc.go.jp/public/statistics/backnumber/2007_en.html (accessed 1 December 2007).

48 Institute of Microbial Chemistry, *Institute of Microbial Chemistry: 1962–1977*; see also, Hamao Umezawa, 'Seiganzai wa Dokomade Kitaka [The Status of Anticancer Drugs]', *Kagaku Asahi* (September 1982): 50–54.

49 Yakugyō Keizai Kenkyūjo, *Yakugyō Keizai Nenkan* [Pharmaceutical Economics Annual] (Tokyo: Yakuji Nippōsha, 1967), 172–173; National Cancer Institute, 'Developmental Therapeutics Program, FDA Approved Drugs', National Cancer Institute, http://dtp.nci.nih.gov/timeline/flash/FDA.htm (accessed 10 November 2007).

50 Ralph Landau, Basil Achilladelis and Alexander Scriabine, eds, *Pharmaceutical Innovation: Revolutionizing Human Health* (Philadelphia: Chemical Heritage Press, 1999), 258–265. Note that brand names of drugs are indicated in capitals while generic names are indicated in lower case. References to generic names are omitted where the brand name and generic name are the same.

51 Yakugyō Keizai Kenkyūjo, *Yakugyō Keizai Nenkan* [Pharmaceutical Economics Annual] (1967), 182–173.

52 PJB Publications, *Scrip: Yearbook* (Richmond: PJB Publications, 1991), 61.

53 Yano Keizai Kenkyūjo, *Iyakuhinshijō Senryaku no tame no Māketingu Dēta Nenpō* [Marketing Data Annual for Strategizing in the Pharmaceutical Market] (Tokyo: Keizai Kenkyūjo, 1985), 296.

54 Yano Keizai Kenkyūjo, *Iyaku Sangyō Nenkan* [Pharmaceutical Industry Annual] (Tokyo: Yano Keizai Kenkyūjo, 1980), 8, 58.

55 Ralph Landau, Basil Achilladelis and Alexander Scriabine, eds, *Pharmaceutical Innovation: Revolutionizing Human Health*, 93.

56 Masanori Fukushima, 'The Overdose of Drugs in Japan', *Nature* 342, no. 21 (December 1989): 850–851; Yano Keizai Kenkyūjo, *Iyaku Sangyō Nenkan* [Pharmacutical Industry Annual] (Tokyo: Yano Keizai Kenkyūjo, 1985).

57 'Iyakuhin Shijō [The Pharmaceutical Market]', *Nikkei Business* 9 December 1985, 10.

58 This has been documented widely. See, for example, 'Kōganzai de 1-chō en no Iryōhi ga Muda, Nihon Byōinkai ga Kenkai [Japan Hospital Association Estimates Waste of 1 Trillion Yen from Two Cancer Drugs]', *Asahi Shimbun* 29 December 1989.

59 Ministry of Health and Welfare, *Yakuji Kōgyō Seisan Dōtai Chōsa Tōkei* [Annual Survey on Production in the Pharmaceutical Industry] (Tokyo: Yakugyō Keizai Kenkyūjo, 1968–2000).

60 Jacqueline L. Longe and Deirdre S. Blanchfield, eds, *Gale Encyclopedia of Medicine*, 636. See also, 'Japanese Drug Companies Pull Ahead in the Race to Innovate'.

61 National Cancer Institute, 'What Is Cancer?' http://www.cancer.gov/cancertopics/what-is-cancer (accessed 10 July 2008).

62 Ministry of Health and Welfare, *Yakuji Kōgyō Seisan Dōtai Chōsa Tōkei* [Annual Survey on Production in the Pharmaceutical Industry] (1968–2000).

63 Chugai Pharmaceutical Co., *Chūgai Seiyaku 75-nen no Ayumi* [A 75-year History of Chugai Pharmaceutical] (Tokyo: Chugai Pharmaceutical Co., 2000).

64 Chugai Pharmaceutical Co., *Yūka Shōken Hōkokusho* [Annual Securities Report] (Tokyo: Ōkurashō Insatsukyoku, 1961), 12.

65 William Bradley Coley, *The Treatment of Malignant Tumors by Repeated Inoculations of Erysipelas: With a Report of Ten Original Cases* (Philadelphia: Lea Brothers & Co., 1893).

66 Jane E. Brody, 'Japanese Study Use of Toxins in Cancer Treatment', *The New York Times* 24 January 1968; Hajime Okamoto, Susumu Shoin, Mikio Minami, Saburo Koshimura and Ryusaku Shimizu, 'Experimental Anticancer Studies Part XXX. Factors Influencing the Streptolysin S-forming Ability of Streptococci Having Anticancer Activity', *Japanese Journal of Experimental Medicine* 36 (1966): 161–174; Hajime Okamoto, Mikio Minami, Susumu Shoin, Saburo Koshimura and Ryusaku Shimizu, 'Experimental Anticancer Studies Part XXXI. On the Streptococcal Preparation Having Potent Anticancer Activity', *Japanese Journal of Experimental Medicine* 36 (1966): 175–186; Hajime Okamoto, Susumu Shoin, Saburo Koshimura and Ryusaku Shimizu, 'Studies on the Anticancer and Streptolysin S-forming Abilities of Hemolytic Streptococci', *Japanese Journal of Microbiology* 11, no. 4 (1967): 323–326.

67 Examples of such side effects were fever, aches and lack of appetite, rather than death. Yakuji Nippōsha, 'Picibanil', in *Saikin no Shinyaku* [New Drugs in Japan] (Tokyo: Yakuji Nippōsha, 1976), 67–73.

68 Yakugyō Jihōsha, *Yakuji Handobukku* [Pharmaceutical Affairs Handbook] (1968–1999).

69 See, for example, 'Nihon no Kusuri, Kuresuchin [Krestin, a Japanese Drug]', *Nikkei Business* 9 December 1985, 9–11.

70 Kureha Chemical Industry Co., *Yūka Shōken Hōkokusho* [Annual Securities Report] (Tokyo: Ōkurashō Insatsukyoku, 1976), 1, 10.

71 These medicinal mushrooms are harvested, dried, ground and reconstituted as tea to boost the immune system.

72 Kureha Chemical Industry Co., *Kureha Kagaku 50-nenshi* [A 50-year History of Kureha Chemical Industry, 419–420.

73 Yakuji Nippōsha, 'Krestin', in *Saikin no Shinyaku* [New Drugs in Japan] (1978), 96–101.

74 In nominal terms, sales of Krestin grew from approximately 10 billion to 32.5 billion yen. Market share is based on production values. Toshihiko Suguro, 'Kureha Kagaku Kōgyō: Daikokubashira "Kuresuchin" Gekigen no Kiki [Kureha Chemical Industry: Sales of Core Product "Krestin" may Plummet]', *Shūkan Tōyō Keizai* 12 May 1990, 139–140. Yano Keizai Kenkyūjo, *Iyaku Sangyō Nenkan* [Pharmaceutical Industry Annual] (Tokyo: Yano Keizai Kenkyūjo, 1985), 537.

75 Peter Marsh, 'Pharmaceutials 6; Optimistic But Still Some Way to Go', *Financial Times* 1 October 1987; PJB Publications, 'The Top-selling Products Worldwide in 1986', *Scrip: Yearbook* (Richmond: PJB Publications,1988), 33.

76 Christopher Dunn, *Scrip's 1994 Review of Cancer Chemotherapy* (Richmond: PJB Publications, 1994), 353. In 1988, Krestin sold $328.1 million, while Nolvadex sold $270 million and Adriamycin sold $253.7 million.

77 Yano Keizai Kenkyūjo, 'Kōryoku ga Yowai kara Tsukawareru, Kuresuchin, Pishibanīru [Krestin and Picibanil Used because of Weak Effects]', *Iyaku Sangyō Nenkan* (1985): 15–18; 'Mukō no Rakuin, Kōganzai Kuresuchin no Unmei [Fate of

Krestin, a Drug Labelled Ineffective]', *Shūkan Shinchō* 15 August 1991, 164–165; Yakuji Nippōsha, 'Krestin', in *Saikin no Shinyaku* [New Drugs in Japan] (Tokyo: Yakuji Nippōsha, 1978), 96–101.

78 'Kōganzai 1-chō en no Kiyasume-ryō [1 Trillion Yen Anticancer Drug for Ease of Mind]', *Aera*, 7 June 1988, 6–11; 'Soshite Ima [And Today]', *Aera* 20 December 1988, 22. See, Isao Nakao, Tadashi Yokoyama, Ichirō Urushizaki, Akira Wakui, Hisashi Furue, Yoshiyuki Koyama, Kiyoji Kimura, Nobuya Ogawa and Tatsuo Saitō, 'Shinkō Igan ni Taisuru PSK no Rinshō Kōka [Clinical Effects of PSK in Advanced Gastric Cancer]', *Oncologia* 14 (1985): 163–170; Minoru Niimoto, Takao Hattori, Ryūichiro Tanida, Koyoshi Inokuchi and Nobuya Ogawa, 'Igan Chiyu Setsujo Shōrei ni Taisuru Maitomaishin C, Futorafūru, Kuresuchin o Mochiita Jutsugo Men'eki Kagaku Ryōhō [Postoperative Immunotherapy for Curatively Resected Gastric Cancer Patients Using Mitomycin C, Ftorafur and Krestin]', *Oncologia* 14 (1985): 171–180. *Oncologia* is a journal sponsored by Kureha.

79 For example, see ' Maruyama Wakuchin o Dō Kangaeruka [What to Think of the Maruyama Vaccine]', *Asahi Shimbun* 12 July 1981.

80 The Research Institute of Vaccine Therapy for Tumors and Infectious Diseases, Nippon Medical School, 'Maruyama Vaccine', http://vaccine.nms.ac.jp/ (accessed 1 December 2007).

81 Zeria Pharmaceutical Co., 'Enkaku (Company History)', Zeria Pharmaceutical Co., http://www.zeria.co.jp/comp/co01.html (accessed 1 December 2007); Datamonitor, 'Chugai Pharmaceutical Co. Ltd', *Company Profile* (London: Datamonitor, 2007).

82 Zeria Pharmaceutical Co., *Yūka Shōken Hōkokusho* [Annual Securities Report] (Tokyo: Ōkurashō Insatsukyoku, 1990), 1.

83 Yoshio Sakurai, Shigeru Tsugakoshi and Kazuo Ōta were involved in the development of Krestin, while Hisashi Furue was involved in the development of Picibanil. See, for example, Japan, House of Representatives, Labour and Welfare Committee, *Official Report of Debates*, 94th Diet, 20th Session, 30 July 1981.

84 Yano Keizai Kenkyūjo, *Iyaku Sangyō Nenkan* [Pharmaceutical Industry Annual] (1980), 446.

85 Japan, House of Representatives, Labour and Welfare Committee, *Official Report of Debates*, 94th Diet, 20th Session, 30 July 1981; Japan, House of Councillors, Labour and Welfare Committee, *Official Report of Debates*, 95th Diet, 3rd Session, 27 October 1981.

86 'O o Hiku Aimaisa: Fushin Maneku Yakuji Gyōsei [The Effects of Ambiguity: Pharmaceutical Administration Invites Mistrust]', *Asahi Shimbun* 16 August 1981.

87 Physicians began to use SSM in 1962. Nippon Medical School, Research Institute of Vaccine Therapy for Tumors and Infectious Diseases, 'Maruyama Vaccine'.

88 An application for SSM was made on November 1976, and was rejected in July 1981. See 'Gan no Maruyama Wakuchin, Shinyaku Ninka Shinsei o Teishutsu [A New Drug Application Filed for the Maruyama Vaccine that Treats Cancer]', *Asahi Shimbun* 30 November 1976; 'Maruyama Wakuchin Kōka Nashi [Maruyama Vaccine Found Ineffective]', *Asahi Shimbun* 11 July 1981.

89 'Kōseishō ga Kyōkyū Keizoku Yōsei: Maruyama Wakuchin, Seiyaku Gaisha ni [MHW Requests Pharmaceutical Firms to Continue to Supply the Maruyama Vaccine]', *Asahi Shimbun* 11 July 1981; 'Maruyama Wakuchin no Kyōkyū Enchō Sara ni 3-nen Mitomeru [3-year Extension Granted to Supply the Maruyama Vaccine]', *Asahi Shimbun* 30 November 1984; 'Maruyama Wakuchin Yūshō Chiken Sara ni 3-nen Enchō [3-year Extension Granted for For-fee Clinical Trials of the Maruyama Vaccine]', *Asahi Shimbun* 21 November 1987; 'Maruyama Wakuchin Sara ni 3-nen Enchō [3-year Extension Granted for Use of the Maruyama Vaccine]', *Asahi Shimbun* 15 November 1990; 'Maruyama Wakuchin Shiyō 4-nenkan no Enchō [4-year Extension Granted for Use of the Maruyama Vaccine]', *Asahi Shimbun* 7 December 1993.

90 See, Nippon Medical School, Research Institute of Vaccine Therapy for Tumors and Infectious Diseases, 'Maruyama Vaccine'. See also, 'Maruyama Wakuchin Seibun Nōshukukyaku: Fukusayō Yokuseizai de Shōnin [Concentrated Maruyama Vaccine: Approved as Remedy for Side Effects]', *Asahi Shimbun* 6 June 1991.

91 Ministry of Health and Welfare, *Saikin no Yakumu Gyōsei* [Recent Trends in Pharmaceutical Administration] (Tokyo: Yaukumu Kōhōsha, 1991), 55–56.

92 In nominal terms, Chugai's sales fell from 23.5 billion yen in 1989 to 8.2 billion yen in 1990. Chugai Pharmaceutical Co., *Yūka Shōken Hōkokusho* [Annual Securities Report] (1991), 19. Sankyo's sales of anticancer drugs fell from 32.5 billion yen in the fiscal year ending March 1990 to 13.0 billion yen in the fiscal year ending March 1991. Sankyo Co., *Yūka Shōken Hōkokusho* [Annual Securities Report] (1991), 23. See also, Toshihiko Suguro, 'Kureha Kagaku Kōgyō, Daikoku Bashira Kuresuchin Gekigen no Kiki [Kureha Chemical Industries' Core Product Krestin Under Threat]', *Shūkan Tōyō Keizai* 12 May 1990, 139–140.

93 Julia Yongue, 'Shinyaku Kaihatsu o Meguru Kigyō to Gyōsei: Chiken o Chūshin ni [Firms and Government in Drug Development: An Examination of Clinical Trials]', in *Kigyō Bunseki to Gendai Shihon Shugi* [Corporate Analysis and Contemporary Capitalism], edited by Akira Kudō and Motoi Ihara (Kyoto: Minerva, 2008), 172–173.

94 Yano Keizai Kenkyūjo, *Iyaku Sangyō Nenkan* [Pharmaceutical Industry Annual] (1980), 8, 58.

95 Todd S. Elwy, Michael D. Fetters, Daniel W. Gorenflo and Tsukasa Tsuda, 'Cancer Disclosures in Japan: Historical Comparisons, Current Practices', *Social Science & Medicine* 46 (September 1998): 1151–1163; David Swinbanks, 'Japanese Doctors Keep Quiet', *Nature* 339 (June 1989): 409.

96 Widely publicized scandals involved drugs such as thalidomide, SMON and chloroquine.

97 Yano Keizai Kenkyūjo, *Iyaku Sangyō Nenkan* [Pharmaceutical Industry Annual] (1985), 17–23.

98 Eric Feldman, 'Medical Ethics the Japanese Way', *The Hastings Center Report* 15, no. 5 (1985): 21–24; William E. Steslicke, 'Doctors, Patients, and Government in Modern Japan', *Asian Survey* 12, no. 11 (1972): 913–931.

99 This was the same reason for the rapid expansion of the antibiotics sector during this period.

100 Physician prescribing incentives from pharmaceutical price differentials were not insignificant. See 'Yakka Kijun Jissei Kakaku yori Ōhabadaka: Saeki 4-wari Chikakumo [Official Drug Prices Much Higher than Actual Drug Prices: Pharmaceutical Price Differentials Account for 40 Per Cent of Drug Prices]', *Asahi Shimbun* 18 July 1978; and 'Yakka Saeki Nen ni 1-chō 300-oku en: Kusuridai Sōgaku no 4-bun no 1 [Pharmaceutical Price Differentials Amount to 1.3 Trillion Yen a Year, or a Quarter of Drug Prices]', *Asahi Shimbun* 9 November 1989. See also, Masanori Fukushima, 'The Overdose of Drugs in Japan'; and 'The Strange Ways of Japanese Medicine Makers', *Fortune* 29 July 1991, 118.

101 Shinnippon Hoki Publishing Co., *Yakka Kijun* [Official Drug List] (Tokyo: Shinnippon Hoki Publishing Co., 1975–1990).

102 Samuel Coleman, *Japanese Science: From the Inside* (London: Routledge, 1999).

103 Even in the early 1990s, Japan's pharmaceutical industry was less research-driven. See David Swinbanks, 'Japan's Foundations Still Building', *Nature* 361 (February 1993): 761–764.

104 Yano Keizai Kenkyūjo, *Iyaku Sangyō Nenkan* [Pharmaceutical Industry Annual] (1985), 18.

105 Ibid., 17–19; The certification of oncologists began in 2007. See Japanese Board of Cancer Therapy, 'Ninteii Seido Kisoku [Certified Oncologist Regulations]', http://www.jbct.jp/sys_regulation01.html (accessed 1 December 2007).

106 See, for example, Lacy Glenn Thomas, 'Spare the Rod and Spoil the Industry: Vigor-
ous Competition and Vigorous Regulation Promote Global Competitive Advantage:
A Ten Nation Study of Government Industrial Policies and Corporate Pharmaceutical
Competitive Advantage', *First Boston Working Paper Series* 90–03 (1990); Gerald
D. Laubach, 'Federal Regulation and Pharmaceutical Innovation', *Proceedings of the
Academy of Political Science* 33, no. 4 (1980): 60–80.

107 Anne Kreuger, 'The Political Economy of the Rent-seeking Society', *American Economic Review* 64 (June 1974): 291–303.

108 'Ososugita Yakujishin Tōshin (Recommendation by the Drug Approval Committee
Long Due)', *Yomiuri Shimbun* 21 December 1989.

109 Yoshio Sakurai and Shigeru Tsugakoshi were involved in both the development and
approval of Krestin. See 'Kōganzai Kuresuchin, Yakujishin no 2 Iin Hantei Ronbun ni
Kanyo [Two Members of the Drug Approval Committee Involved in Drug Develop-
ment]', *Asahi Shimbun* 19 December 1989. See also, Japan, House of Representatives,
Labour and Welfare Committee, *Official Report of Debates*, 94th Diet, 20th Session,
30 July 1981; and Japan, House of Representatives, Labour and Welfare Committee,
Official Report of Debates, 104th Diet, 4th Session, 6 March 1986.

110 David Swinbanks, 'Restrictions Recommended', *Nature* 342 (December 1989): 843.

111 Masanori Fukushuma, 'Clinical Trials in Japan', *Nature Medicine* 1 (1995): 12–13.

112 Sankyo Co., *Sankyo 80-nenshi* [Sankyo, an 80-year History] (Tokyo, Sankyo Co.,
1979), 162.

113 Ministry of Health and Welfare, *Yakuji Kōgyō Seisan Dōtai Chōsa Tōkei* [Annual
Survey on Production in the Pharmaceutical Industry] (1968–2000).

114 Yakugyō Jihōsha, *Yakuji Handobukku* [Pharmaceutical Affairs Handbook]
(1968–1999).

115 In nominal terms, Japan exported 5.0 billion yen and imported 33.2 billion yen worth
of anticancer drugs in 2000. It should be noted that trade figures for anticancer drugs
are not available in the *Tsūshō Hakusho*. Trade data for anticancer drugs were available in Ministry of Health and Welfare, *Yakuji Kōgyō Seisan Dōtai Chōsa Tōkei*
[Annual Survey on Production in the Pharmaceutical Industry] (Tokyo: Yakugyō
Keizai Kenkyūjo, 2006).

116 Yakuji Nippōsha, *Saikin no Shinyaku* [New Drugs in Japan] (1992), 127, 131; ibid.
(2006), 68–77; 'Kaigai de Katsuyaku suru Kokusan Shinyaku no Genjō [The Current
Status of Japanese-origin Drugs Abroad]', *Gekkan Mix* (June 1996): 44–62.

117 Matsuyama Kotone, Tetsuji Sadaike and Masanori Fukushima, 'The Present Approval
State of Anti-tumour Drugs in Japan', *Rinshō Hyōka* [Clinical Evaluation] 31 (2004):
579–586.

118 Jeffrey S. Brown, Brigitta Bienz-Tadmor and Louis Lasagna, 'Availability of Anticancer Drugs in the United States, Europe, and Japan from 1960 through 1991', *Clinical
Pharmacology and Therapeutics* 58 (September 1995): 243–256.

119 Shunsuke Ono, 'The Performance of the Japanese New Drug Review System: From the
Reviewer's Perspective', *Rinshō Hyōka* [Clinical Evaluation] 31 (2004): 557–566.

120 Jon Sigurdson, *Future Advantage Japan?: Chemicals and Pharmaceuticals Report*
(London: Cartermill Publishing, 1996).

121 P. Reed Maurer, interview by author, Tokyo, Japan, 11 July 2007.

122 Patricia Danzon and Mark Pauly, 'Health Insurance and the Growth in Pharmaceutical
Expenditures', *The Journal of Law and Economics* 45, no. s2 (2002): 587–613; Ernst
Berndt, 'Pharmaceuticals in U.S. Health Care: Determinants of Quantity and Price',
The Journal of Economic Perspectives 16, no. 4 (2002): 45–66.

123 Approximately $52.7 billion and $24.1 billion, respectively. Life Insurance Association of Japan, *Seimeihoken Jigyō Gaikyō* [Summary of Life Insurance Business]
(Tokyo: Life Insurance Association of Japan, 1957–2008).

124 Nearly $8,500. Nobuo Koinuma, 'Gan Iryō no Keizaiteki Hyōka [Economic Eval-
utaion of Cancer Treatments]', *Kōshū Eisei* 71, no. 2 (February 2007): 111.

125 About $86. Seimei Hoken Bunka Sentā, *Seimei Hoken ni Kansuru Zenkoku Jittai Chōsa* [National Survey on Life Insurance] (Tokyo: Seimei Hoken Bunka Sentā, 1965–2009).

126 A Health Ministry survey released in 1994 still found that only 18.2 per cent of cancer patients were told of their diagnosis. Ministry of Health and Welfare, *Jinkō Dōtai Shakai Keizaimen Chōsa* [Social and Economic Study of Vital Statistics] (Tokyo: Ministry of Health and Welfare, 1994), 21.

127 Seimei Hoken Bunka Sentā, *Seimei Hoken ni Kansuru Zenkoku Jittai Chōsa* [National Survey on Life Insurance]'. See also Aflac annual reports, http://www.aflac.com/investors/financials/financialannualreports.aspx (accessed 22 November 2010).

128 Cancer insurance policies offer coverage for categories such as surgery, hospitalisation and specific cancer treatments. In 2003, Aflac Japan, the largest provider of cancer insurance in Japan, estimated that pharmaceuticals accounted for 14 per cent of total cancer related expenditures. The amount of insurance used for anticancer drugs, however, is unclear. See Aflac Japan, *Gan no Chiryō ni Kakawaru Keizaiteki Ankēto* [Questionnaire on Economic Costs of Cancer Treatment] (Tokyo: Aflac Japan, 2003).

129 Mamoru Miyamoto, 'Kongō Shinsatsu ni Tsuite [On Mixed Billing]', *Kansai Daigaku Keizai-kei* 226 (September 2006): 77–85.

130 Japanese Board of Cancer Therapy, 'Ninteii Seido Kisoku [Certified Oncologist Regulations]', Japanese Board of Cancer Therapy, 2 May 2007, http://www.jbct.jp/sys_regulation01.html (accessed 30 November 2007).

131 Japanese Society of Medical Oncology, 'Nihon Rinshō Shuyō Gakkai Gan Yakubutsu Ryōhō Senmon'i Ninteisha [JSMO Medical Oncology Certificate List]', http://jsmo.umin.jp/senmoni/lists.html (accessed 9 April 2010); American Board of Medical Specialties, '2008 ABMS Certificate Statistics', http://www.abms.org/ (accessed 9 April 2010); National Health Service, 'Medical and Dental Staff 2008 Detailed Results', http://www.ic.nhs.uk/statistics-and-data-collections/workforce/nhs-staff-numbers/nhs-staff-1998–2008-medical-and-dental (accessed 10 April 2010). Figures refer to total oncologists in the region. Figures for the UK are based on figures for England.

132 Ministry of Health, Labour and Welfare, 'Deaths by Leading Cause of Death, Population and Households', http://www.stat.go.jp/english/data/chouki/02.htm (accessed 1 December 2007).

133 'UFT', *Gekkan Mix* [Monthly Medical Information Express] (December 1996): 61. The top three drugs in 1985 were Krestin, Picibanil and Ftorafur. See Yakugyō Jihōsha, *Yakuji Handobukku*, [Pharmaceutical Affairs Handbook] (Tokyo: Yakugyō Jihōsha, 1987), 266.

134 Tadamasa Matsumoto, 'Wagasha ni Okeru Kōganzai no Kaihatsu', *Kagaku to Kōgyō* (April 1976): 105–107; letter from Valdis Jākobsons, Chairman of the Board, AS Grideks (successor to Latvian Institute of Organic Synthesis) to author, 10 May 2006; Taiho Pharmaceutical Co., 'Taihō Yakuhin no Ayumi', http://www.taiho.co.jp/corporation/history/index.html (accessed 2 December 2007).

135 Yakuji Nippōsha, 'N1(2Tetrahydrofuryl-5-fluouracil)', in *Saikin no Shinyaku* [New Drugs in Japan] (Tokyo: Yakuji Nippōsha, 1974), 53–61. This was a drug for colorectal cancer that was patented in the United Kingdom and the United States in 1969 and 1976, respectively.

136 'UFT', *Gekkan Mix* [Monthly Medical Information Express] (December 1996).

137 S. Fujii, K. Ikenaka, M. Fukushima and T. Shirasaka, 'Effect of Uracil and its Derivatives on Antitumor Activity of 5-fluorouracil and 1-(2-tetrahydrofuryl)-5-fluorouracil', *Gann* 69 (1978): 763–772; See also, Tetsuhiko Shirasaka, *S1 Tanjō* [Creating S-1] (Tokyo: Evidensu, 2006), 74–88.

138 It was approved for a range of cancers from the head, lung and breast, to neck. Yakuji Nippōsha,'.Tegafur-Uracil', in *Saikin no Shinyaku* [New Drugs in Japan] (Tokyo: Yakuji Nippōsha, 1985), 110–113.

139 This value is in nominal terms. 'UFT', *Gekkan Mix* [Monthly Medical Information Express] (December 1996).

140 Merck KGaA, '2006 Online Report: Commercial Unit Oncology', Merck KGaA, http://www.merck.de/servlet/PB/menu/1647870/index.html (accessed 6 December 2007).

141 US Food and Drug Administration, Center for Drug Evaluation and Research, 'Colorectal Cancer Endpoints Workshop Summary, 12 November 2003', US Food and Drug Administration, http://www.fda.gov/cder/drug/cancer_endpoints/colonEndpointsSummary.htm (16 May 2006).

142 Datamonitor, 'Taiho Pharmaceuticals Co Ltd', *Company Profile* (London: Datamonitor, 2007).

143 Yakult Honsha Co., *Yūka Shōken Hōkokusho* [Annual Securities Report] (Tokyo: Ōkurashō Insatsukyoku, 1990), 1; Yakult Honsha Co., 'Enkaku [History]', http://www.yakult.co.jp/front/company/profile/htm/index03.html (accessed 15 November 2007); Datamonitor, 'Yakult Honsha Co., Ltd', *Company Profile* (London: Datamonitor, 2007).

144 Yano Keizai Kenkyūjo, *Iyaku Sangyō Nenkan* [Pharmaceutical Industry Annual] (1980), 12–15.

145 David Drutz, phone interview by author, 15 November 2005.

146 Monroe E. Wall, M.C. Wani, C.E. Cook, Keith H. Palmer, A.T. McPhail and G.A. Sim, 'Plant Antitumour Agents 1: The Isolation and Structure of Campothecin, a Novel Alkaloidal Leukemia and Tumour Inhibitor from Camptotheca Acuminata', *Journal of American Chemical Society* 88 (20 August 1966): 3888–3890; Monroe Wall and Mansukh Wani, 'Camptothecin: Discovery to Clinic', *Annals of the New York Academy of Sciences* 803 (13 December 1996): 1.

147 Yakuji Nippōsha, 'Irinotecan', in *Saikin no Shinyaku* [New Drugs in Japan] (Tokyo: Yakuji Nippōsha, 1995), 72–76.

148 Kiyoshi Terada, 'Ensan Irinotecan', *Fine Chemical* 29 (September 2000): 31–41.

149 Yakuji Nippōsha, 'Irinotecan', 72–76.

150 T. Miyasaka and S. Sawada, 'Anticancer Agent Irinotecan', *Gendai Kagaku* [Current Chemistry] 343 (1999): 58–66.

151 Yakuji Nippōsha, 'Irinotecan', 72–76.

152 Yakult Honsha, Co., '*Yakult Honsha Iyakuhin Jigyō Setsumeikai* [Yakult Honsha Discussion of Pharmaceutical Operations]', 14 June 2006.

153 Rosemary C. Bonney, *SCRIP's Guide to Cancer Therapies: A Biotech Revolution?* (Richmond: PJB Publications, 2001).

154 Yakult Honsha, Co., '*Yakult Honsha Iyakuhin Jigyō Setsumeikai* [Yakult Honsha Discussion of Pharmaceutical Operations]'.

155 Yakuji Nippōsha, 'Oxaliplatin', in *Saikin no Shinyaku* [New Drugs in Japan] (Tokyo: Yakuji Nippōsha, 2006), 68–77.

156 As mentioned earlier, the drug's belated approval in Japan was not simply due to the absence of R&D incentives or fully modern, transparent criteria for drug approval. It was also due to delays to the drug approval process following the HIV blood scandal in the early 1990s. In addition, the Japanese medical system still had much smaller demand for rigorous chemotherapy. Moreover, the infrastructure to develop and approve anticancer drugs remained much less developed compared to the leading Western pharmaceutical markets. The Japanese anticancer drug sector had fewer physicians capable of providing rigorous cancer treatment or coordinating clinical trials. It also had fewer experts capable of evaluating innovative cancer drugs.

157 Yakult Honsha Co., 'Yakult Honsha Iyakuhin Jigyō Setsumeikai Sankō Shiryō [Reference Materials for the Informational Meeting on the Pharmaceutical Business at Yakult Honsha]'.

158 Ministry of Health and Welfare, Mishōninyaku Kentō Kaigi [Committee on Non Approved Drugs in Japan], 'Kako 5-nenkan ni Gakkai/Kanjadantai kara no Sōki

Shōnin no Yōbō ga Ari, katsu Heisei 17-nen 3 gatsu Izen ni Ōbei 4 kakoku de Shōnin Sareta Mishōninyaku [Drugs Requested by Academic/Patient Organiations for Accelerated Approval Within the Past 5 years, that were Approved in the 4 American and European Countries Prior to, During or Before March 2005]', http://www.mhlw.go.jp/shingi/2005/03/s0331-13.html (accessed 1 December 2007).

159 Gankanja Dantai Shien Kikō, 'Shui [Statement]', http://www.canps.net/ (accessed 10 August 2007). Naoko Wakao, Representative of Japan's Cancer Patients Support Organization (CANPS), letter to author, 7 September 2007.

160 P. Reed Maurer, interview by author, Tokyo, Japan, 11 July 2007. While specific definitions vary according to country, orphan diseases refer to life threatening or debilitating conditions that are rare. In general, few remedies are available for orphan diseases, because pharmaceutical firms do not expect to recoup investments on drug R&D through sales.

161 Naoko Wakao, Representative of Japan's Cancer Patients Support Organization (CANPS), letter to author, 7 September 2007.

162 The Law for Promoting University Technology Transfer was introduced in 1998. An assessment of recent changes in legislation has been written by Michael Lynskey, 'The Commercialisation of Biotechnology in Japan: Bioventures as a Mechanism of Knowledge Transfer from Universities', *International Journal of Biotechnology* 6 (2004): 155–185. As noted in Chapter 2, university professors lost their civil servant status in 2004.

163 Bonney, Rosemary C. *SCRIP's Guide to Cancer Therapies: A Biotech Revolution?* (Richmond: Scrip Reports, 2001)

164 Datamonitor, 'Japan – Cancer Drugs', *Industry Profile* (London: Datamonitor, 2002), 8–9; Datamonitor, 'Global – Cancer Drugs', *Industry Profile* (London: Datamonitor, 2002), 9–10.

165 Jürgen Drews, 'Drug Discovery: A Historical Perspective', *Science* 287 (March 2000): 1960–1964.

166 Datamonitor, 'Global – Cancer Drugs', 9–10.

167 US Department of Commerce, International Trade Administration, Market Access and Compliance, 'MOSS Agreement on Medical Equipment and Pharmaceuticals', US Department of Commerce, http://www.mac.doc.gov/japan/source/menu/medpharm/ta860109.html (accessed 15 May 2007).

168 See, for example, Office of Pharmaceutical Industry Research, 'Sōyaku no Ba to shite no Kyōsōryoku Kyōka ni Mukete [Creating a Stronger, More Competitive Environment for Drug Discovery]', *Office of Pharmaceutical Industry Research, Japan Pharmaceutical Manufacturers Association* (November 2005); Office of Pharmaceutical Industry Research, 'Seiyaku Sangyō no Shōrai-zō [The Future Image of the Pharmaceutical Industry]' *Office of Pharmaceutical Industry Research, Japan Pharmaceutical Manufacturers Association* (May 2007).

169 Emiko Ohnuki-Tierney, *Illness and Culture in Contemporary Japan* (Cambridge: Cambridge University Press, 1984), 62.

170 Takeda Pharmaceutical Co., *Takeda 180-nenshi* [A 180-year History of Takeda] (Osaka: Takeda Pharmaceutical Co., 1962); Takeda Pharmaceutical Co., *Takeda 200-nen* [200 Years of Takeda] (Osaka: Takeda Pharmaceutical Co., 1984).

171 Takeda Pharmaceutical Co., *Takeda 180-nenshi* [A 180-year History of Takeda]; Takeda Pharmaceutical Co., *Takeda 200-nen* [200 Years of Takeda].

172 Yakuji Nippōsha, 'Leuprorelin', in *Saikin no Shinyaku* [New Drugs in Japan] (Tokyo: Yakuji Nippōsha, 1993), 127–130.

173 Satoshi Sasaki, Toshihiro Imaeda, Yoji Hayase, Yoshiaki Shimizu, Shizuo Kasai, Nobuo Cho, Masataka Harada, Nobuhiro Suzuki, Shuichi Furuya and Masahiko Fujino, 'A New Class of Potent Nonpeptide Luteinizing Hormone-releasing Hormone (LHRH) Antagonists: Design and Synthesis of 2-phenylimidazo[1,2-a]pyrimidin-5-ones', *Bioorganic & Medicinal Chemistry Letters* 12, (August 2002): 2073–2077.

174 'Kaigai Shijō e Mukau Nihonsei Shinyaku [Japanese-origin Drugs Expanding into Overseas Markets]', *Gekkan Mix* (September 1991): 29; 'Leuprorelin', *Gekkan Mix* (June 1996): 44–45. This joint venture concluded on 30 June 2008. See Takeda Pharmaceutical Co., 'Beikoku Jigyō Saihen ni Tsuite [On the Reorganisation of US Operations]', Takeda Pharmaceutical Co., 2 July 2008, press release, http://www.takeda.co.jp/press/article_28213.html (accessed 30 July 2008).

175 Datamonitor, 'Takeda Pharmaceutical Company Limited', *Company Profile*. (London: Datamonitor, 2007).

176 Rosemary C. Bonney, *SCRIP's Guide to Cancer Therapies: A Biotech Revolution?*, 195.

177 In nominal terms, overseas sales increased from approximately 3 billion yen to 80 billion yen. 'Leuprorelin', *Gekkan Mix* (June 1996): 44–45.

178 In nominal terms, Leuplin's 2004 sales reached 44.5 billion yen. Fuji Keizai, *Iryōyō Iyakuhin Dētabukku* [Prescription Medicine Databook] (Tokyo: Fuji Keizai, 2005), 12.

179 See, for example, Michiyo Nakamoto, 'Global Reach through Tie-ups: Japan', *Financial Times* 30 April 2002; 'Prescription for Change: Looking West', *The Economist* 18 June 2005, 7.

180 'Kaigai Shijō e Mukau Nihonsei Shinyaku [Japanese-origin Drugs Expanding into Overseas Markets]', *Gekkan Mix* (September 1991): 29.

181 In nominal terms, the values of the anticancer drug markets in 2001 in Japan, the United States and the United Kingdom were $3.4 billion, $11.1 billion and $1.6 billion, respectively. Datamonitor, 'Japan – Cancer Drugs', 4; Datamonitor, 'Global – Cancer Drugs', 4; Datamonitor, 'United States – Cancer Drugs', *Industry Profile* (London: Datamonitor, 2002), 4; Datamonitor, 'United Kingdom – Cancer Drugs', *Industry Profile* (London: Datamonitor, 2002), 4.

182 In nominal terms. *Yakuji Handobukku* [Prescription Pharmaceutical Databook] (2009), 370–371.

183 Samuel Coleman, *Japanese Science: From the Inside*, 56; Steven W. Collins, *The Race to Commercialize Biotechnology: Molecules, Markets, and the State in the United States and Japan* (London: RoutledgeCurzon, 2004), 151. See also T. Sugimura, 'Pioneers of Cancer Research in Japan', *Japanese Journal of Cancer Research* 82 (December 1991): 1448–1449.

184 Japan Cancer Association, 'Nihon Gangakkai no Rekishi [History of the Japan Cancer Association]'.

185 In sales. See Takeda Pharmaceutical Co., *Annual Report 2006* (Tokyo: Takeda Pharmaceutical Co., 2006), 2; Pfizer, Inc., *Annual Review 2006* (New York: Pfizer, Inc., 2007), 9; GlaxoSmithKline plc., *Annual Report 2006* (London, GlaxoSmithKline plc., 2007), 2. See also, Ministry of Health, Labour and Welfare, *Iyakuhin Sangyō Jittai Chōsa Hōkoku* [Report on the Status of the Pharmaceutical Industry] (Tokyo: Ministry of Health, Labour and Welfare, 2006).

186 To 1994, Japan Fair Trade Commission, *Shuyō Sangyō ni Okeru Ruiseki Seisan Shūchūdo* [Concentration Ratio of Main Industries] (Tokyo: Japan Fair Trade Commission, 1975–1994), http://www.jftc.go.jp/katudo/ruiseki/ruisekidate.html (accessed 1 June 2008). From 1995, Ministry of Health and Welfare, *Iyakuhin Sangyō Jittai Chōsa Hōkoku* [Report on the Status of the Pharmaceutical Industry] (Tokyo: Ministry of Health and Welfare, 1988–2000); Ministry of Health, Labour and Welfare, *Iyakuhin Sangyō Jittai Chōsa Hōkoku* [Report on the Status of the Pharmaceutical Industry] (Tokyo: Ministry of Health, Labour and Welfare, 2001–2006). Also, US Census Bureau, 'Concentration Ratios in Manufacturing', Economic Census: Concentration Ratios http://www.census.gov/epcd/www/concentration.html, (accessed 1 December 2007).

187 See Steven Collins and Hikoji Wakoh, 'Universities and Technology Transfer in Japan: Recent Reforms in Historical Perspective', *The Journal of Technology Transfer*

25 (June 2000); Kenji Kushida, 'Japanese Entrepreneurship: Changing Incentives in the Context of Developing a New Economic Model', *Stanford Journal of East Asian Affairs* 1 (Spring 2001).

188 Steven W. Collins, *The Race to Commercialize Biotechnology: Molecules, Markets, and the State in the United States and Japan*, 151.

189 For example, Japan Bioindustry Association, *Baiobenchā Tōkei Hōkokusho 2005* [Statistical Report on Bioindustries] (Tokyo: Japan Bioindustry Association, 2006); US Census Bureau, *Scientific Research and Development Services, 2002* (Washington DC: US Census Bureau), http://www.census.gov/prod/ec02/ec0254i07.pdf (accessed 22 November 2009).

190 Takashi Sugimura, 'Gankenkyū ni Kansuru Shomondai to Shohansei [Comments on Cancer Research in Japan]', *Tanpakushitsu Kakusan Kōso* 23, no. 6 (1978): 685–691.

191 The importance of drug approval standards in advancing pharmaceutical industries has been discussed by Lacy Glenn Thomas, who compared the British and French pharmaceutical industries. See, Lacy Glenn Thomas, III, 'Implicit Industrial Policy: The Triumph of Britain and the Failure of France in Global Pharmaceuticals', 451–489.

5 Conclusion: Reconsidering Japan's business in pharmaceuticals

1 Takeda Pharmaceutical Co., 'Takeda Establishes New Global Pharmaceutical R&D Center in US', 25 December 2003, press release, http://www.takeda.com/press/article_801.html (accessed 16 July 2008); 'Asuterasu, Bei ni Shinyaku Kaihatsu Kyoten [Astellas Establishes New Drug Development Centre in the United States]', *Nihon Keizai Shimbun*, 4 March 2008.

2 Alexander Gerschenkron, *Economic Backwardness in Historical Perspective: A Book of Essays* (Cambridge, MA: Harvard University Press, 1962). See also Alice H. Amsden, *The Rise of 'The Rest': Challenges to the West From Late-industrialization Economies* (Oxford: Oxford University Press, 2001); Alice H. Amsden and Takashi Hikino, 'Staying Behind, Stumbling Back, Sneaking Up, Soaring Ahead: Late Industrialization in Historical Perspective', in *Convergence of Productivity: Cross-national Studies and Historical Evidence*, edited by William J. Baumol, Richard R. Nelson and Edward N. Wolff (Oxford: Oxford University Press, 1994), 285–315.

3 Ministry of Health, Labour and Welfare, *Iyakuhin Sangyō Bijon* [Vision Statement on the Pharmaceutical Industry] (Tokyo: Ministry of Health and Welfare, 2002); Ministry of Health, Labour and Welfare, *Shin Iyakuhin Sangyō Bijon* [New Vision Statement on the Pharmaceutical Industry] (Tokyo: Ministry of Health and Welfare, 2007).

4 'Friends for Life: Big Drug Firms Embrace Generics', *The Economist* 8 August 2009, 55–56.

5 'Bei Faizā Kōhatsuyaku Nihon de Sannyū [America's Pfizer to Enter Japan's Generics Market]', *Nihon Keizai Shimbun* 19 November 2009.

6 Simon Frantz, 'The Trouble with Making Combination Drugs', *Nature Reviews Drug Discovery* 5 (November 2006): 881–882; Takeda Pharmaceutical Co., 'Takeda Submits a New Drug Application for a Fixed-dose Combination Tablet of Actos with Sulfonylurea in Japan', 27 July 2009, press release.

Appendices

1 Compiled from Yakugyō Keizai Kenkyūjo, *Yakuji Nenkan* [Pharmaceutical Affairs Annual] (Osaka: Nihon Yakugyō Shimbunsha, 1951, 1957, 1961, 1964); Ministry of Health and Welfare, *Yakuji Kōgyō Seisan Dōtai Chōsa Tōkei* [Annual Survey on Production in the Pharmaceutical Industry] (Tokyo: Yakugyō Keizai Kenkyūjo, 1953–1967); Ministry of Health and Welfare, *Yakuji Kōgyō Seisan Dōtai Chōsa Tōkei*

[Annual Survey on Production in the Pharmaceutical Industry] (Tokyo: Yakugyō Keizai Kenkyūjo, 1968–2000); Ministry of Health, Labour and Welfare, *Yakuji Kōgyō Seisan Dōtai Chōsa Tōkei* [Annual Survey on Production in the Pharmaceutical Industry] (Tokyo: Jihō, 2001–2007). As mentioned in the discussion for sources, values for antitumour drugs have been used as proxy for anticancer drugs.

2 Compiled from Bureau of Statistics, Office of the Prime Minister, *Kagaku Gijutsu Kenkyū Chōsa Hōkoku* [Report on the Survey of Research and Development] (Tokyo: Office of the Prime Minister, 1961–1984); Statistics Bureau and Statistics Centre of the Management and Coordination Agency, *Kagaku Gijutsu Kenkyū Chōsa Hōkoku* [Report on the Survey of Research and Development], (Tokyo: Management and Coordination Agency, 1985–2000); Statistics Bureau, Ministry of Internal Affairs and Communications, ed., *Kagaku Gijutsu Kenkyū Chōsa Hōkoku* [Report on the Survey of Research and Development] (Tokyo: Ministry of Internal Affairs and Communications, 2001–2006).

3 Compiled from Yakugyō Keizai Kenkyūjo, *Yakuji Nenkan* [Pharmaceutical Affairs Annual] (Osaka: Nihon Yakugyō Shimbunsha, 1951, 1957, 1961, 1964); Ministry of International Trade and Industry, *Tsūshō Hakusho* [White Paper on Trade] (Tokyo: Ōkurashō Insatsukyoku, 1958–1973); Ministry of International Trade and Industry, *Tsūshō Hakusho* [White Paper on Trade] (Tokyo: Gyōsei, 1974–2000). From 2001, this data has been available at Ministry of Economy Trade and Industry, *Bōeki Dōkō Dētabēsu* [Database on Trends in Trade], http://www.meti.go.jp/policy/trade_policy/trade_db/index.html (accessed 20 November 2010).

Bibliography

Archival sources

Occupation-period Newspapers and Magazines. Gordon W. Prange Collection. University of Maryland Library, College Park, Maryland, United States.
Papers on the Allied Occupation of Japan. National Diet Library, Tokyo, Japan.
Penicillin Papers. Naito Museum of Pharmaceutical Science and Industry, Kagamihara, Japan.
Selman A. Waksman Papers. Special Collections and University Archives, Rutgers University Library, New Brunswick, New Jersey, United States.

Interviews and personal communications

Drutz, David. Phone interview by author, 15 November 2005.
Jākobsons, Valdis. Letter to author, 10 May 2006.
Maurer, P. Reed. Interview by author, Tokyo, Japan, 11 July 2007.
Nagasaka, Kenjirō. Interview by author, Osaka, Japan, 15 December 2007.
Neimeth, Robert. Letter to author, 31 March 2006.
Shah, Sapan. Phone interview by author, 9 November 2005.
Wakao, Naoko. Letter to author, 7 September 2007.

Other sources: anonymous

'Asuterasu, Bei ni Shinyaku Kaihatsu Kyoten [Astellas Establishes New Drug Development Centre in the United States]'. *Nihon Keizai Shimbun*, 4 March 2008.
'Bei Faizā Kōhatsuyaku Nihon de Sannyū [America's Pfizer to Enter Japan's Generics Market]'. *Nihon Keizai Shimbun*, 19 November 2009.
'Cancer Drug Rejected; U.S. Says Japanese Antibiotic has Significant Side-effects'. *The New York Times*, 22 January 1959.
'Chāchiru Inochi Biroi, Zuruhon zai o Oginau Penishirin [Churchill's Life Is Saved: Penicillin, Instead of Sulfa Drugs, Is the Drug of Choice]'. *Asahi Shimbun*, 27 January 1944.
'Drug Company Mergers: Love Potion No. 9'. *The Economist*, 5 August 1989, 66–67.
'Drug Is Defended by Germany Maker; Thalidomide's Link to Baby Deformities Held Lacking'. *The New York Times*, 4 August 1962.
'Drugs Mergers: Everybody Get Together'. *The Economist*, 8 April 1989, 98.

'Drug Production Begun: Two Plants Now Devoted to Making of Streptomycin'. *The New York Times*, 21 August 1946.

'Friends for Life: Big Drug Firms Embrace Generics'. *The Economist*, 8 August 2009, 55–56.

'Furyō Iyakuhin Torishimari Kyoka: Yamitorihiki wa Genbatsu [Strengthening Regulations Over Unauthentic Medicines: Strict Penalties for Black Market Transactions]'. *Iji Tsūshin* 1 (November 1946): 3.

'Gan no Maruyama Wakuchin, Shinyaku Ninka Shinsei o Teishutsu [A New Drug Application Filed for the Maruyama Vaccine that Treats Cancer]'. *Asahi Shimbun*, 30 November 1976.

'Global Drug Market: 30 Years of Growth'. *Pharma Marketletter*, 4 January 1993.

'Gyōkai Tenbō: Seiyaku Kōgyōkai [Industry Prospects: The Pharmaceutical Industry]'. *Kigyō Chōsa* 63 (September 1948): 3.

'Iyakuhin Shijō [The Pharmaceutical Market]'. *Nikkei Business*, 9 December 1985.

'Japanese Drug Companies Pull Ahead in the Race to Innovate'. *The Economist*, 24 September 1983, 89–90.

'Japan's Medicine Men Take Aim'. *The Economist*, 2 March 1991, 69.

'Kaigai de Katsuyaku suru Kokusan Shinyaku no Genjō [The Current Status of Japanese-origin Drugs Abroad]'. *Gekkan Mix* (June 1996): 44–62.

'Kaigai Shijō e Mukau Nihonsei Shinyaku [Japanese-origin Drugs Expanding into Overseas Markets]'. *Gekkan Mix* (September 1991): 29.

'Kōganzai 1-chō en no Kiyasume-ryō [1 Trillion Yen Anticancer Drug for Ease of Mind]'. *Aera*, 7 June 1988.

'Kōganzai de 1-chō en no Iryōhi ga Muda, Nihon Byōinkai ga Kenkai [Japan Hospital Association Estimates Waste of 1 Trillion Yen from Two Cancer Drugs'. *Asahi Shimbun*, 29 December 1989.

'Kōganzai Kuresuchin, Yakujishin no 2 Iin Hantei Ronbun ni Kanyo [Two Members of the Drug Approval Committee Involved in Drug Development]'. *Asahi Shimbun*, 19 December 1989.

'Kokusaiteki Hitto Shōhin no Jōken [The Criteria for an Internationally Successful Drug]'. *Detailman* (September 1991): 29–45.

'Kōseishō ga Kyōkyū Keizoku Yōsei: Maruyama Wakuchin, Seiyaku Gaisha ni [MHQ Requests Pharmaceutical Firms to Continue to Supply the Maruyama Vaccine]'. *Asahi Shimbun*, 11 July 1981.

'Kyōrin Seiyaku [Kyorin Pharmaceutical]'. *Fain Kemikaru* 31, no. 13 (August 2002): 20–23.

'Leuprorelin'. *Gekkan Mix* (June 1996): 44–45.

'M&A Continues in Pharma/Biotech, but are Mega Acquisitions a Thing of the Past?' *Pharma Marketletter*, 5 January 2009.

'Maruyama Wakuchin Kōkanashi [Maruyama Wakuchin Rejected]'. *Asahi Shimbun*, 11 July 1981.

'Maruyama Wakuchin no Kyōkyū Enchō Sara ni 3-nen Mitomeru [3-year Extension Granted to Supply the Maruyama Vaccine]'. *Asahi Shimbun*, 30 November 1984.

'Maruyama Wakuchin o Dō Kangaeruka [What to Think of the Maruyama Vaccine]'. *Asahi Shimbun*, 12 July 1981.

'Maruyama Wakuchin Sara ni 3-nen Enchō [3-year Extension Granted for Use of the Maruyama Vaccine]'. *Asahi Shimbun*, 15 November 1990.

'Maruyama Wakuchin Seibun Nōshukuyaku: Fukusayō Yokuseizai de Shōnin [Concentrated

Maruyama Vaccine: Approved as Remedy for Side Effects]'. *Asahi Shimbun*, 6 June 1991.

'Maruyama Wakuchin Shiyō 4-nenkan no Enchō [4-year Extension Granted for Use of the Maruyama Vaccine]'. *Asahi Shimbun,* 7 December 1993.

'Maruyama Wakuchin Yūshō Chiken Sara ni 3-nen Enchō [3-year Extension Granted for For-fee Clinical Trials of the Maruyama Vaccine]'. *Asahi Shimbun*, 21 November 1987.

'Merck Introduces Two Drugs in the U.S.'. *Chemical Week*, 26 November 1986.

'Mukō no Rakuin, Kōganzai Kuresuchin no Unmei [Fate of Krestin, a Drug Labelled Ineffective]'. *Shūkan Shinchō*, 15 August 1991.

'Nihon no Kusuri, Kuresuchin [Krestin, a Japanese Drug]'. *Nikkei Business*, 9 December 1985.

'Ofloxacin/Levofloxacin'. *Gekkan Mix* [Monthly Medical Information Express] (December 1996): 55–56.

'O o Hiku Aimaisa: Fushin Maneku Yakuji Gyōsei [The Effects of Ambiguity: Pharmaceutical Administration Invites Mistrust]'. *Asahi Shimbun*, 16 August 1981.

'Ososugita Yakujishin Tōshin [Recommendation by the Drug Approval Committee Long Due]'. *Yomiuri Shimbun*, 21 December 1989.

'Penisirin no Daiikkai Haikyū [The First Ration of Penicillin]'. *Iyaku Tsūshin* 1 (July 1946): 3.

'Penisirin no Seisankeikaku [Production Plan for Penicillin]'. *Akarui Bōeki* 2, no. 2 (1947): 11.

'Penishirin Saihanbai Kyoka [Penicillin Resale Approval]'. *Nihon Iji Shinpō* 10 (May 1946): 11.

'Prescription for Change: Looking West'. *The Economist*, 18 June 2005, 7.

'Soshite Ima [And Today]'. *Aera*, 20 December 1988, 22.

'Teva in Generics JV with Japan's Kowa'. *Pharma Marketletter*, 26 September 2008.

'The Strange Ways of Japanese Medicine Makers'. *Fortune*, 29 July 1991.

'Trade and Industry: Penicillin'. *The Oriental Economist*, 13 September 1947, 749.

'Trade and Industry: Penicillin'. *The Oriental Economist*, 1 May 1948, 352–353.

'Trade and Industry: Penicillin'. *The Oriental Economist*, 3 September 1949, 863.

'Trade and Industry: Pharmaceuticals'. *The Oriental Economist*, 22 February 1947, 140.

'Trade and Industry: Pharmaceuticals'. *The Oriental Economist*, 13 November 1948, 969.

'UFT'. *Gekkan Mix* [Monthly Medical Information Express] (December 1996): 60–61.

'Yakka Kijun Jissei Kakaku yori Ōhabadaka: Saeiki 4-wari Chikakumo [Official Drug Prices Much Higher than Actual Drug Prices: Pharmaceutical Price Differentials Account for 40 Percent of Drug Prices]'. *Asahi Shimbun*, 18 July 1978.

'Yakka Saeki Nen ni Iccho Sanzen oku en [Pharmaceutical Price Differentials Amount to 1.3 Trillion Yen a Year]'. *Asahi Shimbun*, 9 November 1989.

'Yami no Penishirin wa Inchiki [Black Market Penicillin is Fraudulent]'. *Directives and Important Releases of G.H.Q.* 26 (December 1946): 10.

'Yūsei na Kaihatsuryoku de Kyūseicho o Tsuzukeru Zainichi Gaishi [With Stronger Development Capacities, Foreign Firms in Japan Continue to Grow Rapidly]'. *Detailman* (May 1992): 28–35.

Other sources: alphabetical

Aizawa, Minoru, and United Nations Industrial Development Organization. *Review of the Development of Antibiotic Industry in Selected Countries: Technical Report: Antibiotic*

Industry in Japan, History and Development, 74–77. Vienna: United Nations Industrial Development Organization, 1985.

Aflac Japan. *Gan no Chiryō ni Kakawaru Keizaiteki Ankēto* [Questionnaire on Economic Costs of Cancer Treatment]. Tokyo: Aflac Japan, 2003.

American Board of Medical Specialties. '2008 ABMS Certificate Statistics'. http://www. abms.org/ (accessed 9 April 2010).

American Chamber of Commerce in Japan FDI Task Force, 'Pharmaceuticals.' *Specific Policy Recommendation* 3, February 2004, 3.

Amsden, Alice H. *The Rise of 'The Rest': Challenges to the West from Late-industrialization Economies*. Oxford: Oxford University Press, 2001.

Amsden, Alice H., and Takashi Hikino. 'Staying Behind, Stumbling Back, Sneaking Up, Soaring Ahead: Late Industrialization in Historical Perspective'. In *Convergence of Productivity: Cross-national Studies and Historical Evidence*, edited by William J. Baumol, Richard R. Nelson, and Edward N. Wolff, 285–315. Oxford: Oxford University Press, 1994.

Anchordoguy, Marie. *Reprogramming Japan: The High Tech Crisis under Communitarian Capitalism*. Ithaca, NY: Cornell University Press, 2005.

Anegawa, Tomofumi. 'Nihon no Iyakuhin Sangyō: Sono Seikō to Shippai [The Japanese Pharmaceutical Industry: Its Success and Failure]'. *Iryō to Shakai* 12, no. 2 (2002): 49–78.

Aoyagi, Junichi. *Inochi o Kangaete 85-nen: Banyu Seiyaku no Ayumi* [85 Years for Life: The History of Banyu]. Tokyo: Banyu Pharmaceutical, Co. 2000.

Astellas Pharma, Inc. *Annual Report 2009*. Tokyo: Astellas Pharma, Inc., 2009.

——. *Yūka Shōken* Hōkokusho. Tokyo: Ōkurashō Insatsukyoku, 2006.

Ball, Peter. 'The Quinolones: History and Overview'. In *The Quinolones*, edited by Vincent T. Andriole, 1–33. San Diego: Academic Press, Inc., 1988.

Bank of Tokyo-Mitsubishi, Ltd. 'Honkakuteki na Kyōso Jidai o Mukaeru Iyakuhin Gyōkai [The Pharmaceutical Industry to Face an Era of Serious Competition]'. *Chōsa Geppō* [Monthly Research Report] 107 (February 2005): 1–9.

Barral, P.E. *20 Years of Pharmaceutical Research Results Throughout the World*. Antony: Rohne-Poulenc Rorer Foundation, 1996.

Bartholomew, James R. *The Formation of Science in Japan*. New Haven: Yale University Press, 1989.

Berndt, Ernst. 'Pharmaceuticals in U.S. Health Care: Determinants of Quantity and Price'. *The Journal of Economic Perspectives* 16, no. 4 (2002): 45–66.

Bonney, Rosemary C. *SCRIP's Guide to Cancer Therapies: A Biotech Revolution?* Richmond: Scrip Reports, 2001.

Broach, James R., and Jeremy Thorner. 'High-throughput Screening for Drug Discovery'. *Nature* 384 (November 1996): 14–16.

Brody, Jane E. 'Japanese Study Use of Toxins in Cancer Treatment'. *The New York Times*, 24 January 1968.

Brown, Jeffrey S., Brigitta Bienz-Tadmor and Louis Lasagna. 'Availability of Anticancer Drugs in the United States, Europe, and Japan from 1960 through 1991'. *Clinical Pharmacology and Therapeutics* 58 (September 1995): 243–256.

Bud, Robert F. 'Strategy in American Cancer Research after World War II: A Case Study'. *Social Studies of Science* 8 (November 1978): 425–459.

Cancer Research UK. 'Our History'. http://info.cancerresearchuk.org/cancerandresearch/ historyandachievements/ourhistory/ (accessed 1 December 2007).

Carter, Susan B., Scott Sigmund Gartner, Michael R. Haines, Alan L. Olmstead, Richard

Sutch and Gavin Wright, eds. 'Death Rate, by Cause: 1900–1998.' Table Ab929–951. In *Historical Statistics of the United States, Earliest Times to the Present: Millennial Edition*. New York: Cambridge University Press, 2006.

Centre for Medicines Research International. 'Japan in Focus: Strategies for Innovation and Global Drug Development. What Differentiates Japanese Pharma Companies from their Western Counterparts'. *R&D Briefing* 28 (1999): 1–8.

Chandler, Alfred D. *Shaping the Industrial Century: The Remarkable Story of the Modern Chemical and Pharmaceutical Industries*. Cambridge, MA: Harvard University Press, 2005.

Charlton, John, and Mike Murphy, eds. 'Trends in Causes of Mortality: 1841–1994 – An Overview'. In *The Health of Adult Britain*, 30–57. London: Stationery Office, 1997.

Chugai Pharmaceutical Co. *Yūka Shōken Hōkokusho* [Annual Securities Report] Tokyo Ōkurashō Insatsukyoku, 1961, 1971, 1977, 1991.

——. *Chūgai Seiyaku 75-nen no Ayumi* [A 75-year History of Chugai Pharmaceutical]. Tokyo: Chugai Pharmaceutical Co., 2000.

——. 'History'. http://www.chugai-pharm.co.jp/profile/about/history.html (accessed 4 May 2008).

Coleman, Samuel. *Japanese Science: From the Inside*. London: Routledge, 1999.

Coley, Wiliam Bradley. *The Treatment of Malignant Tumors by Repeated Inoculations of Erysipelas: With a Report of Ten Original Cases*. Philadelphia: Lea Brothers & Co., 1893.

Collins, Steven, and Hikoji Wakoh. 'Universities and Technology Transfer in Japan: Recent Reforms in Historical Perspective'. *The Journal of Technology Transfer* 25 (June 2000): 213–222.

Collins, Steven W. *The Race to Commercialize Biotechnology: Molecules, Markets, and the State in the United States and Japan*. London: RoutledgeCurzon, 2004.

Daiichi Pharmaceutical Co. *Daiichi Seiyaku 70-nen no Ayumi* [Daiichi Pharmaceutical, a 70-year History]. Tokyo: Daiichi Pharmaceutical Co., 1986.

——. *Daiichi Seiyaku 80-nenshi* [Daiichi Pharmaceutical, an 80-year History]. Tokyo: Daiichi Pharmaceutical Co., 1996.

——. *Daiichi Seiyaku 90-nenshi* [Daiichi Pharmaceutical, a 90-year History]. Tokyo: Daiichi Pharmaceuticals Co., 2007.

——. *Yūka Shōken Hōkokusho*. Tokyo: Ōkurashō Insatsukyoku, 1986, 1991, 1996.

Daiichi Sankyo, Co. *Annual Report 2009*. Tokyo: Daiichi Sankyo Co., 2009.

——. *Yūka Shōken Hōkokusho*. Tokyo: Ōkurashō Insatsukyoku, 2006.

Dainippon Pharmaceutical Co. *Dainippon Seiyaku 100-nenshi* [A One Hundred Year History of Dainihon Pharmaceutical]. Tokyo: Dainihon Pharmaceutical Co., 1993.

Dainippon Sumitomo Pharma Co. 'Kaisha Enkaku [Company History]'. http://www.ds-pharma.co.jp/profile/history.html (accessed 28 July 2008).

——. *Yūka Shōken Hōkokusho*. Tokyo: Ōkurashō Insatsukyoku, 2006.

Danzon, Patricia, and Mark Pauly. 'Health Insurance and the Growth in Pharmaceutical Expenditures'. *The Journal of Law and Economics* 45, no. s2 (2002): 587–613.

Datamonitor. 'Chugai Pharmaceutical Co. Ltd'. *Company Profile*. London: Datamonitor, 2007.

——. 'Global – Antibacterial Drugs'. *Industry Profile*. London: Datamonitor, 2002.

——. 'Global – Cancer Drugs'. *Industry Profile*. London: Datamonitor, 2002.

——. 'Global Pharmaceuticals'. *Industry Profile*. London: Datamonitor, 2005.

——. 'Japan – Antibacterial Drugs'. *Industry Profile*. London: Datamonitor, 2002.

——. 'Japan – Cancer Drugs'. *Industry Profile*, London: Datamonitor, 2002.

——. 'Japan – Pharmaceuticals'. *Industry Profile*. London: Datamonitor, 2002.

——. 'New Cars in the United States'. *Industry Profile*. London: Datamonitor, 2009.

——. 'Pharmaceuticals in the United States'. *Industry Profile*. London: Datamonitor, 2009.

——. 'Taiho Pharmaceuticals Co., Ltd'. *Company Profile*. London: Datamonitor, 2007.

——. 'Takeda Pharmaceutical Company Limited'. *Company Profile*. London: Datamonitor, 2007.

——. 'United Kingdom – Antibacterial Drugs'. *Industry Profile*. London: Datamonitor, 2002.

——. 'United Kingdom – Cancer Drugs'. *Industry Profile* London: Datamonitor, 2002.

——. 'United States – Antibacterial Drugs'. *Industry Profile* London: Datamonitor, 2002.

——. 'United States – Cancer Drugs'. *Industry Profile* London: Datamonitor, 2002.

——. 'Yakult Honsha Co., Ltd'. *Company Profile*. London: Datamonitor, 2007.

Dees, Bowen C. 'Japanese Science and Technology before 1945'. In *The Allied Occupation and Japan's Economic Miracle: Building the Foundations of Japanese Science and Technology, 1945–52*, 1–11. Richmond: Japan Library, 1997.

Development Bank of Japan. 'Iyakuhin Gyōkai no Genjō to Jenerikku Iyakuhin Shijō [The Current Status of the Pharmaceutical Industry and the Generics Market]'. *Kongetsu no Topikkusu* [Topic of the Month] report no. 145–2 (24 March 2010).

Dibner, M.D. 'Biotechnology in Pharmaceuticals: The Japanese Challenge'. *Science* 229, no. 4719 (1985): 1230–1235.

Drews, Jürgen. 'Drug Discovery: A Historical Perspective'. *Science* 287 (March 2000): 1960–1964.

Dunn, Christopher. *Scrip's 1994 Review of Cancer Chemotherapy*. Richmond: PJB Publications, 1994.

Eisai, Co. *Annual Report 2009*. Tokyo: Eisai, Co., 2009.

Elmsey, John. 'Flourine Helps the Medicine Go Down'. *Independent*, 18 March 1991.

Elwy, Todd S., Michael D. Fetters, Daniel W. Gorenflo and Tsukasa Tsuda. 'Cancer Disclosures in Japan: Historical Comparisons, Current Practices'. *Social Science & Medicine* 46 (September 1998): 1151–1163.

Endō, Hisao, Matsurō Oka, Masaki Ozawa, Yoshiaki Kamoya and Nobuo Tanaka. 'Iryōyō Iyakuhin Shijō ni Okeru Kyōsō Keitai [Forms of Competition in the Ethical Pharmaceutical Market]'. In *Iyakuhin Sangyō Soshikiron* [On the Organisation of the Pharmaceutical Industry], edited by Tsurihiko Nanbu, 49–74. Tokyo: University of Tokyo Press, 2002.

Ennis, Thomas W. 'Dr. Kanematsu Sugiura, 89, Dies; A Pioneer in Cancer Chemotherapy; Research Dates to 1912'. *The New York Times*, 23 October 1979.

European Federation of Pharmaceutical Industries and Associations (EFPIA). *The Pharmaceutical Industry in Figures*. Brussels: EFPIA, 1997, 2005.

Federal Trade Commission, United States. *Economic Report on Antibiotics Manufacture*. Washington: Government Printing Office, 1958.

Federation of Japan Pharmaceutical Wholesalers Association. 'Nihon Iyakuhin Oroshigyō Rengōkai Kaiin Kōseiinsū/Honshasū Suii [Changes in the Number of Member Firms/ Headquarters of the Federation of Japan Pharmaceutical Wholesalers Association]'. Federation of Japan Pharmaceutical Wholesalers Association. http://www.jpwa.or.jp/ jpwa/index.html (accessed 4 May 2007).

Feldman, Eric A. 'HIV and Blood in Japan, Transforming Private Conflict into Public Scandal'. In *Blood Feuds: Aids, Blood and the Politics of Medical Disaster*, 59–94. Oxford: Oxford University Press, 1999.

——. 'Medical Ethics the Japanese Way'. *The Hastings Center Report* 15, no. 5 (1985): 21–24.

Fleming, Alexander. 'On the Antibacterial Action of Cultures of a Penicillium, with Special Reference to Their Use in the Isolation of H. Influenzae'. *British Journal of Experimental Pathology* 10 (June 1929): 226–236.

Foster, Jackson W. 'Three Days' Symposium on Penicillin Production, Held at Welfare Ministry, Tokyo, Japan, November 13–15, 1946'. *Journal of Antibiotics* 1 (March 1947): 1–8.

Frantz, Simon. 'The Trouble with Making Combination Drugs'. *Nature Reviews Drug Discovery* 5 (November 2006): 881–882.

Fuji Keizai. *Iryōyō Iyakuhin Dētabukku* [Prescription Medicine Databook]. Tokyo: Fuji Keizai, 2005.

——. 'Jenerikku Iyakuhin Kokunai Shijō no Shuyō 24 Yakkō Ryōiki o Chōsa [Investigating 24 Therapeutic Sectors in the Domestic Generic Medicines Market]'. https://www.fuji-keizai.co.jp/market/08096.html (accessed 7 May 2010).

Fujii, S., K. Ikenaka, M. Fukushima and T. Shirasaka. 'Effect of Uracil and its Derivatives on Antitumor Activity of 5-fluorouracil and 1-(2-tetrahydrofuryl)-5-fluorouracil'. *Gann* 69 (1978): 763–772.

Fujiki, Hideo, and Mitsuhiro Kida, eds. *Yakuhin Kōgai to Saiban: Saridomaido Jiken no Kiroku kara* [Drug Accidents and Trials: From the Records of the Thalidomide Disaster]. Tokyo: University of Tokyo Press, 1974.

Fujisawa Pharmaceutical Co. *Fujisawa Yakuhin 80-nenshi* [Fujisawa Pharmaceutical, an 80-year History]. Osaka: Fujisawa Pharmaceutical Co., 1976.

——. *Fujisawa Yakuhin 100-nenshi* [Fujisawa Pharmaceutical, a 100-year History]. Osaka: Fujisawa Pharmaceutical Co., 1995.

——. *Yūka Shōken Hōkokusho* [Annual Securities Report]. Tokyo: Ōkurashō Insatsukyoku, 1960–1965, 1972, 1976, 1977.

Fukai, Saburō, ed. *Konnichi no Shinyaku: Kindai Iyakuhin no Hensen* [New Drugs Today: Changes in Modern Pharmaceutials]. Tokyo: Yakuji Jihōsha, 1995.

Fukuhara, Hiroyuki. 'Iyakuhin no Sekai Hatsu Jōshi kara Kakkokuni okeru Jōshi made no Kikan [Time Differences between Initial Global Launches and Domestic Launches of Drugs across Different Countries]'. *Research Paper Series, Office of Pharmaceutical Industry Research, Japan Pharmaceutical Manufacturers Association* 31 (May 2006).

Fukushima, Masanori. 'Clinical Trials in Japan'. *Nature Medicine* 1 (1995): 12–13.

——. 'Sengo no Iyakuhin Ryūtsūshi: Dōran ni Yoru Kakkyō to Ranbai Mondai no Hassei [The History of Distribution in the Pharmaceutical Industry: The Korean War Boom and Emerging Problems with Dumping]'. *Iyaku Jānaru* 11 (June 1972): 40–54.

——. 'Sengo no Iyakuhin Ryūtsūshi: Iyakuhin Kōgyō no Kiki to Dakai e no Mosaku [The History of Distribution in the Pharmaceutical Industry: Seeking Solutions to the Challenges of the Pharmaceutical Industry]'. *Iyaku Jānaru* 11 (September 1972): 44–53.

——. 'Sengo no Iyakuhin Ryūtsūshi: Kajō Seisan ni Taisuru Shijō no Kakudai to Tōsei no Hōsaku [The History of Distribution in the Pharmaceutical Industry: Strategies for Controlling a Market Expanding with Overproduction]'. *Iyaku Jānaru* 11 (July 1972): 58–70.

——. 'The Overdose of Drugs in Japan'. *Nature* 342, no. 21 (December 1989): 850–851.

Galambos, Louis, and Jane Eliot Sewell. *Networks of Innovation: Vaccine Development at*

Merck, Sharp & Dohme, and Mulford, 1895–1995. Cambridge: Cambridge University Press, 1996.

Gankanja Dantai Shien Kikō [Cancer Patients Support Organization]. 'Shui [Statement]'. Gankanja Dantai Shien Kikō http://www.canps.net/ (accessed 10 August 2007).

General Headquarters, Supreme Commander for the Allied Powers, Public Health and Welfare Section, J.M. Bransky Narcotic Investigator, Memorandum for Record, 'Conference Relative to Raising Standards of Pharmaceutical Education', 11 June 1946. Declassified EO 12065 Section 3-402/NNDG no. 775024 (NDL).

——. B.N. Riordan Chief, Supply Division, Memorandum for Record, 'Meeting of Pharmaceutical Education Council', 19 July 1946, 17 January, 14 March 1947, 12 January, 6 July 1951. Declassified EO 12065 Section 3-402/NNDG no. 775024 (NDL).

——. Charles Band Chief, Supply Division. Public Health and Welfare Section, Memorandum for Record, 'Reorganization of the Pharmaceutical and Supply Bureau: Ministry of Welfare', 26 March, 29 March, 1 October 1949. Declassified EO 12065 Section 3-402/NNDG no. 775024 (NDL).

——. *Mission and Accomplishments of the Occupation in the Public Health and Welfare Fields*. Tokyo: Supreme Commander for the Allied Powers. Public Health and Welfare Section, 1949.——. *Public Health and Welfare in Japan. Annual Summary: 1949*. Tokyo: General Headquarters, Supreme Commander for the Allied Powers, Public Health and Welfare Section, 1949.

——. *Public Health and Welfare in Japan. Annual Summary: 1950*. Tokyo: General Headquarters, Supreme Commander for the Allied Powers, Public Health and Welfare Section, 1950.

——. *Public Health and Welfare in Japan. Final Summary: 1951–1952*. Tokyo: General Headquarters, Supreme Commander for the Allied Powers, Public Health and Welfare Section, 1952.

German Cancer Research Center. 'History'. German Cancer Research Center. http://www. dkfz.de/en/dkfz/geschichte.html (accessed 1 December 2007).

Gerschenkron, Alexander. *Economic Backwardness in Historical Perspective: A Book of Essays*. Cambridge, MA: Harvard University Press, 1962.

Gershell, Leland J., and Joshua H. Atkins. 'A Brief History of Novel Drug Discovery Technologies'. *Nature Reviews Drug Discovery* 2 (April 2003): 321–327.

Glaser, Martha. 'Market-share Battle Marks Cardiovasculars, Antiarthritics; 48th Annual Prescription Review'. *Drug Topics* 131 (March 1987): 43.

——. 'Quinolones, Antidepressants Gained in 1988: PDS; Pharmaceutical Data Services'. *Drug Topics* 133 (April 1989): 73.

GlaxoSmithKline plc. *Annual Report*. London: GlaxoSmithKline plc., 2007.

Golec, Joseph, and John Vernon. 'Measuring US Pharmaceutical Industry R&D Spending'. *Pharmacoeconomics* 26, no. 12 (2008): 1005–1017.

Goodman, L.S., M.M. Wintrobe, W. Dameshek, M.J. Goodman, A. Gilman and M.T. McLennan. 'Nitrogen Mustard Therapy. Use of methyl-bis(beta-chloroethyl)amine hydrochloride and tris(beta-chloroethyl)amine hydrochloride for Hodgkin's disease, Lymphosarcoma, Leukemia, and Certain Allied and Miscellaneous Disorders'. *Journal of the American Medical Association* 105 (1946): 475–476.

Great Britain, Business Statistics Office. *Industrial Research and Development Expenditure and Employment: 1975*. London: HMSO, 1979.

Hara, Takuji. *Innovation in the Pharmaceutical Industry: The Process of Drug Discovery and Development*. Cheltenham: Edward Elgar, 2003.

Hashimoto, Takehiko. 'The Hesitant Relationship Reconsidered: University–Industry Cooperation in Post-war Japan'. In *Industrializing Knowledge: University–Industry Linkages in Japan and the United States*, edited by Lewis M. Branscomb, Fumio Kodama and Richard L. Florida, 234–251. Cambridge, MA: MIT Press, 1999.

Hata, Toju, Fumikawa Koga, Yoshimoto Sano, Kokichi Kanamori, Akihiro Matsumae, Ryozo Sugawara, Tadashi Hoshi, Tatsuo Shima, Shinya Ito and Setsuo Tomizawa. 'Carzinophilin, New Tumor Inhibitory Substance Produced by Streptomyces'. *Journal of Antibiotics* 7 (August 1954): 107–112.

Hata, Toju, Yoshimoto Sano, Ryozo Sugawara, Akihiro Matsumae, Kokichi Kanamori, Tatsuo Shima and Tadashi Hoshi. 'Mitomycin, a New Antibiotic from Streptomyces I'. *Journal of Antibiotics, Series A* 9 (July 1956): 141–146.

Hawkins, Elma S., and Michael R. Reich. 'Japanese-originated Pharmaceutical Products in the United States from 1960 to 1989: An Assessment of Innovation'. *Clinical Pharmacology and Therapeutics* 51 (January 1992): 1–11.

Helfand, W. H., H.B. Woodruff, K.M.H. Coleman and D.L. Owen. 'Wartime Industrial Development of Penicillin in the United States'. In *The History of Antibiotics: A Symposium*, edited by John Parascandola, 31–55. Madison: American Institute of the History of Pharmacy, 1980.

Higgs, Gerry. 'Molecular Genetics: the Emperor's Clothes of Drug Discovery?' *Drug Discovery Today* 9 (September 2004): 727–729.

Hillaby, John. 'Cancer Increase is not Clear-cut; World Congress in London Attributes Some of it to Regular Check-ups'. *The New York Times*, 9 July 1958.

Hilts, Philip. *The FDA, Business, and One Hundred Years of Regulation*. New York: Knopf, 2003.

Hirai, Keiji, Akira Ito, Yasuo Abe, Seigo Shizue, Tsutomu Irikura, Matsuhisa Inoue and Susumu Mitsuhashi. 'Comparative Activities of AM-715 and Pipemedic and Nalidixic Acids against Experimentally Induced Systemic and Urinary Tract Infections'. *Antimicrobial Agents and Chemotherapy* 19, no. 1 (1981): 188–189.

Hobby, Gladys L., and Milton Wainwright. *Penicillin: Meeting the Challenge*. New Haven: Yale University Press, 1985.

Holdridge, Geoffrey M., ed. *JTEC/WTEC Annual Report and Program Summary, 1993/1994*. Baltimore: Japan Technology Evaluation Center, 1994.

Hooper, David C., and Ethan Rubinstein. 'Introduction'. In *Quinolone Antimicrobial Agents*, viii–ix. Washington DC: American Society for Microbiology Press, 2003.

Howells, Jeremy, and Ian Neary. *Intervention and Technological Innovation: Government and the Pharmaceutical Industry in the UK and Japan*. Basingstoke: Macmillan, 1995.

Ichikawa, Tokuji. 'Bureomaishin no Shōkai [An Introduction to Bleomycin]'. *Gan no Rinshō* 14, no. 4 (1968): 295–296.

Ikegami, Naoki, and John Creighton Campbell. 'Health Care Reform in Japan: The Virtues of Muddling Through'. *Health Affairs* 18 (May/June 1999): 56–75.

IMS Health, IMS Health Midas, December 2009.

Inagaki, Haruhiko. *Hekiso: Kokusan Penisirin Kaihatsu no Hatafuri, Inagaki Gun'i Shōsa to Ichikōsei Gakuto Dōin* [Hekiso: Pioneering the Development of Penicillin in Japan, Lieutenant Medic Inagaki and the Mobilised Students of the Imperial University]. Tokyo: Nikkei Jigyō Shuppan Sentā, 2005.

Inagaki, Katsuhiko. Interview by Kihachirō Shimizu. 'Nihon ni Okeru Penishirin Kaihatsu no Keii [The Development of Penicillin in Japan]'. *Today's Therapy* 19, no. 2 (1995): 26–34.

——. Interview by Nihon Penishirin Kyōkai. 'Penisirin no Nihon Inyū [The Transfer of Penicillin into Japan]'. In Nihon Penishirin Kyōkai [Japan Penicillin Association]. *Penishirin no Ayumi: 1946–1961* [The History of Penicillin: 1946–1961]. Tokyo: Nihon Penishirin Kyōkai, 1961.

Inoue, Tadashi. 'Iryōyō Iyakuhin Shijō no Tokushusei to Ryūtsū Kaikaku [Special Features of the Prescription Pharmaceutical Market and Distribution Reform]'. *Waseda Shakaigaku Kenkyū* 49 (October 1994): 55–65.

Institute of Microbial Chemistry. *Institute of Microbial Chemistry: 1962–1977*. Tokyo: Center for Academic Publications, 1977.

International Conference on Harmonisation of Technical Requirements for Registration of Pharmaceuticals for Human Use (ICH). http://www.ich.org (accessed 15 May 2007).

Ishidate, M., K. Kobayashi, Y. Sakurai, H. Sato and T. Yoshida. 'Experimental Studies on Chemotherapy of Malignant Growth Employing Yoshida Sarcoma Animals (II). The Effect of N-oxide derivatives of Nitrogen Mustard'. *Proceedings of the Japan Academy* 27 (1951): 493–498.

Ishii, Shinichi. 'Kigyō no Gaiburenkei ni taisuru Ninshiki to Gaiburenkei no Jisshi: Sangakurenkei to Iyakuhin Kigyō o Chūshin to Shita Hikakubunseki [The Perception and Reality of External Collaborations: A Comparative Analysis of University–Industry Collaborations in the Pharmaceutical Industry]'. *Keiei Kenkyū* 53, no. 3 (2002): 205–217.

Ito, Akira, Keiji Hirai, Matsuhisa Inoue, Hiroshi Koga, Seigo Suzue, Tsutomu Irikura and Susumu Mitsuhashi. 'In Vitro Antibacterial Activity of AM-715, a New Nalidixic Acid Analog'. *Antimicrobial Agents and Chemotherapy* 17, no. 2 (1980): 103–108.

Itō, M. 'Nichi-bei-ō ni Okeru Kōkinyaku no Rinshōhyōkahō [A Clinical Evaluation of Antibacterial Agents in the United States, Europe and Japan]'. *Saishin Igaku* 44, no. 12 (1989): 2453–2498.

Japan, House of Councillors, Health and Welfare Committee. *Official Report of Debates*. 93rd Diet, 9th Session, 25 November 1980.

——. *Official Report of Debates*. 95th Diet, 3rd Session, 27 October 1981.

——. *Official Report of Debates*. 126th Diet, 7th Session, 20 April 1993.

——. *Official Report of Debates*. 126th Diet, 11th Session, 30 June 1993.

Japan, House of Representatives, Health and Welfare Committee. *Official Report of Debates*. 94th Diet, 20th Session, 30 July 1981.

——. *Official Report of Debates*. 104th Diet, 4th Session, 6 March 1986.

——. *Official Report of Debates*. 126th Diet, 6th Session, 2 April 1993.

Japan Antibiotics Research Association. 'Honkai no Gaiyō [About Us]'. Japan Antibiotics Research Association. http://www.antibiotics.or.jp/jara/news/jara.htm (accessed 28 April 2008).

Japan Bioindustry Association. *Baiobenchā Tōkei Hōkokusho 2005* [Statistical Report on Bioindustries]. Tokyo: Japan Bioindustry Association, 2006.

Japan Business History Association. *Banyū Seiyaku 85-nenshi* [Banyu Pharmaceutical, an 85-year History]. Tokyo: Banyu Pharmaceutical Co., 2002.

Japan Cancer Association. 'Gangakkai no Rekishi [The History of the Japan Cancer Association]'. Japan Cancer Association. http://www.jca.gr.jp/b01.html (accessed 1 December 2007).

Japanese Board of Cancer Therapy. 'Ninteii Seido Kisoku [Certified Oncologist Regulations]'. Japanese Board of Cancer Therapy. http://www.jbct.jp/sys_regulation01.html (accessed 30 November 2007).

Japanese Society of Medical Oncology. 'Nihon Rinshō Shuyō Gakkai Gan Yakubutsu Ryōhō Senmon'i Ninteisha [JSMO Medical Oncology Certificate List]'. http://jsmo. umin.jp/senmoni/lists.html (accessed 9 April 2010).

Japan External Trade Organisation. *The Survey on Access to Japan: Pharmaceuticals.* Tokyo: Japan External Trade Organisation, 1998.

Japan Fair Trade Commission. *Shuyō Sangyō ni Okeru Ruiseki Seisan Shūchūdo* [Concentration Ratio of Main Industries]. Tokyo: Japan Fair Trade Commission, 1975– 1994. http://www.jftc.go.jp/katudo/ruiseki/ruisekidate.html (accessed 1 June 2008).

Japan Pharmaceutical Association. *Iyakuhin Bungyō Shinchoku Jōkyō* [Progress on the Separation on the Prescribing and Dispensing of Medicines]. Japan Pharmaceutical Association. http://www.nichiyaku.or.jp/contents/bungyo/default.html (accessed 20 April 2008).

Japan Pharmaceutical Manufacturers Association. *JPMA Databook*. Tokyo: JPMA, 2007, 2009.

——. *Seiyakukyō 20-nen no Ayumi* [A 20-year History of the Japan Pharmaceutical Manufacturers Association]. Tokyo: Japan Pharmaceutical Manufacturers Association, 1988.

Jihō. *Iryō Iyakuhin Gyōkai no Ippan Chishiki* [General Information on the Health Care and Pharmaceutical Industries]. Tokyo: Jihō, 2005.

——. *Yakuji Handobukku* [Pharmaceutical Affairs Handbook]. Tokyo: Jihō, 2000–2009.

Johnson, Chalmers A. *MITI and the Japanese Miracle: The Growth of Industrial Policy, 1925–1975*. Stanford, CA: Stanford University Press, 1982.

Kataoka, Ichirō, Mitsuaki Shimaguchi and Mimura Yumiko, eds. *Iyakuhin Ryūtsūron* [Studies on Distrubution in the Pharmaceutical Industry]. Tokyo: University of Tokyo Press, 2003.

Katō, Benzaburō. 'Innen no Dōri ni Rikkyaku Shita Jigyō Keiei [Business Management Based on the Philosophy of Fate]'. In *Gendai Toppu Keiei no Jigyō Tetsugaku* [Business Philosophies among Today's Leading Managers], edited by Nihon Jitsugyō Shuppansha. Tokyo: Nihon Jitsugyō Shuppansha, 1969.

Kazis, Dimitris. *Post-war Industrial Policy and the Electronics Industry in Japan*. Athens: Centre of Planning and Economic Research, 1988.

Keizai Shunjūsha, ed. *Meiji Hyakunen Kigyō no Rekishi* [Company Histories 100 Years after Meiji]. Tokyo: Keizai Shunjūsha, 1968.

Kida, Mitsushiro. *Thalidomide Embryopathy in Japan*. Tokyo: Kodansha, 1987.

Kiese, Manfred. 'Chemotherapie mit Antibakteriellen Stoffen aus Niederen Pilzen und Bakterien'. *Journal of Molecular Medicine* 22 (1943): 505–511.

Kleinfeld, N.R. 'Intense Battle for Antibiotics'. *The New York Times*, 13 June 1983.

Kneller, Robert. 'Autarkic Drug Discovery in Japanese Pharmaceutical Companies: Insights into National Differences in Industrial Innovation'. *Research Policy* 32 (2003): 1805–1827.

——. 'The Beginning of University Entrepreneurship in Japan: TLOs and Bioventures Lead the Way'. *Journal of Technology Transfer* 32 (2007): 435–456.

——. 'University–Industry Collaboration in Biomedical Research in Japan and the United States: Implications for Biomedical Industries'. In *Industrializing Knowledge: University–Industry Linkages in Japan and the United States*, edited by Lewis M. Branscomb, Fumio Kodama and Richard L. Florida, 410–438. Cambridge, MA: MIT Press, 1999.

Koga, Shōsuke. 'Yakujihōsei no Hensen [Changes to the Pharmaceutical Affairs Act]'. *Gekkan Yakuji* 21 (November 1979): 31–40.

Koinuma, Nobuo. 'Gan Iryō no Keizaiteki Hyōka [Economic Evalutaion of Cancer Treatments]'. *Kōshū Eisei* 71, no. 2 (February 2007): 108–112.

Kōseishō 50-nenshi Henshū Iinkai [Editorial Committee for the 50-year History of the Ministry of Health and Welfare]. 'Jiyūka to Kokusaika no Shinten [Progress in Capital Liberalisation and Internationalisation]'. In *Kōseishō 50-nenshi* [A 50-year History of the Ministry of Health and Welfare], 1624–1626. Tokyo: Kōsei Mondai Kenkyūkai, 1988.

Koyama, Yasuo, Akio Kurosasa, Atsushi Tsuchiya and Kinsuke Takakuta. 'A New Antibiotic "Colistin" Produced by Spore-forming Soil Bacteria'. *The Journal of Antibiotics* 3, no. 7 (1950): 457–459.

Kreuger, Anne. 'The Political Economy of the Rent-seeking Society'. *American Economic Review* 64 (June 1974): 291–303.

Kumazawa, Joichi, and Morimasa Yagisawa. 'The History of Antibiotics: The Japanese Story'. *Journal of Infection and Chemotherapy* 8, no. 2 (2002): 125–133.

Kureha Chemical Industry Co. *Kureha Kagaku 50-nenshi* [A 50-year History of Kureha Chemical Industry]. Tokyo: Kureha Chemical Industry Co., 1995.

———. *Yūka Shōken Hōkokusho* [Annual Securities Report]. Tokyo: Ōkurashō Insatsukyoku, 1976.

Kushida, Kenji. 'Japanese Entrepreneurship: Changing Incentives in the Context of Developing a New Economic Model'. *Stanford Journal of East Asian Affairs* 1 (Spring 2001): 86–95.

Kyorin Pharmaceutical Co., *Yūka Shōken Hōkokusho* [Annual Securities Report]. Tokyo: Ōkurashō Insatsukyoku, 1995.

Kyowa Hakko Co. *Bara wa Bara: Kyōwa Hakkō 35-nenshi* [A Rose is a Rose: A 35-year History of Kyowa Hakko]. Tokyo: Kyowa Hakko Co., 1984.

———. *Yūka Shōken Hōkokusho* [Annual Securities Report]. Tokyo: Ōkurashō Insatsukyoku, 1965, 1966.

Landau, Ralph, Basil Achilladelis, and Alexander Scriabine, eds. *Pharmaceutical Innovation: Revolutionizing Human Health*. Philadelphia: Chemical Heritage Press, 1999.

Laubach, Gerald D. 'Federal Regulation and Pharmaceutical Innovation'. *Proceedings of the Academy of Political Science* 33, no. 4 (1980): 60–80.

Laurence, William L. 'Science in Review: Reports of Progress in Fight on Cancer Hold Out Hope of Cutting Death Toll'. *The New York Times*, 13 July 1958.

Liebenau, Jonathan. 'The British Success with Penicillin'. *Social Studies of Science* 17, no. 1 (1987): 69–86.

———. 'Industrial R&D in Pharmaceutical Firms in the Early Twentieth Century'. *Business History* 26, no. 3 (November 1984): 329–346.

Lieberman Marvin B., and David B. Montgomery. 'First-mover Advantages'. *Strategic Management Journal* 9, no. 1 (1988): 41–58.

———. 'First-mover (Dis)advantages: Retrospective and Resource-based View'. *Strategic Management Journal* 19, no. 12 (1998): 1111–1125.

Life Insurance Association of Japan. *Seimeihoken Jigyō Gaikyō* [Summary of Life Insurance Business]. Tokyo: Life Insurance Association of Japan, 1957–2008.

Lipartito, Kenneth. 'Culture and the Practice of Business History'. *Business and Economic History* 24, no. 2 (1995): 1–42.

Lohr, Steve. 'Merck's Big Venture in Japan'. *New York Times*, 13 October 1983.

Longe, Jacqueline L. and Deirdre S. Blanchfield, eds. *The Gale Encyclopedia of Medicine*. 2nd ed. Farmington Hills, MI: Gale Group, 2001.

Low, Morris, Shigeru Nakayama and Hitoshi Yoshioka, eds. *Science, Technology and Society in Contemporary Japan*. Cambridge: Cambridge University Press, 1999.

Lynn, Matthew. *The Billion-dollar Battle: Merck v Glaxo*. London: Mandarin, 1992.

Lynskey, Michael. 'The Commercialisation of Biotechnology in Japan: Bioventures as a Mechanism of Knowledge Transfer from Universities'. *International Journal of Biotechnology* 6 (2004): 155–185.

Macfarlane, Gwyn. *Alexander Fleming: The Man and the Myth*. Oxford: Oxford University Press, 1984.

Maddison, Angus, and Organisation for Economic Co-operation and Development Centre. *The World Economy*. Vol. 2. Paris: Organisation for Economic Co-operation and Development, 2006.

Maeda, K., and H. Umezawa. 'The Crystal Structure of Kanamycin'. *Tetrahedron Letters* 15 (1968): 1875–1879.

Management and Coordination Agency. Statistics Bureau and Statistics Centre. *Kagaku Gijutsu Kenkyū Chōsa Hōkoku* [Report on the Survey of Research and Development]. Tokyo: Management and Coordination Agency, 1985–2000.

Marsh, Peter. 'Pharmaceuticals 6; Optimistic But Still Some Way to Go'. *Financial Times*, 1 October 1987.

Martin, Peter. 'Weak Link in the Chain: Distribution Difficulties Have Meant that Japan's Successes in the West's Car and Consumer Electronics Markets Have Not Been Equalled in Other Industries'. *Financial Times*, 6 March 1997.

Mason, Mark. *American Multinationals in Japan: The Political Economy of Japanese Capital Controls*. Cambridge, MA: Harvard University Press, 1992.

Matsumoto, Tadamasa. 'Wagasha ni Okeru Kōganzai no Kaihatsu'. *Kagaku to Kōgyō* (April 1976): 105–107.

Matsumura, Katsuhiro. 'Seiyaku Kigyō no Keiei Kiban Kyōka Katei, Shōwa 25-nen Zenhan kara 30-nen Goro made [Pharmaceutical Firms Strengthen the Foundations of Business, from the Early 1950s to around 1955]'. *Iyaku Jānaru* 12 (May 1973): 46–52.

——. 'Seiyaku Kigyō no Saihen Seibi to Gōrika Katei, Shōwa 20-nen kara 25-nen zenhan made [The Reorganisation and Rationalisation of the Pharmaceutical Industry, from 1945 to early 1950]'. *Iyaku Jānaru* 12 (March 1973): 42–48.

Matsuo, Katsuichi. 'Korisuchin oyobi Korisuchin Metan Suruhonsan Natoriumu no Kaihatsu [The Development of Colistin and Colistin Methanesulfonate]'. In *Sangyō Gijutsu no Rekishi no Shūtaisei-Taikeika o Okonaukoto ni yoru Inobēshon Sōshutsu no Kankyō Seibi ni Kansuru Chōsa Kenkyu Hōkokusho* [Investigation and Research Report on the Compilation and Organisation on the History of Industrial Technology to Develop an Environment More Suitable for Innovation], edited by Japan Machinery Federation, 74–80, 242–275. Tokyo: Japan Machinery Federation, 2006.

Matsuyama, Kotone, Tetsuji Sadaike and Masanori Fukushima. 'The Present Approval State of Anti-tumour Drugs in Japan'. *Rinshō Hyōka* [Clinical Evaluation] 31 (2004): 579–586.

Maurer, P. Reed. 'Positive News on "Dramatic" Wholesaler Restructuring in Japan Overlooked'. *Pharma Marketletter*, 20 November 2003.

——. 'Why Japanese Pharmaceutical Wholesalers Merge'. *Pharma Marketletter*, 4 June 1999.

Meiji Seika Kaisha, Ltd. *Meiji Seika no Ayumi: Kaukide Tsukutte 60-nen* [A History of Meiji Seika: Selling What We Want to Buy for 60 Years]. Tokyo: Meiji Seika Kaisha, Ltd, 1977.

——. *Meiji Seika no Ayumi: Sōgyō kara 70-nen* [A History of Meiji Seika: 70 Years since Establishment]. Tokyo: Meiji Seika Kaisha, Ltd, 1987.

——. *Meiji Seika no Ayumi: Sōgyō kara 80-nen* [The History of Meiji Seika: 80 Years from Establishment]. Tokyo: Meiji Seika Kaisha, Ltd, 1997.

——. *Yūka Shōken Hōkokusho* [Annual Securities Report]. Tokyo: Ōkurashō Insatsukyoku, 1960.

Merck & Co., *2005 Annual Report*. Whitehouse Station: Merck & Co., 2006.

Merck KGaA. '2006 Online Report: Commercial Unit Oncology'. Merck KGaA. http://www.merck.de/servlet/PB/menu/1647870/index.html (accessed 6 December 2007).

Methé, David T., and Joan D. Pinner-Hahn. 'Globalization of Pharmaceutical Research and Development in Japanese Companies: Organizational Learning and the Parent-Subsidiary Relationship'. In *Japanese Multinationals Abroad: Individual and Organizational Learning*, by Schon Beechler and Allan Bird, 191–210. New York: Oxford University Press, 1999.

Michaels, Adrian. 'Warner Bows to Pfizer Demand for Merger Talks'. *Financial Times*, 14 January 2000.

Ministry of Economy Trade and Industry. *Bōeki Dōkō Dētabēsu* [Database on Trends in Trade], http://www.meti.go.jp/policy/trade_policy/trade_db/index.html (accessed 20 November 2010).

Ministry of Education. *Kyōiku Shihyō no Kokusai Hikaku* [International Comparison of Education Benchmarks]. Tokyo: Office of the Prime Minister, 1985–2005.

Ministry of Education, Culture, Sports, Science and Technology. 'Incorporation of National Universities'. In *FY2003 White Paper on Education, Culture, Sports, Science and Technology*. Tokyo: Ministry of Education, Culture, Sports, Science and Technology, 2004.

Ministry of Health and Welfare. 'Application of Standards for the Implementation of Clinical Trials on Pharmaceutical Products'. Notification no. 445 of Pharmaceuticals and Cosmetics Division/Notification no. 68 of the Safety Division, Pharmaceutical Affairs Bureau, 29 May 1997.

——. 'Densenbyō oyobi Shokuchūdoku no Kanjasū to Shibōshasū [Patients and Deaths of Infectious Diseases and Food Poisoning] (1876–1999)'. Statistics Bureau, Ministry of International Affairs and Communications. http://www.stat.go.jp/data/chouki/24.htm (accessed 20 March 2007).

——. 'Iyakuhin [Pharmaceuticals]'. In *Isei Hyakunenshi* [A 100-year History of Administration in Medicine], 447–451. Tokyo: Gyōsei, 1976.

——. 'Iyakuhin no Kenkyū Kaihatsu no Shien: Gutaiteki na Shiensaku [Supporting R&D in Pharmaceuticals: Specific Support Policies]', in *Kōsei Hakusho* (1988), http://wwwhakusyo.mhlw.go.jp/wpdocs/hpaz198701/b0053.html (accessed 15 November 2010).

——. *Iyakuhin Sangyō Jittai Chōsa Hōkoku* [Report on the Status of the Pharmaceutical Industry]. Tokyo: Ministry of Health and Welfare, 1988–2000.

——. *Jinkō Dōtai Shakai Keizaimen Chōsa* [Social and Economic Study of Vital Statistics]. Tokyo: Ministry of Health and Welfare, 1994.

——. *Kanja Chōsa* [Patient Survey]. Tokyo: Ministry of Health and Welfare, 1953–1985.

——. *Kōsei Hakusho* [White Paper on Health and Welfare]. Tokyo: 1957–2000. Hakusho nado Dētabēsu Shisutemu [Full-text System for White Papers, etc.] http://wwwhakusyo.mhlw.go.jp/wp/index.htm (accessed 8 November 2010).

——. 'Pharmaceutical Business Facilities (C.Y. 1944–1996, F.Y. 1997–2004)'. http://www.stat.go.jp/data/chouki/24.htm (accessed 27 July 2008).

——. *Saikin no Yakumu Gyōsei* [Recent Trends in Pharmaceutical Administration]. Tokyo: Yaukumu Kōhōsha, 1968–1998.

——. 'Standards for the Implementation of Clinical Trials on Pharmaceutical Products'. MHW Ordinance no. 28, 27 March 1997.

——. *Yakkyokuhō, Dairokuji Kaisei* [Japanese Pharmacopoeia, 6th revision]. Tokyo: Ministry of Health and Welfare, 1951.

——. *Yakuji Kōgyō Seisan Dōtai Chōsa Tōkei* [Annual Survey on Production in the Pharmaceutical Industry]. Tokyo: Yakugyō Keizai Kenkyujo, 1953–1967.

——. *Yakuji Kōgyō Seisan Dōtai Chōsa Tōkei* [Annual Survey on Production in the Pharmaceutical Industry]. Tokyo: Yakugyō Keizai Kenkyūjo, 1968–2000.

——. *Yakumu Kōhō* [Bulletin of Pharmaceutical and Supply Bureau]. Tokyo: Yakumu Kōhōsha, 1949–2000.

Ministry of Health, Labour and Welfare. 'Deaths by Leading Cause of Death, Population and Households'. http://www.stat.go.jp/english/data/chouki/02.htm (accessed 1 December 2007).

——. *Iyakuhin Sangyō Bijon* [Vision Statement for the Pharmaceutical Industry]. Tokyo: Ministry of Health, Labour and Welfare, 2002.

——. *Iyakuhin Sangyō Jittai Chōsa Hōkoku* [Report on the Status of the Pharmaceutical Industry]. Tokyo: Ministry of Health, Labour and Welfare, 2001–2006.

——. 'Kako 5-nenkan ni Gakkai/Kanjadantai kara no Sōki Shōnin no Yōbō ga Ari, katsu Heisei 17-nen 3-gatsu Izen ni Ōbei 4-kakoku de Shōnin Sareta Mishōninyaku [Drugs Requested by Academic/Patient Organiations for Accelerated Approval Within the Past 5 Years, that were Approved in the 4 American and European Countries Prior to, During or Before March 2005]'. http://www.mhlw.go.jp/shingi/2005/03/s0331-13.html (accessed 1 December 2007).

——. *Kōsei Rōdō Hakusho* [White Paper on Health, Labour and Welfare]. Tokyo: Ōkurashō Insatsukyoku, 2001–2007. http://www.mhlw.go.jp/wp/hakusyo/index.html (accessed 8 November 2010).

——. *Shin Iyakuhin Sangyō Bijon* [New Vision Statement on the Pharmaceutical Industry]. Tokyo: Ministry of Health and Welfare, 2007.

——. *Yakuji Kōgyō Seisan Dōtai Chōsa Tōkei* [Annual Survey on Production in the Pharmaceutical Industry]. Tokyo: Jihō, 2001–2006.

——. *Yakumu Kōhō* [Bulletin of Pharmaceutical and Supply Bureau]. Tokyo: Yakumu Kōhōsha, 2001–2006.

Ministry of Internal Affairs and Communications, Statistics Bureau. *Kagaku Gijutsu Kenkyū Chōsa Hōkoku* [Report on the Survey of Research and Development]. Tokyo: Ministry of Internal Affairs and Communications, 2001–2006.

——. 'Nenrei Kakusai Danjobetsu Jinkō [Population by Single Years of Age and Sex] (1884–2000)'. http://www.stat.go.jp/data/chouki/02.htm (accessed 20 March 2007).

Ministry of International Trade and Industry. *Tsūshō Hakusho* [White Paper on Trade]. Tokyo: Ōkurashō Insatsukyoku, 1958–1973.

——. *Tsūshō Hakusho* [White Paper on Trade]. Tokyo: Gyōsei, 1974–2000.

Mitsibishi Bank, Ltd. 'Nihon Shijō ni Chūryoku suru Iyakuhin Gaishi [Foreign Pharmaceutical Firms Eye the Japanese Market'. *Mitsubishi Bank Research Report* 369 (January 1986): 22–32.

Mitsubishi Pharma Corp. *Yūka Shōken Hōkokusho*. Tokyo: Ōkurashō Insatsukyoku, 2006.

Miyamoto, Mamoru. 'Kongō Shinsatsu ni Tsuite [On Mixed Billing]'. *Kansai Daigaku Keizai-kei* 226 (September 2006): 77–85.

Miyasaka, Tadashi, and Seigo Sawada. 'Anticancer Agent Irinotecan'. *Gendai Kagaku* [Current Chemistry] 343 (October 1999): 58–66.

Miyata, Shinpei. 'Yoshida Tomizō: Shinjidai o Hiraita Yoshida Nikushu [Tomizo Yoshida: Yoshida Carcinoma and the Beginning of a New Era]'. *Gekkan Gan* 33 (September 2002): 42–45.

Mizuho Corporate Bank, Ltd. 'Ōbei Seiyaku Kigyō no Saihen Dōkō to Wagakuni Seiyakugyōkai e no Inpurikēshon'. *Mizuho Sangyō Chōsa* 17 (March 2005): 1–42.

Motohashi, Kazuyuki. 'Japan's Patent System and Business Innovation: Reassessing Pro-patent Policies'. RIETI Discussion Paper Series 03-E-020, http://www.rieti.go.jp/en/publications/act_dp2003.html (accessed 15 May 2008).

——. 'Baiobenchā no Katsudō ni Kansuru Nichibei Hikakubunseki [A Comparison of Bioventures in Japan and the United States]'. *Iryō to Shakai* 17, no. 1 (2008): 55–70.

Nakagawa, Takeshi. Interview by Shōzō Tsunabuchi in 'Meiji Seika: Ishokudōgen Baio o Mezasu [Meiji Seika Aims to Develop Biotechnology Businesss]'. *Will* (December 1982): 48–51.

Nakajima, Mitsuyoshi. 'Chiken no Shitsuteki Reberuappu no tame no Teian: Kontorōrā no Tachiba kara [Suggestions to Improve the Quality of Clinical Trials: From a Controller's Standpoint]'. *Yakuri to Chiryō* 23, no. 4 (1995): 777–783.

Nakamoto, Michiyo. 'Global Reach through Tie-ups: Japan'. *Financial Times*, 30 April 2002.

Nakamoto, Michiyo, and David Pilling. 'Drugs Market Set for Change: Japan's Pharma Industry is Slowly Opening Up'. *Financial Times*, 3 April 2002.

Nakamura, Yoshiaki, and Hiroyuki Odagiri. 'Nihon no Biobenchā Kigyō: So no Igi to Jittai [Japanese Bioventures: Meaning and Current Status]'. *REITI Discussion Paper Series* 22 (June 2002): 1–52.

Nakane, Chie. *Japanese Society.* Tokyo: Charles E. Tuttle, 1984.

Nakano, Shigeyuki. 'Chiken ni Sanka Suru Hikensha no Meritto [Patient Benefits to Participating in Clinical Trials]'. *Yakuri to Chiryō* 23, no. 5 (1995): 1085–1093.

Nakao, Isao, Tadashi Yokoyama, Ichirō Urushizaki, Akira Wakui, Hisashi Furue, Yoshiyuki Koyama, Kiyoji Kimura, Nobuya Ogawa and Tatsuo Saitō. 'Shinkō Igan ni Taisuru PSK no Rinshō Kōka [Clinical Effects of PSK in Advanced Gastric Cancer]'. *Oncologia* 14 (1985): 163–170.

Nakayama, Shigeru, and Morris Low. 'The Research Function of Universities in Japan'. *Higher Education* 34 (1997): 245–258.

Nanbu, Tsuruhiko. 'Iyakuhin no Sangyō Soshiki: Yakka Kisei no Keizaiteki Kōka [Industrial Organisation in Pharmaceuticals: The Consequences of Price Regulation in Japan]'. *Iryō to Shakai* 7 (January 1997): 1–15.

——, ed. *Iyakuhin Sangyō Soshikiron* [Studies on the Organization of the Pharmaceutical Industry]. Tokyo: University of Tokyo Press, 2002.

National Cancer Center. 'Cancer Statistics in Japan, 2007'. National Cancer Center. http://ganjoho.ncc.go.jp/public/statistics/backnumber/2007_en.html (accessed 1 December 2007).

National Cancer Institute. 'Biological Therapies for Cancer: Questions and Answers'. National Cancer Institute. http://www.cancer.gov/cancertopics/factsheet/Therapy/biological#q3 (accessed 26 May 2008).

——. 'Developmental Therapeutics Program, FDA Approved Drugs'. National Cancer Institute. http://dtp.nci.nih.gov/timeline/flash/FDA.htm (accessed 10 November 2007).

——. 'Dictionary of Cancer Terms'. National Cancer Institute. http://www.cancer.gov/dictionary/ (accessed 20 March 2007).

——. 'Dictionary of Cancer Terms: Antitumor Antibiotic'. http://www.cancer.gov/templates/db_alpha.aspx?CdrID=44488 (accessed 26 May 2008).

——. 'The National Cancer Institute Act, 1937–2007: Celebrating 70 Years of Excellence in Cancer Research'. National Cancer Institute. http://www.cancer.gov/aboutnci/ncia (accessed 1 December 2007).

——. 'What Is Cancer?' http://www.cancer.gov/cancertopics/what-is-cancer (accessed 10 July 2008).

National Health Service. 'Medical and Dental Staff 2008 Detailed Results'. http://www.ic.nhs.uk/statistics-and-data-collections/workforce/nhs-staff-numbers/nhs-staff-1998–2008-medical-and-dental (accessed 10 April 2010).

National Science Foundation (United States). *Survey of Industrial Research and Development Historical Database 1953–1998*. http://www.nsf.gov/statistics/iris (accessed 13 November 2009).

Neimeth, Robert. 'Japan's Pharmaceutical Industry Postwar Evolution'. In *The Changing Economics of Medical Technology*, edited by Annetine Gelijns and Ethan Halm, Committee on Technological Innovation in Medicine, Institute of Medicine, 155–168. Washington DC, National Academies Press, 1991.

Neu, Harold C. 'The Crisis in Antibiotic Resistance'. *Science* 257, no. 5073 (1992): 1064–1073.

Nihon Kōgakukai [Japan Federation of Engineering Societies]. *Meiji Kōgyōshi* [History of Industry in the Meiji Period]. Tokyo: Nihon Kōgakukai, 1925.

Nihon Penishirin Kyōkai [Japan Penicillin Association]. *Penishirin no Ayumi: 1946–1961* [The History of Penicillin: 1946–1961]. Tokyo: Nihon Penishirin Kyōkai, 1961.

Nihon Yakushi Gakkai [The Japanese Society for the History of Pharmacy]. *Nihon Iyakuhin Sangyōshi* [The History of the Japanese Pharmaceutical Industry]. Tokyo: Yakuji Nippōsha, 1995.

Niimoto, Minoru, Takao Hattori, Ryūichiro Tanida, Koyoshi Inokuchi and Nobuya Ogawa. 'Igan Chiyu Setsujo Shōrei ni Taisuru Maitomaishin C, Futorafūru, Kuresuchin o Mochiita Jutsugo Men'eki Kagaku Ryōhō [Postoperative Immunotherapy for Curatively Resected Gastric Cancer Patients Using Mitomycin C, Ftorafur and Krestin]'. *Oncologia* 14 (1985): 171–180.

Nippon Kayaku Co. *Nippon Kayaku no Ayumi: Kono 10-nen o Chūshin ni Shite* [The History of Nippon Kayaku: With Special Attention to the Past 10 Years]. Tokyo: Nippon Kayaku Co., 1976.

——. *Yūka Shōken Hōkokusho* [Annual Securities Report]. Tokyo: Ōkurashō Insatsukyoku, 1950, 1951, 1974, 1979.

Nippon Medical School, Research Institute of Vaccine Therapy for Tumors and Infectious Diseases. 'Maruyama Vaccine'. Nippon Medical School. http://vaccine.nms.ac.jp/ (accessed 1 December 2007).

Nishida, Minoru, Tadao Matsubara, Takeo Murakawa, Yasuhiro Mine, Yoshiko Yokota, Sachiko Goto and Shogo Kuwahara. 'Cefazolin, a New Semisynthetic Cephalopsorin Antibiotic II. In Vitro and In Vivo Antimicrobial Activity'. *The Journal of Antibiotics* 23, no. 3 (1970): 137–148.

Nishikawa, Takashi. *Kusuri Kara Mita Nihon; Shōwa 20-nendai no Genfūkei to Konnichi* [Looking at Japan from 'Medicine': Scenes from the 1940s to the Present]. Tokyo: Yakuji Nippōsha, 2004.

Nishimura, Sey. 'Censorship of Medical Journals in Occupied Japan'. *Journal of the American Medical Association* 274, no. 6 (August 1995): 454–456.

Nishimura, Shūzō. 'Iryō Sangyō [The Healthcare Industry]'. In *Sengo Nihon Sangyōshi* [A History of Japanese Industries in the Post-war Period], edited by Sangyō Gakkai [The Society for Industrial Studies], 769–786. Tokyo: Tōyō Keizai Shinpōsha, 1995.

Nitta, Kazuo, Kuniichiro Yano, Fumio Miyamoto, Yoshiharu Hasegawa, Toshihisa Sato, Noriko Kamoto and Shintaro Matsumoto. 'A New Antibiotic, Josamycin. II: Biological Studies'. *The Journal of Antibiotics Series A* 20, no. 3 (1967): 181–187.

Nitta, Shinji. 'Iyakuhin no Shinsa Gyōsei [Administering the Examination of Pharmaceuticals]'. *Gekkan Yakuji* 21 (November 1979): 53–65.

Oberlaender, Christian. 'The Rise of Western "Scientific Medicine" in Japan: Bacteriology and Beriberi'. In *Building a Modern Japan: Science, Technology and Medicine in the Meiji Era and Beyond*, edited by Morris Low, 11–36. New York: Palgrave Macmillan, 2005.

Odagiri, Hiroyuki. 'Iyakuhin Sangyō ni okeru Araiansu [Alliances in the Pharmaceutical Industry]'. *Iryō to Shakai* 17, no. 1 (2008): 3–18.

——. 'Nihon no Biobenchā Kigyō: Sono Igi to Jittai [Japanese Bioventures: Meaning and Current Status]'. *REITI Discussion Paper Series* 02-J-007 (June 2002).

Office of Pharmaceutical Industry Research. 'Seiyaku Sangyō no Shōraizō [The Future Image of the Pharmaceutical Industry]'. *Office of Pharmaceutical Industry Research, Japan Pharmaceutical Manufacturers Association* (May 2007).

——. 'Sōyaku no Ba to shite no Kyōsōryoku Kyōka ni Mukete [Creating a Stronger, More Competitive Environment for Drug Discovery]'. *Office of Pharmaceutical Industry Research, Japan Pharmaceutical Manufacturers Association* (November 2005).

Office of the Prime Minister, Bureau of Statistics. *Kagaku Gijutsu Kenkyū Chōsa Hōkoku* [Report on the Survey of Research and Development]. Tokyo: Office of the Prime Minister, 1961–1984.

Ohnuki-Tierney, Emiko. *Illness and Culture in Contemporary Japan*. Cambridge: Cambridge University Press, 1984.

Okamoto, H., M. Minami, S. Shoin, S. Koshimura and R. Shimizu. 'Experimental Anticancer Studies Part XXXI. On the Streptococcal Preparation Having Potent Anticancer Activity'. *Japanese Journal of Experimental Medicine* 36 (1966): 175–186.

Okamoto, H., S. Shoin, M. Minami, S. Koshimura and R. Shimizu. 'Experimental Anticancer Studies Part XXX. Factors Influencing the Streptolysin S-forming Ability of Streptococci Having Anticancer Activity'. *Japanese Journal of Experimental Medicine* 36 (1966): 161–174.

Okamoto, Hajime, Susumu Shoin, Saburo Koshimura and Ryusaku Shimizu. 'Studies on the Anticancer and Streptolysin S-forming Abilities of Hemolytic Streptococci'. *Japanese Journal of Microbiology* 11, no. 4 (1967): 323–326.

Okimoto, Daniel I. *Between MITI and the Market: Japanese Industrial Policy for High Technology*. Stanford, CA: Stanford University Press, 1989.

Ono, Shunsuke. 'The Performance of the Japanese New Drug Review System: From the Reviewer's Perspective'. *Rinshō Hyōka* [Clinical Evaluation] 31 (2004): 557–566.

Organisation for Economic Co-operation and Development. *Health at a Glance 2009: OECD Indicators*. Paris: Organisation for Economic Co-operation and Development, 2009.

——. *International Trade by Commodities Statistics Database*, http://www.sourceoecd.org (accessed 20 May 2010).

——. *Pharmaceuticals: Gaps in Technology*. Paris: Organisation for Economic Cooperation and Development, 1969.

Osono, Takashi, Yoshihiko Oka, Shunichi Watanabe, Yōzō Numazaki, Kiruko Moriyama, Hitoshi Ishida, Kiyoshi Suzaki, Yoshirō Okami and Hamao Umezawa. 'A New Antibiotic Josamycin I: Isolation and Physicochemical Characteristics'. *The Journal of Antibiotics Series A* 20, no. 3 (1967): 174–180.

Otsuka Pharmaceutical Co. *Kessan Jōhō* [Financial Information]. http://www.otsuka.co.jp/company/profile/finance/ (accessed 10 May 2009).

——. 'The Extent and History of Foreign Direct Investment in Japan'. *Foreign Direct Investment in Japan*. Cambridge: Cambridge University Press, 2008.

Parascandola, John, ed. *History of Antibiotics: A Symposium*. Madison: American Institute of the History of Pharmacy, 1980.

Pharmaceutical Research and Manufacturers of America. *Pharmaceutical Industry Profile 2008*. Washington DC: Pharmaceutical Research and Manufacturers of America, March 2008.

Pfizer, Inc. *Annual Review*. New York: Pfizer, Inc., 2006.

PJB Publications. *Scrip's Antibacterial Report*. London: PJB Publications, 1990.

——. *Scrip: Pharmaceutical Company League Tables*. Richmond: PJB Publications, 1991.

——. *Scrip: Yearbook*. Richmond: PJB Publications, 1988, 1991.

Podolsky, M. Lawrence, and Daniel E. Koshland. 'The Oxford Incidents'. In *Cures out of Chaos: How Unexpected Discoveries Led to Breakthroughs in Medicine and Health*, 177–224. Amsterdam: Harwood, 1997.

Rapoport, Carla. 'Chugai – a Portfolio of Pills'. *Financial Times*, 22 September 1983.

Reich, Michael. 'Why the Japanese Don't Export More Pharmaceuticals: Health Policy as Industrial Policy'. *California Management Review* 32, no. 2 (1990): 124–150.

Rhoads, C.P. 'Nitrogen Mustards in the Treatment of Neoplastic Disease: Official Statement'. *Journal of the American Medical Association* 131 (1946): 656–658.

Sams, Crawford F. Interview by Darryl Podoll, 3 May 1979. Interview OH037, transcript, Washington University School of Medicine Oral History Project, Bernard Becker Medical Library, St Louis, Missouri, http://beckerexhibits.wustl.edu/oral/interviews/sams.html (accessed 8 November 2010).

Sams, Crawford F., and Zabelle Zakarian, *'Medic': The Mission of an American Military Dofctor in Occupied Japan and Wartorn Korea*. London: M.E. Sharpe, 1998.

Sankyo Co. *Sankyo 80-nenshi* [Sankyo, an 80-year History]. Tokyo, Sankyo Co., 1979.

——. *Sankyō 100-nenshi* [Sankyo, a 100-year History]. Tokyo: Sankyo Co., 1999.

——. *Yūka Shōken Hōkokusho* [Annual Securities Report]. Tokyo: Ōkurashō Insatsukyoku, 1960, 1991.

Saruta, Takao. 'Chiken no Shitsuteki Reberuappu no tame no Teian: Tantōi no Tachiba kara [Suggestions to Improve the Quality of Clinical Trials: From a Physician's Standpoint]'. *Yakuri to Chiryō* 23, no. 3 (1995): 561–564

Sasaki, Satoshi, Toshihiro Imaeda, Yoji Hayase, Yoshiaki Shimizu, Shizuo Kasai, Nobuo Cho, Masataka Harada, Nobuhiro Suzuki, Shuichi Furuya and Masahiko Fujino. 'A New Class of Potent Nonpeptide Luteinizing Hormone-releasing Hormone (LHRH) Antagonists: Design and Synthesis of 2-phenylimidazo[1,2-a]pyrimidin-5-ones'. *Bioorganic & Medicinal Chemistry Letters* 12 (August 2002): 2073–2077.

Sato, K., Y. Matsuura, M. Inoue, T. Une, Y. Osada, H. Ogawa and S. Mitsuhashi. 'In Vitro and In Vivo Activity of DL-8280, a New Oxazine Derivative'. *Antimicrobial Agents and Chemotherapy* 22, no. 4 (1982): 548–553.

Schatz, Albert, Elizabeth Bugie and Selman Waksman. 'Streptomycin, a Substance Exhibiting Antibiotic Activity against Gram-positive and Gram-negative Bacteria'. *Proceedings of the Society for Experimental Biology and Medicine* 55 (1944): 66–69.

Schmitt, Eric. 'What's Hot in Imported Products; Antibiotics Made Jointly'. *The New York Times*, 30 November 1986.

Seimei Hoken Bunka Sentā. *Seimei Hoken ni Kansuru Zenkoku Jittai Chōsa* [National Survey on Life Insurance]. Tokyo: Seimei Hoken Bunka Sentā, 1965–2009.

Seiyaku Kigyō Kondankai [Council of Pharmaceutical Firms], *Seiyaku Kigyō no Genjō to Kōsatsu* [An Evaluation of the Current Status of Pharmaceutical Firms]. Tokyo: Seiyaku Kigyō Kondankai, 1965.

Shimizu, Kihachirō. 'Nihon ni Okeru Penishirin Kaihatsu no Keii [The Development of Penicillin in Japan]'. *Today's Therapy* 19, no. 2 (1995): 26–34.

Shionogi & Co. *Yūka Shōken Hōkokusho* [Annual Securities Report]. Tokyo: Ōkurashō Insatsukyoku, 1960.

Shinnippon Hoki Publishing Co. *Yakka Kijun* [Official Drug List]. Tokyo: Shinnippon Hoki Publishing Co., 1977–1990.

Shirasaka, Tetsuhiko. *S1 Tanjō* [Creating S-1]. Tokyo: Evidensu, 2006.

Sigurdson, Jon. *Future Advantage Japan?: Technology Strategies for Pharmaceutical and Chemical Corporations*. London: Cartermill, 1996.

Sneader, Walter. *Drug Discovery: A History*. Chichester: John Wiley & Sons, 2005.

Sōda, Hajime. 'Ishinki no Seiyaku [Manufacturing Pharmacy during the Times of the Meiji Restoration]'. *Iyaku Jānaru* 11 (August 1972): 38–42.

———. 'Ishinki no Seiyaku [Manufacturing Pharmacy during the Times of the Meiji Restoration]'. *Iyaku Jānaru* 11 (September 1972): 57–60.

———. 'Ishinki no Seiyaku [Manufacturing Pharmacy during the Times of the Meiji Restoration]'. *Iyaku Jānaru* 11 (November 1972): 58–63.

Sugimura, Takashi. 'Gankenkyū ni Kansuru Shomondai to Shohansei [Comments on Cancer Research in Japan]'. *Tanpakushitsu Kakusan Kōso* 23, no. 6 (1978), 685–691.

Sugimura, T. 'Pioneers of Cancer Research in Japan'. *Japanese Journal of Cancer Research* 82 (December 1991): 1448–1449.

Steslicke, William E. 'Doctors, Patients, and Government in Modern Japan'. *Asian Survey* 12, no. 11 (1972): 913–931.

Sugawara, Ryozo, and Toju Hata. 'Mitomycin C, a New Antibiotic from Streptomyces II'. *Journal of Antibiotics, Series A* 9 (July 1956): 147.

Suguro, Toshihiko. 'Kureha Kagaku Kōgyō: Daikokubashira "Kuresuchin" Gekigen no Kiki [Kureha Chemical Industry: Sales of Core Product "Krestin" May Plummet]'. *Shūkan Tōyō Keizai*, 12 May 1990, 139–141.

Sumitomo Trust & Banking Co. 'Kakudai suru Jenerikku Iyakuhin Gyōkai no Yukue [The Future of the Expending Generics Market]'. *Chōsa Geppō* (January 2006).

Sunday Times Insight Team. *Suffer the Children: The Story of Thalidomide*. London: Andre Deutsch, 1979.

Swinbanks, David. 'Japanese Doctors Keep Quiet'. *Nature* 339 (June 1989): 409.

———. 'Restrictions Recommended'. *Nature* 342 (December 1989): 843.

———. 'Japan's Foundations Still Building'. *Nature* 361 (February 1993): 761–764.

Tabuchi, Kaoru. 'GMP no Ayumi to sono Tenbō [History and Prospects of GMP]'. *Gekkan Yakuji* 21 (November 1979): 243–247.

Taiho Pharmaceutical Co. 'Taihō Yakuhin no Ayumi [A History of Taiho Pharmaceutical]'. Taiho Pharmaceutical Co. http://www.taiho.co.jp/corporation/history/index.html (accessed 2 December 2007).

Takahashi, Hidenao. 'Iyakuhin no Juyō no Kakaku Danryokusei no Suikei [The Price Elasticity of Demand in Pharmaceuticals: An Examination of the Biennial Price Reductions]'. *Hitotsubashi University COE Working Paper* 12 (August 2005).

Takahashi, Hisashi, Isao Hayakawa and Takeshi Akimoto. 'The History of the Development and Changes of Quinolone Antibacterial Agents'. *Yakushigaku Zasshi* 38, no. 2 (2003): 161–179.

Takahashi, Takao. 'Medical Business Ethics: The HIV-tainted Blood Affair in Japan'. In *Taking Life and Death Seriously: Bioethics from Japan*, edited by Takao Takahashi, 253–273. Amsterdam: Elsevier, 2005.

Takeda, Chōbei. 'Wagakuni no Iyakuhin Kōgyō to Bōeki [Pharamceutical Industry and Trade in Our Country]'. *Kankeiren* 16 (January 1949): 19–21.

Takeda Pharmaceutical Co. *Annual Report 2006*.Tokyo: Takeda Pharmaceutical Co. 2006.

——. *Annual Report 2009*. Osaka: Takeda Pharmaceutical Co., 2009.

——. 'Beikoku Jigyō Saihen ni Tsuite [On the Reorganisation of US Operations]'. 2 July 2008. Press release. http://www.takeda.co.jp/press/article_28213.html (accessed 30 July 2008).

——. *Takeda 180-nenshi* [A 180-year History of Takeda]. Osaka: Takeda Pharmaceutical Co., 1962.

——. *Takeda 200-nen* [200 Years of Takeda]. Osaka: Takeda Pharmaceutical Co., 1984.

——. 'Takeda Establishes New Global Pharmaceutical R&D Center in US'. 25 December 2003. Press release. http://www.takeda.com/press/article_801.html (accessed 16 July 2008).

——. 'Takeda no Rekishi [A History of Takeda]'. Takeda Pharmaceutical Co. http://www.takeda.co.jp/about-takeda/history/article_79.html (accessed 30 November 2007).

——. 'Takeda Submits a New Drug Application for a Fixed-dose Combination Tablet of Actos with Sulfonylurea in Japan'. 27 July 2009. Press release.

——. *Yūka Shōken Hōkokusho* [Annual Securities Report]. Tokyo: Ōkurashō Insatsukyoku, 1960.

Takemae, Eiji. *Inside GHQ: The Allied Occupation of Japan and its Legacy*. London: Continuum, 2002.

Takeuchi, Yutaka, Yoshiaki Takebayashi, Makoto Sunagawa, Yutaka Isobe, Yukari Hamazume, Akura Uemura and Tetsuo Noguchi. 'The Stability of a Novel Carbapenem Antibiotic, Meropenem (SM-7338), in a Solid State Formulation for Injection'. *Chemical & Pharmaceutical Bulletin* 41, no. 11 (1993): 1998–2002.

Tanaka, Shūmei. 'Iyakuhin no Ryūtsu o Meguru Mondaiten [Problems in Pharmaceutical Distribution]'. In *Shakai Yakugaku Nyūmon*, 156–168. Tokyo: Nankōdō, 1987.

Tatsuta, Kuniaki, and Morimasa Yagisawa. *Kōseibusshitsu: Seisan no Kagaku* [Antibiotics: The Science of Production]. Tokyo: Nihon Kagakukai [The Chemical Society of Japan], 1994.

Teff, H., and C.R. Munro. *Thalidomide: The Legal Aftermath*. Farnborough: Saxon House, 1976.

Terada, Kiyoshi. 'Ensan Irinotekan [Irinotecan Hydrochloride]'. *Fine Chemical* 29 (September 2000): 31–41.

Thomas, III, Lacy Glenn. 'Implicit Industrial Policy: The Triumph of Britain and the Failure of France in Global Pharmaceuticals'. *Industrial and Corporate Change* 3, no. 2 (1994): 451–489.

——.'Spare the Rod and Spoil the Industry: Vigorous Competition and Vigorous Regulation Promote Global Competitive Advantage'. First Boston Working Paper Series 90–03, 1990.

——. *The Japanese Pharmaceutical Industry: The New Drug Lag and the Failure of Industrial Policy*. Northampton: Edward Elgar, 2001.

Thomson Reuters. *The Japanese Generic Drug Market: Opportunities and Strategies for Success*. London: Thomson Reuters, 2009.

Thompson, Nigel. *International Price Comparison: Japan*. Tokyo: Japan Pharmaceutical Manufacturers Association Long Term Vision Research Council, 1999.

Timmermans, Stefan, and Valerie Leiter. 'The Redemption of Thalidomide: Standardizing the Risk of Birth Defects'. *Social Studies of Science* 30, no. 1 (February 2000): 41–71.

Todaka, Kōji. '"GRP"; Nihon ni okeru Yakuzai Kaihatsu no Infura to shite no Ishi no Yakuwari ["GRP"; The Role of Physicians in Helping to Develop Drugs in Japan]'. *Rinshō Hyōka* 31, no. 3 (2004): 567–571.

Tokai Bank, Ltd. 'Hanbai-mō no Kyōka o Isogu Iyakuhinkai [The Pharmaceutical Industry Rushes to Strengthen its Distribution Network]'. *Tokai Ginkō Chōsa Geppō* 222 (January 1966): 17–26.

Travis, John. 'Reviving the Antibiotic Miracle?' *Science* 264, no. 5157 (1994): 360–362.

Tsunematsu, Kinoichi. 'Saihen Katei no Iyakuhin Sangyō [The Pharmaceutical Industry under Reorganisation]'. *Iyaku Jānaru* 9 (September 1970): 20–23.

——. 'Senryōka ni Okeru Yakuji Eisei Taisaku [Public Health and Welfare Policy under the Occupation]'. *Iyaku Jānaru* 9 (July 1970): 56–58.

Tsunoda, Fusako. *Hekiso: Nihon Penishirin Monogatari* [Hekiso: The Story of Penicillin in Japan]. Tokyo: Shinchōsha, 1978.

Ueda, Eiji. 'Wagakuni no Chiken no Genjō to Mondaiten [The Current Environment and Issues around Clinical Trials in Japan]'. *Modan Media* 50, no. 2 (2004): 10–13.

Umezawa, Hamao. 'Kanamycin', in *Saikin no Shinyaku* [New Drugs in Japan], edited by Yakuji Nippōsha (Tokyo: Yakuji Nippōsha, 1959), 13–17.

——. 'Kanamycin: Its Discovery'. *Annals of the New York Academy of Sciences* 76, no. 2 (1958): 20–26.

——. 'Kōsei Busshitsu no Kenkyūshi (1) [A History of Research in Antibiotics (1)]'. *Shizen* 17, no.2 (1962): 83–89.

——. 'Kōsei Busshitsu no Kenkyūshi (2) [A History of Research in Antibiotics (2)]'. *Shizen* 17, no. 3 (1962): 78–89.

——. 'Kōsei Busshitsu o Motomete (1): [Searching for Antibiotics (1)]'. *Shokun* 1, no. 1 (1980): 282–299.

——. 'Kōsei Busshitsu o Motomete (2): Kanamaishin no Hakken [Searching for Antibiotics (2): The Discovery of Kanamycin]'. *Shokun* 1, no. 2 (1980): 294–305.

——. 'Kōseibusshitsu o Motomete (3): Michi no Ryōiki Gan e no Chōsen [Searching for Antibiotics (3): Challenging Cancer]'. *Shokun* 12, no. 3 (1980): 230–244.

——. 'Seiganzai wa Dokomade Kitaka [The Status of Anticancer Drugs]'. *Kagaku Asahi* (September 1982): 50–54.

Umezawa, Hamao, Kenji Maeda, Tomio Takeuchi and Yoshiro Okami. 'New Antibiotics, Bleomycin A and B'. *Journal of Antibiotics, Series A* 19 (September, 1966): 200–209.

Umezawa, Hamao, Masahiro Ueda, Kenji Maeda, Koki Yagishita, Shinichi Kondo, Yoshiro Okami, Ryozo Itahara, Yasuke Osato, Kazuo Nitta and Tomio Takeuchi. 'Production and Isolation of a New Antibiotic, Kanamycin'. *The Journal of Antibiotics Series A* 10 (September 1957): 181–188.

US Congress, Office of Technology Assessment. *Commercial Biotechnology: An International Assessment*. Washington DC: US Government Printing Office, 1984.

US Department of Commerce. *Pharmaceutical Price Controls in OECD Countries: Implications for US Consumers, Pricing, Research and Development, and Innovation*. Washington DC: US Department of Commerce, 2004.

US Department of Commerce, Bureau of the Census. *Statistical Abstract of the United States 1940*. Washington DC: US Government Printing Office, 1941.

——. 'Concentration Ratios in Manufacturing'. US Census Bureau. http://www.census.gov/epcd/www/concentration.html (accessed 1 December 2007).

——. *Scientific Research and Development Services, 2002*, Washington, DC: US Census Bureau. http://www.census.gov/prod/ec02/ec0254i07.pdf (accessed 22 November 2009).

US Department of Commerce, International Trade Administration, Market Access and Compliance. 'MOSS Agreement on Medical Equipment and Pharmaceuticals'. United States Department of Commerce. http://www.mac.doc.gov/japan/source/menu/medpharm/ta860109.html (accessed 15 May 2007).

US Department of Commerce, International Trade Administration, Office of Japan Market Access and Compliance. 'U.S.–Japan Structural Impediments Initiative (SII)'. United States Department of Commerce. http://www.mac.doc.gov/japan/market-opening/market-opening.htm (accessed 2 May 2008).

US Food and Drug Administration, Center for Drug Evaluation and Research. 'CDER Drug and Biological Approval Reports'. http://www.fda.gov/cder/rdmt/default.htm (accessed 4 May 2008).

——. 'Colorectal Cancer Endpoints Workshop Summary, 12 November 2003'. US Food and Drug Administration. http://www.fda.gov/cder/drug/cancer_endpoints/colonEndpointsSummary.htm (accessed 16 May 2006).

——. 'FDA Oncology Tools Approval Summary for Bleomycin'. US Food and Drug Administration. http://www.accessdata.fda.gov/scripts/cder/onctools/summary.cfm?ID=208 nnk (accessed 10 November 2007).

——. 'FDA Oncology Tools Approval Summary for Mitomycin C'. US Food and Drug Administration. http://www.accessdata.fda.gov/scripts/cder/onctools/summary.cfm?ID=273 (accessed 10 November 2007).

——. 'Label and Approval History'. US Food and Drug Administration. http://www.accessdata.fda.gov/scripts/cder/drugsatfda/index.cfm?fuseaction=Search.Label_ApprovalHistory#apphist (accessed 8 May 2008).

Vogel, Steven Kent. *Japan Remodeled: How Government and Industry are Reforming Japanese Capitalism*. Ithaca, NY: Cornell University Press, 2006.

Wakaki, Shigetoshi. 'Tōsha ni Okeru Seiganzai no Kenkyū to Kaihatsu no Genjō [The Status of Anticancer Drug R&D at Our Company]'. *Kagaku Kōgyō* (April 1976): 96–98.

Wakaki, S., H. Marumo and K. Tomioka. 'Isolation of New Fractions of Antitumour Mitomycins' *Antibiotics and Chemotherapy* 8, no. 8 (1958): 228–240.

Wakasugi, Ryūhei and Harue Wakasugi. 'Iyakuhin no Kenkyū Kaihatsu to Hōseido [Pharmaceutical R&D and the Legal System]'. *Mitagakkai Zasshi* 99, no. 1 (April 2006): 57–74.

Wall, Monroe E. and M.C. Wani. 'Camptothecin: Discovery to Clinic'. *Annals of the New York Academy of Sciences* 803 (13 December 1996): 1–12.

Wall, Monroe E., M.C. Wani, C. E. Cook, Keith H. Palmer, A.T. McPhail and G.A. Sim. 'Plant Antitumour Agents 1: The Isolation and Structure of Campothecin, a Novel Alkaloidal Leukemia and Tumour Inhibitor from Camptotheca Acuminata'. *Journal of American Chemical Society* 88 (20 August 1966): 3888–3890.

Westney, Eleanor. 'Country Patterns in R&D Organization: The United States and Japan'. In *Country Competitiveness: Technology and the Organizing of Work*, edited by Bruce Kogut, 36–53. Oxford: Oxford University Press, 1993.

White, G. Philip. *Antibiotics: Market Review and Development Trends*. London: FT Healthcare, 1999.

Wilson, Jenny. *Antibacterial Products and Markets, Scrip Reports*. Richmond: PJB Publications, 1997.

Woodruff, Barry. 'A Soil Microbiologist's Odyssey'. *Annual Review of Microbiology* 35 (1981): 1–28.

World Health Organization. Global TB Database. http://www.who.int/tb/country/global_ tb_database/en/index.html (accessed 1 November 2007).

Yagisawa, Morimasa. 'Antibiotics, Chemotherapeutics and Other Microbial Products Originated from Japan'. Unpublished document.

——. 'Biseibutsu Taisha Sanbutsu Tansaku Kenkyū no Dōkō [Trends in Exploratory Research of Microbial Metabolite Part 2; 20 Years after Antibiotics]'. *Baiosaiensu to Indasutorī* 58, no. 2 (2000): 89–94.

Yagisawa, Yukimasa. 'Early History of Antibiotics in Japan'. In *The History of Antibiotics: A Symposium*, edited by John Parascandola, 69–90. Madison: American Institute of the History of Pharmacy, 1980.

——. 'Shinbunya o Kirihiraita Kōseibusshitsu [A New Field Created by Antibiotics]'. *Iyaku Jānaru* 9 (February 1970): 20–23.

Yakugai Konzetsu Fōramu. *Yakugai Eizu wa Naze Okitaka* [Why the HIV Drug Tragedy Occurred]. Tokyo: Kirishobō, 1996.

Yakugyō Jihōsha. *Nihon no Iyakuhin Sangyō* [The Japanese Pharmaceutical Industry]. Tokyo: Yakugyō Jihōsha, 1973.

——. *Yakuji Handobukku* [Pharmaceutical Affairs Handbook]. Tokyo: Yakugyō Jihōsha, 1968–1999.

Yakugyō Keizai Kenkyūjo. *Yakugyō Keizai Nenkan* [Economics of the Pharmaceutical Industry Annual]. Tokyo: Yakuji Nippōsha, 1967, 1971, 1979, 1984, 1987.

——. *Yakuji Nenkan* [Pharmaceutical Affairs Annual]. Tokyo: Nihon Yakugyō Shimbunsha, 1951, 1957, 1961, 1964.

Yakuji Kenkyūkai. *Saikin no Yakumu Gyōsei* [Recent Trends in Pharmaceutical Administration]. Tokyo: Yakumu Kōhōsha. 1999–2005.

Yakuji Nippōsha. *Saikin no Shinyaku* [New Drugs in Japan]. Tokyo: Yakuji Nippōsha, 1950–2006.

——. *The Japanese Pharmaceutical Industry in the New Millennium*. Tokyo: Yakuji Nippōsha, 2001.

Yakult Honsha Co. 'Enkaku [History]'. Yakult Honsha Co. http://www.yakult.co.jp/front/ company/profile/htm/index03.html (accessed 15 November 2007).

——. 'Yakult Honsha Iyakuhin Jigyō Setsumeikai Sankō Shiryō [Reference Materials for the Informational Meeting on the Pharmaceutical Business at Yakult Honsha]'. Tokyo: Yakult Honsha Co., 14 June 2006.

——. *Yūka Shōken Hōkokusho* [Annual Securities Report]. Tokyo: Ōkurashō Insatsukyoku, 1990.

Yakuseki Nippōsha. *Yakugyō Nenkan* [Pharmaceutical Industry Annual]. Tokyo: Yakuseki Nippōsha, 1935, 1938.

Yamanouchi Pharmaceutical Co. *Yamanouchi Seiyaku 50-nenshi* [A 50-year History of Yamanouchi Pharmaceutical]. Tokyo: Yamanouchi Pharmaceutical Co., 1975.

——. *Yūka Shōken Hōkokusho* [Annual Securities Report]. Tokyo: Ōkurashō Insatsukyoku, 1950, 1961, 1971, 1976, 1981.

Yamazaki, Tōru. 'Sengo Yakugyōshi [A Postwar History of the Pharmaceutical Industry] (1)'. *Yakkyoku* 16, no. 8 (August 1965): 3–8.

——. 'Sengo Yakugyōshi [A Postwar History of the Pharmaceutical Industry] (2)'. *Yakkyoku* 16, no. 9 (September 1965): 7–12.

——. 'Sengo Yakugyōshi [A Postwar History of the Pharmaceutical Industry] (3)'. *Yakkyoku* 16, no. 10 (October 1965): 7–12.

——. 'Sengo Yakugyōshi [A Postwar History of the Pharmaceutical Industry] (4)'. *Yakkyoku* 16, no. 11 (November 1965): 7–12.

Yano Keizai Kenkyūjo. *Iyaku Sangyō Nenkan* [Pharmaceutical Industry Annual]. Tokyo: Yano Keizai Kenkyūjo, 1975, 1980, 1985.

——. *Iyakuhinshijō Senryaku no tame no Māketingu Dēta Nenpō* [Marketing Data Annual for Strategizing in the Pharmaceutical Market]. Tokyo: Yano Keizai Kenkyūjo, 1985.

——. 'Kōryoku ga Yowai kara Tsukawareru, Kuresuchin, Pishibanīru [Krestin and Picibanil Used because of Weak Effects]'. *Iyaku Sangyō Nenkan* (1985): 15–18.

Yasuda, Kuniaki. 'Nihon ni Okeru Shiniyakuhin no Shōnin Shinsa Kikan [Approval Times for New Drugs in Japan]'. *Research Paper Series, Office of Pharmaceutical Industry Research, Japan Pharmaceutical Manufacturers Association* 35 (December 2006).

Yongue, Julia. 'Research Culture in the Pharmaceutical Industry'. *Kenkyū Gijutsu, Keikaku* 8, no. 3 (1993): 239–248.

——. 'Origins of Innovation in the Japanese Pharmaceutical Industry: The Case of Yamanouchi Pharmaceutical Company (1923–1976)'. *Japanese Research in Business History* 22 (2005): 109–136.

——. 'Shinyaku Kaihatsu o Meguru Kigyō to Gyōsei: Chiken o Chūshin ni [Firms and Government in Drug Development: An Examination of Clinical Trials]'. In *Kigyō Bunseki to Gendai Shihon Shugi* [Corporate Analysis and Contemporary Capitalism], edited by Akira Kudō and Motoi Ihara, 166–191. Kyoto: Minerva, 2008.

Yoshida, T., H. Sato and M. Ishidate. 'Yoshida Nikushu ni yoru Akusei Shuyō Kagakuryōhō no Jikkenteki Kenkyū 1 [Experimental Studies on Chemotherapy of Malignant Growth Employing Yoshida Sarcoma 1'. *Gann* 41 (1950): 93–96.

Yoshida, Tomizō. 'Cancer Research in Japan'. *Cancer Research* 16, no. 11 (1956): 1007–1008.

Yoshitomi Pharmaceutical Industries, Ltd. *Yoshitomi Seiyaku 50-nen no Ayumi* [A 50-year History of Yoshitomi Pharmaceutical]. Tokyo: Yoshitomi Pharmaceutical Industries, Ltd, 1990.

——. *Yūka Shōken Hōkokusho* [Annual Securities Report]. Tokyo: Ōkurashō Insatsukyoku, 1949, 1960, 1961.

Zeria Pharmaceutical Co. 'Enkaku [Company History]'. Zeria Pharmaceutical Co. http://www.zeria.co.jp/comp/co01.html (accessed 1 December 2007).

——. *Yūka Shōken Hōkokusho* [Annual Securities Report]. Tokyo: Ōkurashō Insatsukyoku, 1990.

Index

Taylor & Francis

eBooks

FOR LIBRARIES

ORDER YOUR FREE 30 DAY INSTITUTIONAL TRIAL TODAY!

Over 23,000 eBook titles in the Humanities, Social Sciences, STM and Law from some of the world's leading imprints.

Choose from a range of subject packages or create your own!

Benefits for you

▶ Free MARC records
▶ COUNTER-compliant usage statistics
▶ Flexible purchase and pricing options

Benefits for your user

▶ Off-site, anytime access via Athens or referring URL
▶ Print or copy pages or chapters
▶ Full content search
▶ Bookmark, highlight and annotate text
▶ Access to thousands of pages of quality research at the click of a button

For more information, pricing enquiries or to order a free trial, contact your local online sales team.

UK and Rest of World: **online.sales@tandf.co.uk**

US, Canada and Latin America:
e-reference@taylorandfrancis.com

www.ebooksubscriptions.com

ALPSP Award for BEST eBOOK PUBLISHER 2009 Finalist

Taylor & Francis eBooks
Taylor & Francis Group

A flexible and dynamic resource for teaching, learning and research.